WITH

D1228881

The Poetry of Tennyson

Alfred Tennyson. Chalk drawing by M. Arnault, 1864.
Reproduced by permission of the National Portrait Gallery, London.

The Poetry of Tennyson

A. Dwight Culler

New Haven and London   Yale University Press

1977

Designed by John O. C. McCrillis
and set in Baskerville type.
Printed in the United States of America by
The Alpine Press, South Braintree, Mass.

Published in Great Britain, Europe, Africa, and
Asia (except Japan) by Yale University Press,
Ltd., London. Distributed in Latin America by
Kaiman & Polon, Inc., New York City; in
Australia and New Zealand by Book & Film
Services, Artarmon, N.S.W., Australia; and in
Japan by Harper & Row, Publishers, Tokyo
Office.

Library of Congress Cataloging in Publication Data

Culler, Arthur Dwight.
    The poetry of Tennyson.

    Includes bibliographical references and index.
    1. Tennyson, Alfred Tennyson, Baron, 1809–1892—
Criticism and interpretation.

PR5588.C8   821'.8   76-48899
ISBN 0-300-02084-8

For Jonathan and Beth

Contents

Acknowledgments

This is a good moment to be writing on Tennyson, for the great collections of his letters and papers, so long in private hands or under restriction, are now available to the public and may be quoted. I am deeply grateful to Sir Charles Tennyson, who has done so much to bring this about, and to Lord Tennyson, who has given me permission to quote from unpublished material. To the Librarians and Directors of the Tennyson Research Centre at Lincoln, the Trinity College Library, the Cambridge University Library, the Houghton Library at Harvard, the Henry E. Huntington Library, the Yale University Library, and the British Library, I offer my thanks. They provided me with every facility and every courtesy. For giving me a pre-publication view of his edition of Tennyson's letters I am deeply indebted to Cecil Lang, and to Jack Kolb I owe the same favor with respect to his edition of the letters of Arthur Hallam. I am especially indebted to Christopher Ricks, whose superb edition of Tennyson's *Poems,* in the Longmans Annotated English Poets Series, greatly lightened my labors.

Although at this date it is quite impossible for me to distinguish between what I have taught my students and what I have learned from them, I am sure I have learned a great deal, and I would particularly like to mention those who have written dissertations on Tennyson under my direction: Marguerite Stewart, Perry Nodelman, David Goslee, and Elizabeth Francis. I am grateful to Doris Nelson, administrative assistant of the Yale English Department, for typing the final draft of the manuscript and for serving so ably as my assistant during a period of administrative chores. Of my wife I said in my book on Newman that she had shed both sweetness and light upon the problem of composing it. I can only add here that she has not changed her ways: she has typed, checked, researched, and advised, and for all this I am deeply grateful. To the authorities of Yale University, my academic home during most of my life, I am indebted for generous leaves in which to do the research and writing for this book. I am also indebted to the John Simon Guggenheim Memorial Foundation for the award of a Fellowship, not given in support of this book, but into which the writing of this book has slightly encroached.

A portion of the material has appeared elsewhere in a different form: a part of chapter 4 in my essay, "Tennyson, we cannot live in art," *Nineteenth-Century Literary Perspectives: Essays in Honor of Lionel Stevenson,* ed. Clyde de L. Ryals (Durham: Duke University Press, 1974); and a passage from chapter 9 in my article, "Monodrama and the Dramatic Monologue," *PMLA,* 90 (May 1975). They are used again by permission of the Duke University Press and the Modern Language Association.

A.D.C.

1

"Tennyson, Tennyson, Tennyson"

> Accustom yourself to reflect on the words you use. . . . For if words
> are not THINGS, they are LIVING POWERS, by which the things
> of most importance to mankind are actuated, combined, and
> humanized.
>
> Coleridge, *Aids to Reflection*

In 1858 John Tyndall, the scientist, visited Tennyson at Farringford and had a conversation with him which, he said, "pres-
ently became intensely interesting." It concerned a state of consciousness into which Tennyson said he could throw himself by
thinking intently of his own name. It was impossible to describe
the state, for "language seemed incompetent to touch it," but it
was apparently an isolation of the spirit from the body. "By God
Almighty," declared Tennyson, "there is no delusion in the matter! It is no nebulous ecstasy, but a state of transcendent wonder,
associated with absolute clearness of mind."[1] A fuller account of
this experience is given by Tennyson himself in the *Memoir* composed by his son:

> A kind of waking trance I have frequently had, quite up from
> boyhood, when I have been sitting alone. It has generally
> come upon me thro' repeating my own name two or three
> times to myself, till all at once, as it were out of the intensity of
> the consciousness of individuality, the individuality itself
> seemed to dissolve and fade away into boundless being, and
> this is not a confused state but the clearest of the clearest, the
> surest of the surest, the weirdest of the weirdest, utterly
> beyond words, where death was an almost laughable impossi-
> bility, the loss of personality being no extinction but the only
> true life.[2]

This experience was of great significance to Tennyson, for it
provided evidence for one of his most deeply held convictions, the
unreality of the material universe and the reality of the unseen
world. It also indicated to him that nothing could be known about

that world that was communicable to others in the concepts of ordinary speech. And yet it suggested there was one kind of speech, the quasi-mystical word uttered as a kind of chant or incantation, that did have the power to transport the soul at least to the verges of that world. Poetry, of course, was the larger name of that speech, and one has the feeling that this experience lay at the very source of Tennyson's power as a poet.

What is the nature of the experience? We today are perhaps in a better position to understand it than earlier generations because of our interest in transcendental meditation.[3] This practice, which, according to its founder, derives from the ancient Vedic tradition of India, centers upon a mantra, or Sanskrit word, which is chosen by the initiator especially for the meditator and which he is admonished never to reveal. Consisting of soft vowel and consonantal sounds, meaningless to him, it provides a focus for his meditation, and as he repeats it to himself, banishing all distracting thoughts and breathing slowly and deeply, he enters into a profoundly restful state in which he seems to float off into the serene. It seems likely that Tennyson, without having any knowledge of this tradition, stumbled upon a meditative technique similar to that of the great Eastern religions. One cardinal difference was that he was meditating upon his own name, whereas the traditional techniques emphasized a more impersonal approach. One Zen Buddhist practice, for example, combines inhalations with rhythmic counting. A fourteenth-century Christian mystical treatise counsels the reader to attain union with God by banishing all physical activities and excluding worldly thoughts, and as a means of doing this it suggests that a single-syllable word, such as "God" or "love," be repeated over and over again. In Judaism a method was developed which involved contemplating the letters of the Hebrew alphabet that formed God's name (YHWH), and in the Shinto religion, in Taoism, and in Islamic Sufism other methods were employed. All of them involved a quiet calm environment, a passive attitude, a comfortable position so that one's muscular activity was reduced to a minimum, and a mental device. For Tennyson this device was apparently the sound of his own name, and if one's mantra is supposed to be chosen with reference to the individual alone, so that in repeating it he is meditating upon his own soul, then in this instance it was obviously well chosen.

William James discusses Tennyson's trance in *The Varieties of Religious Experience,* and though James is too rationalistic to do justice to its poetic quality, he is helpful in setting it in the context of nineteenth-century attitudes toward language. In his view it is to be classed among those lower orders of mystical experience in which some word or phrase that has long been familiar to the individual suddenly strikes him with a force totally fresh and new. He instances the impact upon Newman of St. Augustine's phrase, *Securus judicat orbis terrarum,* which Newman had known for years but which had never particularly impressed him until it was pointed out by a friend in Wiseman's article. Or there is the impact upon Martin Luther of the familiar words of the Creed, "I believe in the forgiveness of sins." Of John Foster, the essayist, it is said that "single words (as *chalcedony*), or the names of ancient heroes, had a mighty fascination over him," and that "at any time the word *hermit* was enough to transport him." There is also, as Edmund Wilson reminds us, the story of the old woman who, in the exercise of reading her Bible, derived such comfort from "that blessed word *Mesopotamia*," and James mentions an old German lady who longed all her life to visit "Philadelphiā," simply because the name had haunted her imagination.[4] *Chalcedony, Mesopotamia, Philadelphia*—clearly, the musical quality of Tennyson's name had something to do with its power to induce a trance. Had his name been Wragg, poor thing! it is unlikely that he would have experienced such transports.

If Tennyson could not communicate the quality of his experience in prose, perhaps he could in verse, and on one occasion he did attempt it. In *The Ancient Sage,* a "very personal" poem written near the end of his life, the Sage, obviously a figure of Tennyson himself, is addressing a young skeptic who might almost stand for John Tyndall. He is trying to convince him that the soul of man does occasionally have "gleams . . . / Of more than mortal things."

>   for more than once when I
> Sat all alone, revolving in myself
> The word that is the symbol of myself,
> The mortal limit of the Self was loosed,
> And past into the Nameless, as a cloud
> Melts into Heaven. I touch'd my limbs, the limbs

> Were strange not mine—and yet no shade of doubt,
> But utter clearness, and thro' loss of Self
> The gain of such large life as match'd with ours
> Were sun to spark—unshadowable in words,
> Themselves but shadows of a shadow-world.[5]

The experience is still ineffable, but in the heightened language of poetry there is increased emphasis upon the paradox that the trance is both produced by words and yet is beyond words. By meditating upon his own name the poet passes into "the Nameless." By "revolving in myself / The word that is the symbol of myself," he achieves a state "unshadowable in words, / Themselves but shadows of a shadow-world."

This paradox reminds us that there are two different conceptions of language to be found in Tennyson's work and indeed throughout the nineteenth century. On the one hand, there was the view that words were the poor husks of reality, abstract denotative counters which were the product of the understanding generalizing upon sense experience. Such words corresponded to classes of objects in the phenomenal world but to nothing more. On the other hand, there was still alive something of the older conception of language as a magical instrument, a means of incantation or ritual, which gave one power over reality or revealed its true nature. By this view words were proper names, containing the ontological secret of a thing. Thus, in antiquity the true or secret name of the city of Rome was jealously guarded from its enemies, and Adam by naming things knew their nature. Carlyle held that ordinary language was but the old clothes of the mind, but he believed that by penetrating to the true, original meaning of words one could gain a true conception of the thing. Thus, a king is not properly one who lounges upon a throne but one who has *can-ning* (ability), and a duke is one who leads (*dux*).[6] Tennyson in repeating his own name was meditating upon his own nature, and what he discovered is that his was an immortal soul, unrelated to the body. The only mistake he made was in trying to explain this ineffable experience to a scientist like Tyndall. Had he treated it in a lyric, he would simply have induced a trancelike state in the reader by chanting, "Tennyson, Tennyson, Tennyson."

That Tennyson's poems do have this purely lyric element we know. Whitman says, "To me, Tennyson shows more than any poet I know (perhaps has been a warning to me) how much there is in finest verbalism. There is such a latent charm in mere words, cunning collocutions, and in the voice ringing them, which he has caught and brought out, beyond all others—as in the line, 'And hollow, hollow, hollow, all delight.' "[7] R. H. Horne says too, "Perhaps the first spell cast by Mr. Tennyson, the master of many spells, he cast upon the ear. . . . Nay, he will write you a poem with nothing in it except music, and as if its music were everything, it shall charm your soul."[8] Examples of this "finest verbalism" are to be found in Mariana's refrain, "I am aweary," in the refrain "dying, dying, dying" in the Bugle Song, and in the magic moment in *The Princess* when the wind arises and whispers to the Prince, "Follow, follow, and win." Tennyson's son tells us that his father's poems "were generally based on some single phrase like 'Someone had blundered': and were rolled about, so to speak, in his head, before he wrote them down."[9] Out of their own music they rose up into poems. Every lyric is thus in some sense an act of transcendental meditation, operating upon a particular word or phrase and inducing in the reader who can savor its shape and sound a state of transcendent wonder. The most famous instance of this is the lyric *Far–Far–Away*.

Speaking of his early childhood, Tennyson says, "The words 'far, far away' had always a strange charm for me."[10] So strange was this charm that in this lyric, written at the very end of his life, he was still trying to fathom its nature. To understand it we must realize that the words, as Tennyson pronounced them, were spaced out into three separate feet and were sounded quietly and with a "dying fall." Presumably, they were attenuated almost to a whisper. The images he associated with them in the poem were the distant horizon, where earth and heaven meet, and the "lin-lan-lone" of evening bells, which imitates their rhythm. Both by their form and by their meaning they suggest a world beyond life and death where the antinomies of this world will be reconciled. There, birth and death, joy and pain, the human and divine, will be one, but how this will happen is as mysterious as the phrase itself. The manuscript shows that Tennyson had infinite difficulty with this lyric, and indeed, as an effort in analysis, it ultimately confesses its failure.

What charm in words, a charm no words could give?
O dying words, can Music make you live
        Far—far—away?

The poem is written "For Music," and the thought is that the refrain line, with its infinite diminuendo, will somehow express what the longer lines of the couplet cannot. But it is doubtful whether even music can resolve the central paradox of the poem, that language has a power which language itself cannot express.

Tennyson's sensitivity to the sound and shape of words is very early evident. Speaking of his education at Louth School, he says, "The only good I ever got from it was the memory of the words, 'sonus desilientis aquae,' and of an old wall covered with wild weeds opposite the school windows."[11] Actually, the words he must have been referring to are Ovid's *ex alto desilientis aquae*[12] (water leaping down from on high), and it is evidence of the auditory quality of his imagination that in his memory he imported the sound (*sonus*) of the water into the phrase. Also from the school he got "such pictures as that conjured up by the Greek word *Tanupeplos* of the women floating through the streets of Troy with their long dresses flying out behind them."[13]

Another phrase that seems to have moved Tennyson deeply as a boy is the phrase "No more," for an early poem of that title has all the marks of an authentic experience.

> Oh sad *No More!* Oh sweet *No More!*
>   Oh strange *No More!*
> By a mossed brookbank on a stone
> I smelt a wildweed-flower alone;
> There was a ringing in my ears,
> And both my eyes gushed out with tears.
> Surely all pleasant things had gone before,
> Lowburied fathomdeep beneath with thee, NO MORE![14]

Wordsworth said that "the meanest flower that blows can give / Thoughts that do often lie too deep for tears." Dr. Arnold, despite his great love for flowers, thought this sentiment excessive, but now the youthful Tennyson experiences an almost physical reaction at the thought of the passing of a wildweed-flower. What is even more strange, as he laments the passing of the flower, the very phrase of his lamentation displaces the flower and is itself elevated to the status of a mythical person, who is buried along with the flower that it seems to lament. In the parallel myth of Hyacinthus the more plastic Greek imagination imprinted upon the petals of the flower the marks of the Greek letters, AI ("Alas"). But Tennyson, more auditory in approach, hypostatized the phrase itself, which he made at once the theme, the refrain, and the mythical figure of his poem.

All the things that we have been saying seem to be gathered together in another passage in *The Ancient Sage* which, like that describing the boyhood trance, is presented as evidence that the mind, at least in childhood, does have gleams of "more than mortal things."

> for oft
> On me, when boy, there came what then I call'd,
> Who knew no books and no philosophies,
> In my boy-phrase 'The Passion of the Past.'
> The first gray streak of earliest summer-dawn,
> The last long stripe of waning crimson gloom,
> As if the late and early were but one—
> A height, a broken grange, a grove, a flower
> Had murmurs 'Lost and gone and lost and gone!'
> A breath, a whisper—some divine farewell—
> Desolate sweetness—far and far away—
> What had he loved, what had he lost, the boy?
> I know not and I speak of what has been.

Here are the flower (also the broken grange which will later appear in *Mariana*), the phrase "far far away," the reconciliation of opposites, and the sense of a divine sadness or desolate sweetness which seems imprinted on all things in nature. Like the child in the Immortality Ode, this boy has a dim and fading memory of something infinitely sweet and infinitely beautiful which he once knew, perhaps in another world, but which is now "lost and gone." Oddly enough, he embodies this feeling in the phrase "The Passion of the Past," which, as he says in a comment on the poem, represented "more especially my own personal feelings."[15] Tennyson talked freely to his contemporaries about this phrase, but it is not at all clear what it means. To James Spedding it merely conveyed the fact that Tennyson was always dissatisfied with the present, never cared for it till it was past. For Hallam too it apparently connoted Tennyson's strong feeling *for* the past, for he says, "I . . . am not without some knowledge and experience of your passion for the past."[16] But as Tennyson uses the phrase, it is not the passion of a modern subject *for* the past, but the passion *of* the past itself—its yearning, its suffering, its desire to recover itself and be. Denotatively, the phrase is not perhaps a very good one—certainly it is not at all clear. But it is apparent that for Tennyson its power lay in the instrinsic qualities of the phrase itself, particularly its alliteration and the sense of dissonance between *Passion* and *Past*. Doubtless there were also purely personal associations which we cannot now recover.

At what point did Tennyson become aware of this magical power of language? "The first poetry that moved me," he says, "was my own at 5 years old. It was one windy day, I stood and stretched out my arms to the wind, and said aloud, 'I hear a voice that's speaking in the wind.' It moved me wonderfully. I thought it grand."[17] Wordsworth too listened to "notes that are / The ghostly language of the ancient earth, / Or make their dim abode in distant winds." But whereas Wordsworth added, "Thence did I drink the visionary power," Tennyson was moved by his own line of verse. It is not too much to say that language and poetry played for Tennyson the same role that nature played for Wordsworth. Where Wordsworth roamed the fields, Tennyson ranged the English poets, reading them in his father's library and imitating them with astonishing facility.

> According to the best of my recollection [he wrote], when I was about eight years old, I covered two sides of a slate with Thomsonian blank verse in praise of flowers, for my brother Charles, who was a year older than I was, Thomson then being the only poet I knew. . . . About ten or eleven, Pope's *Homer's Iliad* became a favorite of mine and I wrote hundreds and hundreds of lines in the regular Popeian metre, nay even could improvise them, so could my two elder brothers, for my father was a poet and could write metre very skillfully. . . . At about twelve and onward I wrote an epic of six thousand lines à la Walter Scott with Scott's regularity of octosyllables and his occasional varieties. Though the performance was very likely worth nothing I never felt myself more truly inspired, I wrote as much as seventy lines at one time, and used to go shouting them about the fields after dark.[18]

At fourteen he wrote an Elizabethan play, *The Devil and the Lady*, which was more Elizabethan than the Elizabethans themselves, and in *Armageddon* he imitated Milton. *The Coach of Death* was a gothic ballad, and in *Poems by Two Brothers* (1827), the work of himself and Charles, he drew upon a whole range of late eighteenth- and early nineteenth-century poets. "Accept then, soul of my soul," he wrote dramatically to his sister's governess, "these effusions, in which no Ossianic, Miltonic, Byronic, Milmanic, Moorish, Crabbic, Coleridgic etc. fire is contained."[19] He was wrong: such fire was contained in most of his productions until, arriving at his own time, he discovered his own voice. Surely this is a remarkable development. Every poet is imitative in his youth, but not many recapitulate the entire history of English poetry. Unlike the youthful Keats, Tennyson did not remain silent upon a peak in Darien—rather he plunged volubly into its thickets and claimed province after province for his own.

The work that chiefly bears witness to the presence in Tennyson of a magical conception of language is *The Devil and the Lady*, a fragmentary drama which Tennyson wrote at the age of fourteen. It is an astonishing production for a boy of that age, not only in poetic power but also in attitude and information. "Where could the whelp have learned all this?" was Jowett's reaction, and the answer is, from the Elizabethans. The play is eloquent testimony to the impact which the literature and especially the language of the great Elizabethans had on the youthful Tennyson. The concordance to *The Devil and the Lady* shows that in the three acts of this fragmentary drama Tennyson used over four thousand different words, which is more than half the number in the entire poetical works of Milton. It is obvious that he was simply intoxicated with the power of language, and as he allows his characters to run on for forty or fifty lines at a time and then draw themselves up short in mild astonishment at their own verbosity, it almost seems as if he is parodying the form even while he is employing it. Of course he is not: it is merely that he feels such delight in his new toy, and in his absolute mastery over it, that he cannot resist displaying it in an exaggerated form. But one effect of this is that he has seized very clearly on a central point in the Elizabethan drama, namely, the magical power of the word, and has made this into a major theme in his own play.

The story is that of a necromancer, Magus, who is called away upon a journey and who entrusts his wife, Amoret, to the Devil to keep her chaste and pure while he is gone. The Devil, though shrinking from so formidable a task, disguises himself as the Lady and in that shape fends off a whole series of would-be lovers—a Lawyer, an Apothecary, a Sailor, a Mathematician or Astronomer, a Soldier, and a Monk. The relationship between these characters is established almost entirely by their relative power of language. It is by a cabalistic spell that the Magus conjures up the Devil and forces him to do his bidding, and it is because his powers do not extend to reading the secret thoughts of his Lady that he is forced to depend upon his familiar. The Lady laments her lack of Latin with which to exorcise the Devil, and the Devil simply overwhelms the Lady by the sheer torrent of his abuse. With the entrance of the lovers the play becomes, if possible, even more linguistic, for each speaks exclusively in the jargon of his own profession. The Lawyer's speech is larded with mittimuses and writs, the Apothecary's with boluses and gallipots, the Mathematician's with cosines and surds, and the Sailor's with cockleboats and ballast. It is with these terms that they abuse and berate one another. Further, although the drama breaks off at this point, it is clear that this act is to culminate in a scene in which each suitor will sing a song in praise of his lady (presumably the very quintessence of his own professional lingo) and the "Lady" will then unveil herself to the one she likes best. Just at this point the prearranged signal will be given, the Magus will rush in, and bastinadoes will follow.

What further was to come is uncertain. Hallam Tennyson, in a note at the end of the Trinity College manuscript, says: "This scene would probably have ended with wild dance and revel of all the characters in the play and many he-devils and she-devils—and many thunders and lightnings—all singing a mad chorus—like this—" and he then quotes from *The Vision of Sin:*

> Fill the can and fill the cup!
> All the windy ways of men
> Are but dust that rises up
> And is lightly laid again.

"Perhaps the final scene," Hallam continues, "might have been as in this Vision, a fair landscape with a great sun rising over it—. . . . Flames start from the earth and consume the [*illegible*: lovers? characters?]—the devil exultant."[20] Hallam is undoubtedly repeating something his father had told him, though whether it represents his father's boyhood intention is uncertain. For one is inclined to ask, what about the Lady? Surely, in accordance with the spirit of comedy, the implications of the title (which give her a role equal to the Devil's), and hints in the drama itself, she is somehow to recover her tongue and have her revenge upon these excessively articulate men. Professor Paden has suggested that when

the Devil conducts Magus to the Lady's bechamber to show him
how well he has fulfilled his task he will find a seventh lover
already nearing his goal.[21] The suggestion is an attractive one,
and I would only add that, if so, the lover ought to be a Poet, for
only a poet would have the verbal power to triumph in this drama
of linguistic virtuosity.

Actually, however, there is considerable evidence that the Lady
was to be vindicated in a more decorous way. For there is a serious,
poetic side to the drama which is evidenced by several long descriptive passages and particularly by the Magus's account of his
attempt to voyage over the ocean in a shallop and of his being
driven back by a storm. This storm Magus attributed to "Some
spells of darker Gramarie than mine, / [which] Rul'd the dim
night and would not grant me passage." There is, then, a power
superior to the magic of the necromancer, and one can only
assume that it is the Omnipotent Love which is invoked by Magus
at the beginning of the drama, for Love is the "Tyrant o' th' earth
and sea," "whose boundless sway / And uncontroll'd dominion
boweth down / The Spirits of the Mighty." It is, moreover, responsible for the storm actually raging at the moment. Amoret it
is, of course, who later attempts to raise a storm against her
husband—"The big waves shatter thy frail skiff! the winds / Sing
anything but lullabies unto thee!"—and thus we must assume that
her prayer is answered by the Omnipotent Love with which she,
by her name, is associated. Both the storm with which the play
opens and that which drives the necromancer back come out of
the North (Satan's quarter), and as Magus stations himself at the
"Northern casement" to spy upon his wife, it must be assumed
that he is to be visited by tempest one final time. Indeed, his wife,
in repudiating his imputations upon her chastity, urges him to
"cleave to th' sunny side o' the wall"[22] and attributes his "Illiberal
innuendos and dark hints" to suspicion, gendered of a "diseased
vision." In this she is right, for when the storm drives him back it
takes the form of his own unclean imaginings: "dim Phantasies,"
"unutterable things," a black shape clinging to his boat, a sullen owl
on the prow, and melancholy sprites white as their shrouds. Indeed, Magus himself in invoking Omnipotent Love has acknowledged that she was only "to be understood by those / Who feel
thee and aid thy purpose," of which he was not one. He, says
Amoret, is the "antidote to love," the "bane of Hope," which
consumes "the green promise of my youth" so that "I never more

can hope and therefore never / Can suffer Disappointment."
Both are unknown to her. This is surely why Tennyson prefixed
to his drama the Latin motto, *Spes alit juventutem et poesin, vituperatio praemit et laedit.* (Hope nourishes youth and poetry, abuse
represses and injures it.) Sir Charles Tennyson has noted that the
motto provides a curious foretaste of Tennyson's well-known sensitivity to criticism,[23] but its application to the drama is that Amoret
is the poet-figure associated with love, youth, and hope, whereas
Magus and his ally the Devil, whose harsh abuse and dark suspicions are the product of his own unclean mind, are the critics. The
Devil and the Lady, in full accord with Tennyson's later work,
may be translated the Critic and the Poet, and though the critic's
vituperatio has the magical power that abuse and satire tradition-
ally have, it is to be supposed that the poetry of Amoret, in
harmony with Omnipotent Love, will be enough to dispel the
storm which has brooded over the whole drama and cause the sun
to rise over the fair landscape as promised. Then it will not be
inappropriate for law, medicine, mathematics, religion, and even
the military and nautical professions to pay their homage to
Poetry in the way they proposed. But it may be that Tennyson was
uncertain whether he should have this happy ending or the
ghoulish one appropriate to the malefactors in the drama.

   The Vision of Sin, which Hallam Tennyson has associated with
The Devil and the Lady, ends with the suffering characters asking of
the inscrutable mountain height, "Is there any hope?"

> To which an answer peal'd from that high land,
> But in a tongue no man could understand;
> And on the glimmering limit far withdrawn
> God made Himself an awful rose of dawn.

If we are to interpret these lines in the light of *The Devil and the
Lady,* then the question, "Is there any hope?" would refer to the
hope that nourishes youth and poetry, and although the answer
comes in a tongue no man could understand, it is to be presumed
that poetry would come nearer to understanding it than any
other. For although Tennyson is quite clear that "matter-moulded
forms of speech" cannot compass the divine, and that the "mystic
gleams" we have of "something felt, like something here; / Of
something done, I know not where?" are "Such as no language
may declare,"[24] still the language of poetry comes nearer to it than

any other. It mediates between the human and the divine. Through its music and song, through its phrases which have their power in themselves, and especially through the Love which is its animating soul, it speaks to us of that which is "lost and gone" or "far far away."

2

The Poetry of Apocalypse

It was a time when one madman printed his dreams, another his day-visions; one had seen an angel come out of the sun with a drawn sword in his hand, another had seen fiery dragons in the air, and hosts of angels in battle array.

Southey, *Letters from England*

Tennyson's Aunt Mary Bourne used to look across the street at Spilsby and say, "This reminds me of the great gulf which shall divide the wicked from the blessed."[1] Among the latter she included herself, for she would often weep with emotion at the goodness of God. "Has He not," she would exclaim, "damned most of my friends? But *me, me* He has picked out for eternal salvation, *me* who am no better than my neighbours!" Among the damned she apparently included her nephew, for on one occasion she said, "Alfred, Alfred, when I look at you, I think of the words of Holy Scripture—'Depart from me, ye cursed, into everlasting fire.' "[2] Aunt Mary was not an eccentric but one of a type that was common in England from the time of the great Evangelical revival until well into the nineteenth century. During this period it was widely believed that the world was rapidly approaching its end, that a last terrible battle between the forces of good and evil was impending, that the Second Coming of Christ was at hand, and that when he came he would judge all men and set up his Kingdom on earth, which would last for a thousand years.

This apocalyptic temper was not limited to the religious imagination but was to be found in all departments of life. In geology, for example, scientists were divided into two diametrically opposed schools, those who held that the earth had assumed its present form as a result of violent catastrophes, such as earthquakes, volcanoes, and deluges, and those who believed that it was rather by slower and more gradual processes continued over a longer period of time. The former were known as "catastrophists," the latter as "uniformitarians."[3] The uniformitarian view was initially put forward by James Hutton, a Scot, in 1785, and as it is the modern scientific view, one cannot but believe that it would have quickly triumphed over its rival, championed by the German, Abraham Gottlob Werner, had not the French Revolution occurred just at this time. But the Revolution—surely, said Burke, the most momentous event the world has ever known—followed by the earth-shaking Napoleonic wars, did seem to confirm the fact that it was by violent cataclysm and titanic convulsions that change, at least in the political realm, was wrought. If so, why not also in the natural? And so, though Hutton's theory had been reinforced for a while by the gradualism of Lamarck, in 1812, on the very eve of that "world-earthquake, Waterloo," Georges Cuvier, the comparative anatomist, published his *Discours sur les révolutions de la surface du globe,* which had the effect, along with the work of his English disciple, William Buckland, of confirming England and France in catastrophism for two decades. It was only with the publication of Lyell's *Principles of Geology* in 1830–33 that this view was gradually displaced and the uniformitarian hypothesis substituted. It is no accident, one feels, that Lyell's work appeared just at the time when England, by passing the First Reform Bill, elected gradualism rather than catastrophism as its mode of effecting political change.

These concepts of catastrophism and uniformitarianism are useful in discriminating among literary figures in the nineteenth century. Carlyle, for instance, is a catstrophist writer, whereas George Eliot is generally uniformitarian, though she falls into catastrophism in her final chapters. Catastrophism obviously implies the visionary imagination, since it is only through that faculty that the great catastrophes at the beginning or the end of the world can be seen. So much is indicated by the evolution of the word *apocalypse,* which initially meant "revelation" but, because of the peculiar character of what was revealed in the Apocalypse of St. John, ultimately became associated with violent catastrophe. On the other hand, if it is only by divine revelation that the great final catastrophes can be seen, it is only by patient observation and analysis that one can detect subtle change. This is the forte of the great Victorians, and to move from the Romantic to the Victorian period is, with many exceptions and qualifications, to move from catastrophism to literary uniformitarianism. Newman, in moving from Evangelicalism to Roman Catholicism, exemplified it, and so too did Tennyson. Beginning as a catastrophist under the shadow of Milton and the great Romantics, he moved in his middle years toward uniformitarianism but then, as darkness settled over his vision, moved back toward catastrophism again.

Certainly his earliest work was visionary or apocalyptic in character. The Poet, he says, in an 1830 work of that title, "in a golden clime was born."

> He saw thro' life and death, thro' good and ill,
>   He saw thro' his own soul.
> The marvel of the everlasting will,
>   An open scroll,
>
> Before him lay.

Of the Mystic, also 1830, it is said, "Angels have talked with him, and showed him thrones," and, as the Daughters of Time hold aloft the cloud that hangs over the gates of birth and death, he sees far through them and beholds the great serene abstractions of Time, Space, and Eternity. "You tell me that to me a Power is given," says the speaker in *Perdidi Diem*, "An effluence of serenest fire from Heaven, / Pure, vapourless, and white, / As God himself in kind." The finest expression, however, of this conception of the poet is to be found not in Tennyson's poetry but in a prose passage which was printed by Hallam Tennyson as a fragment of an essay on *Ghosts*. The title is a misnomer, for it is actually a description of the visionary or mystical poet.

> He who has the power of speaking of the spiritual world, speaks in a simple manner of a high matter. He speaks of life and death, and the things after death. . . . He unlocks with a golden key the iron-grated gates of the charnel house, he throws them wide open. And forth issue from the inmost gloom the colossal Presences of the Past, *majores humano*; some as they lived, seemingly pale, and faintly smiling; some as they died, still suddenly frozen by the chill of death. . . .
>
> The listeners creep closer to each other, they are afraid of the drawing of their own breaths, the beating of their own hearts. The voice of *him* who speaks alone like a mountain stream on a still night fills up and occupies the silence. He stands as it were on a vantage ground. He becomes the minister and expounder of human sympathies. His words *find* the heart like the arrows of truth. Those who laughed long before, have long ago become solemn, and those who were solemn before, feel the awful sense of unutterable mystery. The speaker pauses:
>
> "Wherefore," says one, "granting the intensity of the feel-

ing, wherefore this fever and fret about a baseless vision?"
"Do not assume," says another, "that any vision *is* baseless."[4]

Out of this assumption, that no vision is baseless, came in Tennyson's earliest years a series of apocalyptic or visionary poems which are far bolder in conception, though of course less perfect in execution, than anything he ever attempted later. Among them are a translation of the opening lines of Claudian's *Rape of Proserpine,* the related poems *Armageddon* and *Timbuctoo,* and *The Coach of Death.*

One hardly knows why Tennyson should have been attracted to translate *The Rape of Proserpine* by the late classical poet Claudian. Perhaps he already felt that love for the myth of Demeter which his son says was so strong a feeling of his later years, for the myth is a beautiful expression of the theme "lost and gone" or "far far away." Or it may be that he was simply attracted by Claudian's powerful and somber conception of the poet as presented in the invocation, for it is to this portion of the poem that his translation is largely limited. The poet in Claudian is presented as a priest of the Eleusinian mysteries, and that Tennyson entered into this conception is evident from the fact that in his translation he not only reproduces but even intensifies the element of divine ecstasy. Where the original says, "My full heart bids me boldly sing" (*audaci prodere cantu / mens congesta iubet*), Tennyson translates, "With senses rapt in holy thought I sing": and he dramatizes the driving away of the uninitiate with the cry, "Away! away! profane ones!" What follows is a ritual in which the priest enacts the process of his own inspiration. "Seraphic transports through my bosom roll, / All Phoebus fills my heart and fires my soul," and, to manifest this state, "The God—the God appears!" The priest then summons up the Demons of the underworld who are to "explain" to him "The dread Arcana of the Stygian reign," and these arcana are the substance of his poem. It should be clear that there is nothing here so secular as a muse. There is only a poet-priest whose inspiration is one with the ritual he is performing and whose poem is the utterance of sacred mysteries not open to the uninitiate. Coleridge perhaps hit on the reason for Claudian's popularity in the early nineteenth century (he was translated three times between the years 1814 and 1823) when he observed that in his work there was "an oscillation between the objective poetry of the ancients and the subjective mood of the moderns."[5]

In *Armageddon,* which unites the influence of Milton with that of the Book of Revelation, the poet is no longer a priest but a Hebrew prophet or seer. More specifically, he is a youth who, through the favor of a seraph or angel of God, is granted an apocalyptic vision comparable to that of St. John so that he can prophesy of the Latter Times. Of himself he could not do this. "Thy sense is clogg'd with dull Mortality," says the angel. "Open thine eyes and see!" Then, says the youth, in one of the most remarkable passages in all of Tennyson,

> I felt my soul grow godlike, and my spirit
> With supernatural excitation bound
> Within me, and my mental eye grew large
> With such a vast circumference of thought,
> That, in my vanity, I seem'd to stand
> Upon the outward verge and bound alone
> Of God's omiscience. Each failing sense,
> As with a momentary flash of light,
> Grew thrillingly distinct and keen. I saw
> The smallest grain that dappled the dark Earth,
> The indistinctest atom in deep air,
> The Moon's white cities, and the opal width
> Of her small, glowing lakes, her silver heights
> Unvisited with dew of vagrant cloud,
> And the unsounded, undescended depth
> Of her black hollows. Nay—the hum of men
> Or other things talking in unknown tongues,
> And notes of busy Life in distant worlds,
> Beat, like a far wave, on my anxious ear.
>
> I wondered with deep wonder at myself:
> My mind seem'd winged with knowledge and the strength
> Of holy musings and immense Ideas,
> Even to Infinitude. All sense of Time
> And Being and Place was swallowed up and lost
> Within a victory of boundless thought.
> I was a part of the Unchangeable,
> A scintillation of Eternal Mind,
> Remix'd and burning with its parent fire.
> Yea! in that hour I could have fallen down
> Before my own strong soul and worshipp'd it.

It is true that even before the descent of the seraph the youth, standing upon the mountain that overlooks the valley of destruction, has had a vision of the coming of Armageddon which is horrific in its splendor. It is, indeed, comparable in imaginative power to visionary passages in Milton, Dante, Shelley, and the Bible, and one cannot say that the quality of the vision which follows the angel's descent is noticeably better, or more spiritual, than that which precedes. The reason for this is not far to seek. The passage describing the dilation of the youth's powers is an imaginative rendering of the trancelike state which Tennyson says he knew from a boy. In the description of this state quoted in chapter 1, we are told that it consisted in two things: a sense of the loss of personality—a merging of the soul in God—and absolute clarity of mind. So here the youth's failing sense grew wondrously distinct and keen, so that he saw the indistinctest atom in earth, air, and moon. He also felt himself upon "the outward verge and bound alone / Of God's omniscience. . . . / I was a part of the Unchangeable, / A scintillation of Eternal Mind." Of course, in this poem the state is not induced by the youth's repeating his own name, which would be inappropriate, but it does result in his wishing to fall down before his own strong soul and worship it, which, in the circumstances, would be more inappropriate still. It is evident that self-contemplation and orthodox Christianity do not mix, and when the poem breaks off with the vision of Armageddon still to come, we are not really surprised. Knowing *Hyperion: A Fragment,* we would say that this is always where such poems break off. Ostensibly an apocalyptic vision, the poem is really about the experience of apocalypse, and once that experience is over there is no place else for the poem to go.

Unless, indeed, it should go to Timbuctoo, and that, in fact, is what happened. *Armageddon* was written about 1824, when Tennyson was a youth of fifteen. Four years later, when he was at Cambridge, he was requested by his father to compete for the Chancellor's Gold Medal by writing a prize poem on the subject "Timbuctoo." Unwilling, apparently, to compose an entirely new poem for the occasion, Tennyson sent home for the manuscript of *Armageddon* and out of the second half of it quarried *Timbuctoo.* To the parsimonious or thrify poet it is an object lesson in quarrying. By the change of the single word *tents* to *spires* he was able to turn a twenty-five-line description of the cohorts and palaces of Jehovah

into an account of the pinnacles and battlements of Timbuctoo.[6]
But despite the fact that *Timbuctoo* has nearly half of its 248 lines
in common with the revised version of *Armageddon,* all is turned to
such different purpose that it is, in structure and conception,
quite a different poem. Standing now upon Mt. Calpe, instead of
on the mountain overlooking the valley of destruction, and looking south across the Strait of Gibraltar to Africa, instead of north,
east, and west at the assembling powers of God and Satan, the
youth is no longer a Hebrew prophet but a Romantic poet. As
evidence of this, he is musing upon the "legends quaint and old"
which "had their being in the heart of man"—Atlantis, El Dorado,
and the islands of the Hesperides. Is there really, he cries, buried
amid the hills of Africa, a city so fair as Timbuctoo, or is it but a
dream? At this a young seraph appears beside him and, explaining that he is the Spirit of Fable, who has taught men to attain by
shadowing forth the Unattainable, frees his sense of dull mortality
so that he can see not only the towers and battlements of Timbuctoo, not only the pillared front of its golden shrine, but also, far
within, the "snowy skirting of a garment" thronged about with
worshipers. Only for a moment he sees it, however, and then
"Thick night / Came down upon my eyelids, and I fell." That such
too will be the fate of the city is indicated by the seraph, for just as
the river which mirrors its mystic battlements cannot endure to
carry their image through the world but buries itself in sand, so

> The time is well-night come
> When I must render up this glorious home
> To keen *Discovery.*

Then the brilliant towers of the city will darken and shrink into a
cluster of mud huts, "Black specks amid a waste of dreary sand."

   That the seraph who in *Armageddon* represented the Spirit of
Prophecy, should in *Timbuctoo* have become the Spirit of Fable is
particularly interesting because in the former poem the youth,
following Milton, had said that "No fabled Muse"—that is, no
pagan muse of a fabulous religion—could enable him to express
what he had seen. Divine inspiration was necessary. But now it is
precisely this objective, divine inspiration that is replaced by the
subjective power of the imagination. One may say that this change
was made necessary by the change in topic, and so in part it was.
But the Trinity College manuscript of *Armageddon,* which is later
than the version we have hitherto been discussing, reveals that

Tennyson had already been moving in this direction.[7] The manuscript is part of a notebook dated January 10, 1828, and it shows that Tennyson revised the poem, still under the title *Armageddon*, in a way which brought it much nearer to the form it was to assume in *Timbuctoo*. Essentially, he did two things. At the end he greatly elaborated the vision of the tents of the Lord and the City of God, and in the section immediately following the youth's awakening by the angel he added a long passage analyzing the swarm of conflicting thoughts and images that were crowding through his mind. This emphasis upon the youth's subjectivity has some psychological interest, but it is injurious to the poem as a whole because it tends to destroy the sense of clarity, serenity, and mental power which had made the youth so impressive a figure. He is now all turned in upon himself. Moreover, in revising this revision for *Timbuctoo*, Tennyson omitted the section in which the youth felt himself one with the Unchangeable and wished to fall down before his own strong soul and worship it. Admittedly, this is rather strong language for one who is only going to see Timbuctoo, not Armageddon, and doubtless the change may be explained on that basis. Still, it is part of the series of alterations that take us from the priest of Claudian to the prophet of *Armageddon* to the more inward and humane conception of Romantic poet.

Ultimately, the difference between the two poems is the difference between their cities—the fact that the one deals with the City of God at the moment when it is about to triumph over its enemies and be established forever, and the other with a city of the imagination which is about to be exposed to the harsh touch of reality and destroyed. Actually, the former topic had already been made into a Romantic commonplace by artists and poets who, drawing on the religious catastrophism of the day, depicted in lurid detail the destruction of the cities of the ancient world. Bulwer Lytton's *Last Days of Pompeii* (1834) is merely the latest and mildest work in this genre, for he had been preceded by Edwin Atherstone, the religious poet, who wrote an epic in thirty books on *The Fall of Nineveh* (1828) and a shorter but more impressive *Last Days of Herculaneum* (1821). More important was the work of John Martin, the painter, who, in the decade 1820–30, produced a series of paintings depicting the lost cities of the ancient world in the apocalyptic hour of their destruction. The most important of these were *The Fall of Babylon, Belshazzar's Feast, The Destruction of*

Pompeii and Herculaneum, and *The Fall of Nineveh.*[8] Winifred Gérin
has shown that reproductions of these paintings penetrated to the
Haworth parsonage and influenced the "Glass Town" world of the
Brontë children.[9] Perhaps they also penetrated to Somersby, for
in the *Poems by Two Brothers* (1827) there are some eight or ten
poems which deal with this same theme of the fall of empire or
the destruction of cities. There are apostrophes to Persia on the
destruction of Persepolis, lamentations of the Peruvians at the
slaying of Ataliba, God's denunciations of Pharaoh-Hophra,
prophecies of woe against Rome for laying waste the groves of the
Druids, and descriptions of the expedition of Nadir Shah into
Hindustan. Even the prize poem that Tennyson had attempted
the year before *Timbuctoo,* on *Napoleon's Retreat from Moscow,*[10] had
taken this form, for Moscow is represented as the "Holy City," the
"Jerusalem of Russia," and Napoleon, if not actually Satanic, is at
least a hero of the Satanic school. All these cities, historical and
visionary, may be reduced to two, Jerusalem and Babylon, the
City of God and the City of Wrath, and all the conflicts between
them to miniature versions of Armageddon.

Not so with Timbuctoo, which is a city of the imagination. The
reason why Timbuctoo had been selected by the Cambridge authorities as the subject of the 1829 competition is that this fabulous city, which had tantalized men's imaginations ever since the
fourteenth century but had never yet been seen by any European,
was just then the object of intensive exploration. Beginning in the
late eighteenth century the Association for the Promotion of the
Discovery of Africa had sent out several expeditions with the sole
object of finding Timbuctoo. The most famous of these was that
of Mungo Park, a Scottish ship's doctor, who, though he did not
reach Timbuctoo, performed incredible exploits which he nar-
rated in his popular *Travels in the Interior Districts of Africa* (1799).
Then, in December 1824, the Geographical Society of Paris announced a prize of 7,000 francs to be given to the first person to
reach Timbuctoo and return, and it became a kind of race between the French and the English to see who would get there first.
Two English expeditions, one from the south and one from the
north, were mounted. That of Hugh Clapperton failed, but Major
A. Gordon Laing actually reached the city on August 13, 1826, the
first European to do so. Tragically, he was killed as he started
back, and so, though the news of his accomplishment reached
London in April 1828, the city remained as mysterious as ever.

But then, just as the authorities were announcing the topic for their poem,[11] reports began to filter out that an obscure Frenchman, René Caillié by name, by the desperate expedient of getting himself carried there disguised as a slave, had reached Timbuctoo and returned. And in 1830, when his account of his travels was published, it revealed, just as Tennyson had predicted, that the city was indeed "nothing but a mass of ill-looking houses built of earth."[12] Such was the fate of this particular legend which "had its being in the heart of man."

After *Timbuctoo* Tennyson did not write many visionary or apocalyptic poems, and in the few that he did write it is curious how perfunctory the visionary apparatus has become. In *The Vision of Sin* it is reduced to a single line: "I had a vision when the night was late," and what follows does not impress us as a vision but a moral allegory. In *A Dream of Fair Women* Tennyson is combining Chaucer's *Legend of Good Women* with the techniques of Dante, but it is now 1832 and so he modernizes the medieval dream-vision by comparing the poet to a balloonist, who is "Self-poised, nor fears to fall." But then, in a revised version, he eliminates the balloon and is held above his subject by his knowledge of Chaucer's art—a knowledge, however, which does not give him command of his subject but rather makes him hesitate to speak. The principal exception in this decline of the visionary mode is *The Palace of Art,* for in its courts and gilded galleries, its "huge crag-platform, smooth as burnish'd brass," one recognizes an English Gothic version of Nineveh or Babylon. And in the latter part of the poem, when the biblical allusions increase and "Mene, Mene" is written on the wall, we are aware that we are once again at Belshazzar's Feast. Yet it is significant that Tennyson does not destroy the Palace:

> Yet pull not down my palace towers, that are
>   So lightly, beautifully built:
> Perchance I may return with others there
>   When I have purged my guilt.

It is not merely that the Palace is a more ambiguous symbol than the cities of earlier days, but also that Tennyson now prefers the milder method of reformation.

Finally, in *St. Simeon Stylites* Tennyson places that Eastern ascetic on a pillar forty cubits high, which is exactly the kind of vantage point he had previously reserved for his own mystical persona.

But now he makes this figure into a grotesque and clearly implies that the slight panic he is beginning to feel about his own salvation may be justified. St. Simeon is undoubtedly a wicked allusion to the Rev. Charles Simeon, leader of the Evangelicals at Cambridge in Tennyson's day. "Every body knows," writes a contemporary, "that at Trinity Church, Cambridge, there has been, evangelizing the gownsmen for the last half century, a great saint called Simeon."[13] "The gownsmen were much divided respecting him," writes another. "Among the thoughtless or evil part of them there was bitter dislike to his strictness in religion. All who were known to attend his church, and much more his evening parties, were called Simeonites by their less thoughtful brother students; and the reading men of them who remained at Cambridge during the long vacation were called 'the remnant of the Simeonites.' Many other humorous and harmless little sarcasms of a like kind might be heard."[14] One of their number, John Allen, used to pray with Thackeray and FitzGerald to bring them to a more lively apprehension of their sins, and he apparently induced Thackeray to weep.[15] Tennyson does not narrow his poem to a local allusion and it is not unmitigated satire. But it is clear that by 1833 he was more impressed with the dangers than the virtues of the apocalyptic method.

Even before that time, however, Tennyson felt some difficulty about the method, for it is notable that not a single one of his early poems, with the exception of the prize poem *Timbuctoo*, was completed. Often their materials are taken up and reutilized in the next effort, but even then they remain fragmentary. This is true of *The Rape of Proserpine, The Devil and the Lady, Armageddon, The Coach of Death, Pierced through with knotted thorns of barren pain,* and *Perdidi Diem*. Of course, one could say simply that the subjects were momentous and that Tennyson was a very young man: he had bitten off more than he could chew. But there is something more to it than that. There is the fact that all seems to be going well right up to the crucial moment, but then he turns aside, or breaks off, or something intervenes. Sometimes he turns aside into subjectivity—into the experience of apocalypse rather than apocalypse itself—and sometimes he gets diverted into Timbuctoo. He is obviously fascinated with Armageddon, and yet the battle is never joined, the sinners are never judged, the vision is never completed. Poetry of apocalypse we may call it, but there is also a kind of evasion of apocalypse which one would willingly understand.

Part of the explanation may lie in the relation of the apocalyptic method to Tennyson's religious views. For even as he was writing these poems he must have been moving away from the more graphic version of Christianity in which he had been raised toward a liberal or Broad Church position which rejected all forms, creeds, or definitions of the divine. By this view he would have had no doubt about the existence of God, but of his name, nature, and attributes he would have known nothing. In the late poem *The Ancient Sage* he calls God the "Nameless," and in the early *The "How" and the "Why"* he says, with an almost pathetic inarticulateness, "I feel there is something; but how and what? / I know there is somewhat; but what and why?" All is "behind the veil," and as is the way with the goddess Isis, who is Tennyson's symbol for religious mystery, if one veil is lifted, there is another underneath. In the early essay *Ghosts* he says, "He [the visionary poet] lifts the veil, but the form behind it is shrouded in obscurity. He raises the cloud, but he darkens the prospect."[16] Writing to his fiancée in 1838–40, he speculated, "Who knows whether revelation be not itself a veil to hide the glory of that Love which we could not look upon without marring our sight, and our onward progress?"[17] Since all creeds and doctrines are human in origin, they are but imperfect approximations of a truth that is far wider, nobler, and purer than anything the human mind can conceive. It follows from this that vagueness and indeterminacy are of the essence of Tennyson's religion. His typical images of God—"the Power in darkness that we guess"—are the veiled statue, the stairway mounting up through the mist, and the mountain peak swathed in cloud. He is what one might call a formal agnostic.

As a result, after about 1830 Tennyson hesitates to use the word "vision" of our apprehension of God. In *Armageddon* the youth boldly says, "I stood upon a mountain . . . and I saw," but in *Timbuctoo* it is rather "I gazed," "I mused," "methought I saw." Even then, of course, the object is secular not divine, and the function of the Spirit of Fable is not to enable man to see, rather to feel:

> to sway
> The heart of man: and teach him to attain
> By shadowing forth the Unattainable;
> And step by step to scale that mighty stair
> Whose landing-place is wrapt about with clouds
> Of glory, of Heaven.

"Few there be," he adds, "So gross of heart who have not felt and known / A higher than they see." In the Prologue of *In Memoriam* Tennyson will go further and deny even knowledge to religion: "We have but faith: we cannot know; / For knowledge is of things we see"—and we do not see God.

For a person of T. S. Eliot's generation, for whom "the spirit killeth but the letter giveth life," this element of indeterminacy in Tennyson's religion created a problem. It meant that if Tennyson attempted a poetry of statement, he could not make a precise statement about God, and if he attempted visionary poetry, he could not have a clear vision. The most he could offer was a mountain peak veiled in mist or cloud. Macaulay, on the other hand, felt that this was all a nineteenth-century poet ought to offer. In his famous essay on Milton in the *Edinburgh Review* he developed an extended contrast between the "exact details" of Dante and the "dim intimations" of Milton and declared that, whichever was better as poetry, the latter was the more appropriate for representing supernatural beings. "What is spirit?" he asked. "We . . . infer that there exists something which is not material. But of this something we have no idea. We can define it only by negatives. We can reason about it only by symbols. We use the word; but we have no image of the thing; and the business of poetry is with images, and not with words. The poet uses words indeed; but they are merely the instruments of his art, not its objects. They are the materials which he is to dispose in such a manner as to present a picture to the mental eye." Now the great mass of men, declared Macaulay, demand pictures, and doubtless in the Middle Ages the sharp images of Dante did no violence to men's conception of religion. But "Milton wrote in an age of philosophers and theologians. It was necessary therefore for him to abstain from giving such a shock to their understanding as might break the charm which it was his object to throw over their imaginations. This is the real explanation of the indistinctness and inconsistency with which he has often been reproached."[18] But if this were true in the seventeenth century, what would be the case in the nineteenth? Macaulay's essay was published in August 1825, in between the writing of *Armageddon* and its conversion into *Timbuctoo*, and if Tennyson had read it, it would certainly have given him pause. Even if he had not read it, it was an indication of what brisk young men were thinking about poetry in 1825, and Tennyson would have become conscious of this the moment he got to Cambridge.

That he did become conscious of it and felt that some sense other than the visual might be his means of apprehending spirit is suggested by two short poems he wrote about this time. The first is simply entitled *Stanzas:*

> What time I wasted youthful hours,
> One of the shining wingèd powers
> Show'd me vast cliffs, with crowns of towers.
>
> As towards that gracious light I bow'd,
> They seem'd high palaces and proud,
> Hid now and then with sliding cloud.
>
> He said, "The labour is not small;
> Yet winds the pathway free to all;—
> Take care thou doest not fear to fall!"

That Tennyson clearly envisioned the dangers of apocalyptic poetry is evident, and that he suffered some kind of Icarian fall in moving from *Armageddon* to *Timbuctoo* is apparent. But in another poem, also dealing with a city of legend, he saw another way.

> Ilion, Ilion, dreamy Ilion, pillared Ilion, holy Ilion,
> City of Ilion when wilt thou be melody born?

As Tennyson reminds us in *Tithonus*, Troy was built by the music of Apollo's lyre: "Like that strange song I heard Apollo sing, / While Ilion like a mist rose into towers." But as the one city rose out of mist into solid form, so the other was "hid now and then by sliding cloud." The one is a City of God which the poet is simply to envision, but the other is a city of the imagination which he is to create by the sound of his own music. So in *Gareth and Lynette*, when Gareth and his companions come to the plain of Camelot and see the city appearing and disappearing through the mist, they are afraid and think it unreal. And Merlin does indeed tell them that it is a city in process and must be built by each man for himself.

> "For an ye heard a music, like enow
> They are building still, seeing the city is built
> To music, therefore never built at all,
> And therefore built for ever."

In *Ilion, Ilion* the means by which the city is built is not formally the lyre of Apollo but the two rivers, Scamander and Simois, which flow down from the heart of Ida, rippling over the meadow

and murmuring the refrain, "When wilt thou be melody born?" It
is the stream, then, which, in the language of one of Tennyson's
later poems, is the "voice" of the "Peak." In that poem the poet
looks up to the silent mountain height and cries, "Hast thou no
voice, O Peak, / That standest high above all?" And the answer
comes from the stream, "I am the voice of the Peak, / I roar and
rave for I fall."[19] It is *because* the stream falls that it roars, *because* it
feels upon it the power of the deep that it is troubled and makes
its moan, whereas the Peak, not feeling this power, remains silent.
This is a new idea. It is not because of his Icarian flight that the
poet sings but because of his Icarian fall. It is because of his
declension from a divine to a human condition that he has a
message to the world. This is why the words "far far away" and
"lost and gone" had such a power for Tennyson, because they
hinted at mystic gleams which he had once seen and then had lost
in cloud. In *Merlin and the Gleam* Tennyson represents himself as
following the Gleam through the various phases of his life, and if
one understands that he followed at a distance and seldom saw,
then that is a correct statement. But, by an incongruous image, the
Gleam is represented as floating upon a stream of melody, and
when it is, that represents more truly the Tennysonian method.
For except for a few years in his youth Tennyson's method was
not, like the deluded knights in *The Holy Grail,* to follow the Gleam
till it led to an apocalyptic vision of a Heavenly City, but to allow
the stream of melody which descended from the heights to well
up in his being and create the "city built to music."

3

The Solitary Singer

> Like a high-born maiden
> In a palace-tower
> Soothing her love-laden
> Soul in secret hour
> With music sweet as love, which overflows her bower:
>
> Shelley, *To a Skylark*

"Standing on Earth, not rapt above the Pole, / More safe I sing." So Tennyson might have said in 1830, for by this date he had already reached the conclusion which he expressed in *Milton: Alcaics* that although he admired the Milton of the grand style, it was the pastoral Milton that he loved. As a result he changed his own image. He is no longer a youth standing upon a mount and seeing a vision but a maiden seated by a stream whose melody, as it descends from a cloud-capped mountain, is an imperfect but beautiful rendering of the voice on high. Since the voice on high, according to *The Vision of Sin*, spoke in "a tongue no man could understand," the voice of the stream is not easily intelligible to all. Neither is it joyful, for it is not happy to be leaving its ethereal regions, and as it reemerges in the garden below, as a fountain or spring tended by the maiden, it becomes indistinguishable from the melody of her song and the river of her tears. In this form it flows out of the garden past the great city of the plain, and the question now is not how accurately it reproduces the cadence of the divine but how sympathetically it will be received in the haunts of men. Will the people of the city hearken to its song and rebuild their city in harmony with its music, or will they reject it with hostility and disdain?

The earliest version of this image appears in *The Poet's Mind* in the *Poems, Chiefly Lyrical* of 1830. The poet's mind is there represented as a sacred garden, and the "dark-brow'd sophist" is urged to come not near, for "All the place is holy ground." If he were to enter, the flowers would wither, the singing bird would fall to the ground, and the fountain would cease to play. For ever in the middle of the garden leaps a fountain which is drawn

29

> From the brain of the purple mountain
> Which stands in the distance yonder.
> It springs on a level of bowery lawn,
> And the mountain draws it from Heaven above,
> And it sings a song of undying love.

And yet, says the poet to the dark-browed sophist,

> tho' its voice be so clear and full,
> You never would hear it, your ears are so dull;
> So keep where you are: you are foul with sin;
> It would shrink to the earth if you came in.

It is true that in this poem the inhabitant of the garden is probably a priest rather than a maiden, for here there are still elements of the earlier apocalyptic view. Indeed, the poem boldly states the *procul, o procul este, profani* theme of the translation of Claudian. Still, the poet is standing on a level with mankind, not above it, and he is aware that his garden can be invaded and destroyed. So, while looking back to *Armageddon,* the poem more clearly looks forward to *Claribel, Mariana*, and *The Lady of Shalott,* which will weave a variation on this theme from 1830 to 1842.

What are the elements from which this new symbol of the poet derives? As one examines the early poems which lead into the volume of 1830, it appears that there are three: the concept of an interior landscape or "garden of the mind," nature poetry which gradually takes on a mythical character, and the so-called "lady" poems.

In the first group are *Ode: O Bosky Brook, Recollections of the Arabian Nights, Ode to Memory,* and *The Lover's Tale. O Bosky Brook,* as Sir Charles Tennyson says,[1] is divided into three rather disconnected parts, of which the first is addressed to the brook, the second to the moon, and the third to darkness or night. But the parts are not really so disconnected as they appear, for it is the brook that leads the poet into the moonlit scene, and the moon, "Pale Priestess of grey Night," who leads him on to the temple of Athor, the god of Night, where he will perform his act of worship. "I savour of the Egyptian," he cries, "and adore / Thee, venerable dark! august obscure! / Sublimest Athor!" Not because of any affinity between thy glooms and mine, but rather,

> That as thou wert the parent of all life,
> Even so thou art the mother of all thought,

> Which wells not freely from the mind's recess
> When the sharp sunlight occupies the sense.

It is Night as the undifferentiated expanse which the mind can people with its own creations that he prizes, and of this he has already found a symbol in the black mountain tarn to which the brook had led him. Peering down into its silent depths, he finds, peering back up at him, "The abiding eyes of Space," which from "the grave / Of that black Element, / Shine out like wonderful gleams / Of thrilling and mysterious beauty." Naturalistically, he has seen the reflection of his own eyes; mythically, he has seen the eyes of Athor; poetically, he has found in the natural world a realm so congenial to the imagination that, when he wandered up the brook at eventide and saw the sun set, he felt the same dilation of mind which he felt in *Armageddon* when the seraph freed his sense of dull mortality. But here, unaided by the seraph, he has himself spanned the distance between an English brook and an Egyptian god.

The poem is fragmentary and therefore, as in the apocalyptic poems, Tennyson does not attempt the difficult feat of what we, in the space age, have come to call reentry. Perhaps it is approached by the qualification in the last lines that not absolute dark or utter silence is best for the imagination, but that "Rare sound, spare light" will best prepare the soul for that combination of observation with reverie which he calls "awful muse and solemn watchfulness." At least this must be the mood—not in which he had started following the bosky brook, for then he was overwhelmed by impressions of sense—but which he had reached at eventide, in the twilight world between day and dark.

In *Recollections of the Arabian Nights* and *Ode to Memory* Tennyson both enters and leaves the world of imagination, and perhaps the most interesting thing about both poems is the way he does it. *Recollections of the Arabian Nights* begins as follows:

> When the breeze of a joyful dawn blew free
> In the silken sail of infancy,
> The tide of time flow'd back with me,
>   The forward-flowing tide of time;
> And many a sheeny summer-morn,
> Adown the Tigris I was borne,
> By Bagdat's shrines of fretted gold,
> High-walled gardens green and old;

> True Mussulman was I and sworn,
> For it was in the golden prime
> Of good Haroun Alraschid.

Just as in infancy the poet was borne backward through historic
time to the days of Haroun Alraschid and became a Mussulman in
imagination, so now through recollection he is borne backward
through personal time and recovers his childhood experience.
The poem is thus a double voyage—back through memory and
back through history—and part of its interest is the way the
vehicle of imagination coalesces with the tenor of experience. For
the "tide of time" that carries him backward becomes the actual
river (the Tigris) on which he voyaged, and so both his original
imagination and his memory of it take the form of a Shelleyan
voyage in a "shallop" which moves through a series of exotic and
lovely scenes, giving a sense of deeper and deeper penetration
into a remote and sensuous world: the river, the broad canal
which leads aside, the lake into which it widens, the flower-lined
walks on the shore of the lake, the bulbul whose song possessed
the night (it is entirely a "night voyage"), the garden, the dazzling
Pavilion of the Caliphate, and therein the beautiful argent-lidded
Persian girl. In any true Shelleyan poem she would be the object
of the quest, and so she seems to be here. But at the last moment
she is displaced by the jovial, rollicking king himself. Not she is on
the throne, but he—

> his deep eye laughter-stirr'd
> With merriment of kingly pride,
> Sole star of all that place and time,
> I saw him—in his golden prime,
> THE GOOD HAROUN ALRASCHID.

Part of the pleasure of this is the way Tennyson has solved the
problem of how to stop his poem, by bringing the Caliph up out of
the refrain into the narrative itself. But it also brings the reader
down out of the narrative into the broad light of day, for in the
185th Tale of *The Arabian Nights,* on which Tennyson's poem is
chiefly based, there is nothing that the young Prince, who has
secretly stolen to an assignation with the Caliph's favorite, would
less rather see than the Caliph himself. Yet this is what Tennyson
has him do, and so the heady, amorous vision dissolves in boyish
laughter.

The high point of the poem, however, comes not with the Caliph or the argent-lidded Persian girl but with the song of the bulbul in the central stanza. Or, as the poet says,

> Not he, but something which possess'd
> The darkness of the world, delight,
> Life, anguish, death, immortal love,
> Ceasing not, mingled, unrepress'd,
>   Apart from place, withholding time,
>   But flattering the golden prime
>   Of good Haroun Alraschid.

There are no bulbuls in *The Arabian Nights* any more than there are shallops. The Persian nightingale, one suspects, comes from Keats, and it is in this vision of an ecstatic song possessing the beauty of the night that Tennyson expresses his childhood delight in imaginative experience. Thus, at the center of the poem and as the true object of its quest stands, not an amorous object, but the voice of the artist. Tennyson has led up to this moment by taking us from daylight into night, from night to "another night in night" as we enter the embowering trees, and finally to the "closest coverture" where the airs of "middle night" died round the bulbul as he sang. As in Keats's *Ode,* it is in the absence of sensory experience that one pours forth one's soul in such an ecstasy.

The *Ode to Memory* is generally recognized to be Tennyson's version of the *Immortality Ode.* Its verse probably owes something to Wordsworth's irregular stanza, and its theme, though lacking the metaphysical boldness of the great ode, is similar: the memories of earliest childhood support us in our later years. This is reiterated in the cry at the beginning, middle, and end of the poem:

> O, strengthen me, enlighten me!
> I faint in this obscurity,
> Thou dewy dawn of memory.

The poet is situated, then, in spiritual darkness, and Memory is conceived as a goddess robed in orient light, whose floating locks are garlanded with flowers and who leads by the hand her infant Hope. The model is evidently the odes of Collins, but the mythological element is unsatisfactory, and in stanza v Tennyson abandons it and represents Memory as an artist.[2] "Great artist Memory," he calls her, who in her "various gallery" has numerous

"sketches" of which the earliest is set round with "royal framework
of wrought gold." Three of these sketches are described: the
landscape around Somersby, the seacoast near Marblethorpe, and
the garden of the rectory itself. At least these are the biographical
equivalents. Great emphasis is placed upon the humble character
of the scene. Memory is not nursed by flaunting vines or exotic
waterfalls, rather it thrives upon familiar rural scenes such as
might appear in a landscape by Constable or a painting of the
Dutch school. But the strange thing is that whereas the first two
scenes are sketches of earliest childhood which Memory has reproduced, the third subtly turns into an image of Memory itself. It
becomes one with "the garden of the mind" which has been
mentioned in stanza iii, and whereas previously the artist had
"retired" in the sense of standing back to look at his sketches, now
he retires in the sense of withdrawing from the world to live in the
garden.

> Whither in after life retired
> From brawling storms,
> From weary wind,
> With youthful fancy re-inspired,
> We may hold converse with all forms
> Of the many-sided mind,
> The few whom passion hath not blinded,
> Subtle-thoughted, myriad-minded.

The "we" is obviously the poet and Memory, who are withdrawing
into themselves and holding converse with the forms of their own
mind. But we are told by Tennyson that the lines which follow,

> My friend, with thee to live alone,
> Methinks were better than to own
> A crown, a sceptre, and a throne! [119–21]

were written later and were addressed to Arthur Hallam. This can
only have been between April 1829, when Tennyson first met
Hallam, and June 1830, when the poem was published with the
lines in question. It seems clear, however, that no contemporary
reader could have known to read the lines in that sense.[3] The
subtitle, "Addressed to————," and the little space which now
separates these lines from the rest of the poem were not added
until 1872, and since an ode to Memory is presumably addressed to
Memory—and Memory is in fact the figure addressed in this

poem, being spoken of as "thou" from the first line to the last—a reader would naturally identify this friend with the artist Memory, with whom the poet has just expressed a wish to retire. One hesitates to challenge the accuracy of Tennyson's memory (especially about an ode to Memory), but one wonders whether his remark (made very late in life) does not refer, not to the original composition of the lines, but rather to the way he came to understand them after Hallam's death—and also, one might add, to his revision of them for the edition of 1842. For in that edition he made two small but significant changes. In the first line (119) he changed the archaic "thee" to "you" and in the second "Methinks were better" to "Were how much better." Since everywhere else in the poem Memory is addressed as "thou" or "thee" and the poem as a whole is conducted entirely in terms of pseudo-Miltonic poetic diction, the effect of these changes is not only to differentiate the friend from Memory but also to draw these lines up out of the poem and into the modern world. In other words, the poet, having written a deliberately archaic ode to Memory, now turns to his human friend and dedicates or addresses it to him. We have here a slight anticipation of the frame device Tennyson will employ in later years.

There is no space to give a full account of the blank verse narrative *The Lover's Tale*. Tennyson says that he wrote the first three parts of it in his nineteenth year, that is, in 1828–29. He continued to be occupied with it up until 1832, when he intended to publish it but at the last minute withdrew it because of its many imperfections. It is, nonetheless, a very beautiful poem, so Shelleyan that one can hardly believe Tennyson's assertion that it was written before he had read Shelley. It is a tale, told by the youth himself, of a poet-lover (Julian) who was brought up in close companionship with his foster sister (Camilla), whom he hoped to marry. One day Camilla, who was unconscious of more than a brotherly affection on Julian's part, confided to him that she loved Lionel, their friend. The youth fell senseless at her feet and, when he revived, left their home to wander distracted through the land. At this point the poem breaks off, the youth being unable to tell his friends of the momentous "event" toward which the entire narrative moves. This much Tennyson had written in 1828–29. Forty years later he added a sequel, *The Golden Supper*, based on a story by Boccaccio, of which one can only say that it is so little in harmony with the first three parts of the tale that one can hardly

believe that this is the way it was supposed to end.[4] For not only
does the "event" lack the horror we had come to expect, but also
The Golden Supper is a purely external narrative of actions, whereas
the first three parts of the tale are concerned exclusively with the
world of emotion.

Parts I–III, indeed, are not properly a tale but a Romantic
exploration of the psychology of the teller. They show the speaker
in the very process of recalling his past, of reexperiencing his
narrative even as he narrates it. He begins more or less involuntarily, as he feels the Goddess of the Past, that "great Mistress of the
ear and eye," breathe upon him and draw the sail of his thought
back to the morning star and East of Life. He knows that by
closing his eyes "the memory's vision hath a keener edge," and
when he does a "cloud of unforgotten things, / That sometimes on
the horizon of the mind / Lie folded" sweeps across it, flash upon
flash. Beginning quietly, in accordance with the quiet beginning
of his life, he gradually works himself up into a frenzy until he
finally rushes forth in the same distracted state that he had known
before. The real subject of the poem is not the things that happened to him in the past but the things that happen to him now, as
he relives the past.

It follows from this that the speaker in the poem sees the
natural world as the physiognomy of a mind, as the emblem of
spiritual states. Just as Shelley in *Prometheus Unbound* used imagery
"drawn from the operations of the human mind"[5] to characterize
the natural world, rather than the reverse, so too does he. The
quiet bay in which his life began, called Lover's Bay, is "Like to a
quiet mind in the loud world," and its breakers sink powerless, "as
anger falls aside . . . on the breast of peaceful love." The Hill of
Woe the lovers think to rename the Hill of Hope, and it is an ill
omen that they do not, for this is a world in which thought
modifies circumstance as much as circumstance thought.

> Alway the inaudible, invisible thought,
> Artificer and subject, lord and slave,
> Shaped by the audible and visible,
> Moulded the audible and visible.

Thus, the true subject of the poem is the great spiritual abstractions, Love, Hope, and Memory, and the true narrative is how,
when the two sisters, Love and Hope, were parted, Love did not
die but, after sorrowing long,

> sought out Memory, and they trod
> The same old paths where Love had walk'd with Hope,
> And Memory fed the soul of Love with tears.

The narrator's retelling of the tale under the aegis of the Goddess of the Past is the retreading of the paths previously walked with Hope. It is clear that for a number of years Tennyson thought of Memory as the faculty principally ministering to the poetic imagination.

The idea of the "garden of the mind" which we have been tracing in these early poems undergoes in other poems a development until it becomes a symbol of the cosmic mind. As a boy at Marblethorpe, on the Lincolnshire coast, Tennyson used to climb up onto the tussocked dunes which ran between the marsh and the sea. "I used to stand on this bank," he said, "and think that it was the spine-bone of the world." Then he would listen to the voice of this prostrate giant, "for the sound," wrote Hallam Tennyson, "is amazing. All around there is a kind of hoarse whisper."[6] *Poems, Chiefly Lyrical* is largely an attempt to see how much of nature can be captured through its sounds. "The wheatears whisper to each other: / What is it they say?"[7] In a poem entitled simply *Song* both the winds and the streams seem to say, "We are free." But the one says it by breathing mellow preludes and the other by caroling and tinkling low like a bell, so that the poet is able to modulate his vowel and consonant sounds into a highly ordered work of art. In another *Song* "Worn Sorrow sits by the moaning wave," but a few lines later it is not the wave that moans but Sorrow herself: "Ever alone / She maketh her moan"; and so the process of myth-making in this landscape has begun. It is continued with the autumn fields:

> A spirit haunts the year's last hours
> Dwelling amid these yellowing bowers:
>   To himself he talks;
> For at eventide, listening earnestly,
> At his work you may hear him sob and sigh
>   In the walks.

From here it is only a step to *Claribel* and *Mariana,* but first one must account for another group of poems that ornament (or disfigure) the volumes of 1830 and 1833, the so-called "lady" poems.

The lady poems are a group of a dozen or fifteen poems which bear the titles *Lilian, Isabel, Madeline, Adeline, Rosalind, Eleänore, Kate,* and so on, and which are character sketches or portraits of the ladies in question. They constitute both a puzzle and an embarrassment to the admirer of Tennyson. What is one to make of such a series of vapid female figures? There seems to be no real literary precedent for them, not even, as is sometimes said, in the Literary Annuals—the *Forget-Me-Nots* and *Friendship's Offerings* —which began to appear in the mid 1820s.[8] Of course, earlier English poetry is full of "Celias" and "Delias," but these are love poems, addressed to the ladies in question, not portraits of them. Neither, apart from *Isabel*, which is said to be modeled on the poet's mother, and *Lilian*, who may embody traits of Sophia Rawnsley,[9] do they seem to be portraits, fancy or otherwise, of Tennyson's acquaintances. Tennyson himself said, "All these ladies were evolved, like the camel, from my own consciousness."[10] But if so, are we then driven to some deep psychological explanation? Is it true, as Lionel Stevenson has suggested, that the ladies are to be identified with the poet's own *anima* and that, in accordance with the Jungian theory in which the *anima* is of the opposite sex from the individual himself, the poet was producing images of his own soul?[11] One cannot altogether deny suggestions of this sort, neither should one forget that the poems began, very suddenly, with the onset of puberty and stopped, very suddenly, with the access of judgment. Still, granting all this, it remains true that the most striking feature of these poems is their highly formal character. Each is unique in metrical form and the forms vary from stanza to stanza. It is as if the young poet had wished to run through a series of finger exercises and, not caring to invent a new subject or theme for each one, had simply taken the varying moods of the feminine soul as an analogue of the kind of beauty he was attempting to produce. There is a parallel to this in the work of an obscure German composer, Erasmus Widmann. Widmann wrote galliards and dances in the service of the Count of Hohenlohe which he published in 1613 in his *Musikalischer Tugendtspiegel* (Musical Mirror of Virtue). "Widmann's special conceit," says Edward Tatnall Canby, "was to write his dances individually, instead of in the more usual pairs or groups, and to give each of them a girl's name, like today's hurricanes and typhoons. . . . The dances are in the familiar two-part form, each half optionally repeatable. *Johanna* is a lively dance in duple time,

Margaretha moves more rapidly, *Christina* is slower with a pleasing sequence of scale passages, *Anna* lilts jauntingly, like the 'walking' tunes of old Ireland; *Regina* is her sister, moving at a slower jaunt. *Felicitas* is the only dance in triple time, matronly and well ornamented. *Sophia*, most dignified of all, moves with an elegant grace, a figurative bow to one side and the other, recalling the formal Playford county dances of a slightly later time."[12] There is no likelihood that Tennyson ever heard of Erasmus Widmann, but his lady poems can be described in the same terms as Widmann's dances. Alexander Pope, speaking of the "ruling passions" of men, said that "Most women have no character at all," but Tennyson's ladies are highly individualized in their traits and these are often embodied in a refrainlike phrase. "Airy, fairy Lilian," for example, is the feminine coquette whose arch-innocence and gaiety ultimately so wearies the poet that he threatens to crush her. Isabel is the ideal union of opposing qualities, Wordsworth's "perfect woman nobly planned." Madeline is almost an opposition piece to her, because whereas on Isabel's lips "perpetually did reign / The summer calm of golden charity," "No tranced summer calm is thine, / Ever varying Madeline." Madeline is, indeed, a study in change. Adeline and Margaret are also paired, the former "faintly smiling" and the latter characterized by a "tearful grace" that is equally mysterious. Rosalind is "my frolic falcon," and Eleänore is the epitome of rich, luxuriant beauty. Kate is a modified version of Shakespeare's Shrew. And so on, with Marion, the "uncommon commonplace," "trim Lisette," and Amy, whose name betokens love. The best criticism of these poems (aside from FitzGerald's, who cut all but *Isabel* out of his copy of the *Poems* of 1842)[13] is that of R. H. Horne in the *New Spirit of the Age* (1844). He says that Tennyson's "characters, with few exceptions, are generalizations, or refined abstractions, clearly developing certain thoughts, feelings, and forms, and bringing them home to all competent sympathies." His Claribels, etc., "do not belong to the flesh-and-blood class . . . [but] are transcendentalisms of the senses; examples of the Homeric εἰδωλα, or rather . . . the descendants of those εἰδωλα, as modified by the influence of the romantic ages. Standing or seated, flying or floating, laughing or weeping, sighing or singing, pouting or kissing, they are lovely underbodies, which no German critic would hesitate for a moment to take to his visionary arms; but we are such a people for 'beef.' "[14] In short, the poems are efforts to explore different aspects of formal beauty through the metaphor of the feminine soul or form.

This does not rescue them from being bad poems, and the thing that turns what FitzGerald calls "the tiresome Gallery" of Adelines, Madelines, and Eleänores into the very effective Claribels, Marianas, and Œnones is that Tennyson stopped painting them and allowed them to speak. He endowed them with the soul of lonely places, with the sobbing quality which he found in nature, and he placed them in the garden of the mind. In so doing he transformed them from an art object into a symbol of the artist. One cannot say that Tennyson invented the feminine image, which is so important a symbol for later pre-Raphaelite and aesthetic writers. It was invented for modern times by Richardson and the second generation of Romantic poets. But it was so developed by Tennyson that it was established as a major poetic resource, and the poem in which this was first done, in which the three elements of nature myth, the lady poems, and the garden of the mind are drawn together, is *Claribel*, the piece with which *Poems, Chiefly Lyrical* opens.

What is *Claribel*? John Stuart Mill has said that it might almost as well be called "A solitary Place in a Wood,"[15] and in truth one does not know whether this poem is more about the lady who "lowlieth" or the place in which she lies low. It is perfectly clear that the work, with its "moss'd headstone," belongs to the tradition of English churchyard poetry, and the beetle who "boometh" in the second stanza may be traced from Gray's *Elegy* to Collins's *Ode to Evening* to John Clare's *Summer Evening*, where he "booms" for the first time. But just as one decides that it hardly matters whether the dead lady be considered the emanation of the melancholy scene or the scene the objective equivalent of one's grief for the dead lady, one realizes that the really obvious thing about the poem is its elaborate verbal pattern. Claribel is certainly so called because her name contains two *l*'s and an *r*, and the thirteen -eth rhymes are there not because the sound suggests the sighing or soughing of death but because of the peculiar softness of the feminine endings. Paradoxically, to modern ears the poem would perhaps be better without the -eths, but then it would not be what its subtitle calls it, *A Melody*. It is a melody in which the mournful sounds of an English churchyard are elaborated into a musical composition. In the opening stanza these sounds are discriminated into alto and basso profundo, into the light and airy sounds made by the breezes and the falling rose leaves and, on the other hand, the "ancient melody / Of an inward agony" made by the solemn oak tree that has not lost its leaves. In the second stanza there are three groups of three details each, the first being times of day with their (predominantly) insect noises, the second the songs of birds, and the third the sound of running water. All this happens, as the refrain line says, "Where Claribel low lieth," and that is what the "Melody" is. If it were set to music, its meaning would be clearer, and one would then begin to apprehend that these sounds of the churchyard are really sung by Claribel herself, who is the *genius loci* or spirit of the place.

With *Mariana* and its companion poem, *Mariana in the South,* Tennyson turns more particularly to the immured maiden—the maiden who finds herself in the "closed situation" of the moated grange, the isle and castle of Shalott, the vale of Ida, or the Palace of Art. In every case, however, there is an opening or aperture through which she may look out upon the world—the window in the moated grange, the magic mirror of the Lady of Shalott, the gallery of the Palace of Art, and the "gorges, opening wide apart," which "reveal / Troas and Ilion's column'd citadel." Into this distant city so revealed, Troy or Camelot, the lady's lover has disappeared, and as her thoughts follow him across the glooming flats, or down the river, or through the gorge, she makes her moan, and her song, "overflowing the vale profound," is ultimately carried to the city, where its reception, though varied, is far less sympathetic than that of Wordsworth's Solitary Reaper. Tennyson is not by any means saying the same thing or even very similar things in these poems, but in the situation of the abandoned maiden who is waiting for death or dying and who, from her isolated situation, pours forth a lament which sweeps over the world and is rebuffed by the world, he obviously found a symbol for one part of his imaginative experience.

Like Claribel, Mariana seems so much a *genius loci* that lovers of Tennyson have been very reluctant to admit that there was not somewhere a moated grange of which Mariana was the mythical embodiment. But Tennyson has said that the grange was "no particular grange, but one which rose to the music of Shakespeare's words,"[16] and he prefixed to the poem the epigraph,

"Mariana in the moated grange (Measure for Measure)." Actually, of course, these words do not occur in Shakespeare. Shakespeare's words are: "There, at the moated grange, resides this dejected Mariana" (III.i. 276), which Tennyson's imagination transformed into the alliterative and metrical form on which it could work. It is out of this inner music, then, that the poem arises, and one feels that Mariana is less an emanation of the moated grange than the grange is an exhalation of her consciousness. For although the grange is described by the poetic speaker, only the refrain being put into Mariana's mouth, one has the impression that the entire poem is spoken by Mariana. The reason for this is that the grange is described for us as Mariana sees it. It is her perception of the grange, the phenomenology of it, that we are given. Partly this is done through the images of brokenness and decay, of darkness and shadow, of emptiness and desolation, which are also the images of her mind. But partly, too, it is done through a prolonged sense of interior time. Rossetti is the poet who has made peculiarly his own the situation in which the neurasthenic hero or heroine waits in anxiety or dread for an event that is not to happen, but Tennyson has anticipated him here by building this poem out of strain, immobility, and frustration. The technical means by which this is done—chiefly the alternation of night and day, the use of verbs in the customary or habitual mode, the slight variations in the refrain which but emphasize its essential sameness, and the retardation of the meter—are deftly handled. But the chief resource in fusing subject and object is the utter absence in the poem of any guiding, organizing, or generalizing intelligence. The description consists entirely of isolated, atomistic detail.[17] In *Maud* the hero takes it as a token of madness that he focuses so obsessively upon a tiny shell, that, when Maud's brother lay dying as a result of the duel, it was not upon the tragedy of his death that he dwelt but upon the tiny ring that glinted upon his finger. Here too the moated grange does not consist for Mariana of organized interior space but of a mouse shrieking in the wainscot, of a rusted nail hanging from the gable wall, of a fly singing in the pane, even of the absence of the sound of a clinking latch. All these things did "confound her sense," but, with a genius which saw that the only possible way to culminate a poem that had to be completely static (and in conformity with what the statisticians have told us, that most suicides occur not on a gloomy

Monday morning but on a pleasant Friday afternoon), Tennyson added:

> but most she loathed the hour
> When the thick-moted sunbeams lay
> Athwart the chambers.

For in this image of dust suspended in the air we have the essence of his particularist method. *Mariana* is an extremely original poem, and in it, together with three or four poems by Coleridge, Keats, and Browning, we can see the birth of the early pre-Raphaelite method of realizing a state of consciousness through the intense use of atomistic detail.

It becomes even clearer what Tennyson has accomplished in this poem when one sees how he fell away from his achievement in *Mariana in the South*. Tennyson often wrote "pendants" to poems, and so here, having written a *Mariana* in terms of cold and wet, he thought to write another in terms of hot and dry. But he neglected to consider that, having changed the environment, he ought also to change the state of consciousness. Hot and dry is more appropriate to an oppressive emotion than to desolation. Beyond that, he failed to enter into his subject's consciousness, and although Arthur Hallam says that this was required by the essential and distinguishing conception of the poem,[18] one fails to see why it was. And finally, Tennyson has abandoned his method of minute, unrelated detail. Instead, he regularized and rationalized his poem into a well-laid-out landscape, a coherent description of the lady, and an orderly narrative moving through a single day whose stages are marked out by the moving shadow of the hour. There is also an element of religious consolation that is quite foreign to the central concept of the poem. For the first *Mariana* is totally static, ending exactly where it began except in heightened frustration. But Mariana in the South is never really desolate because she has the comfort of her Catholic religion, and at the end she escapes from her closed situation by going out onto the balcony, looking up to the heavens, and finding in Christ a Bridegroom to replace the one who had gone away. Some of this process of rationalization took place in the revision of the poem for the edition of 1842 and so illustrates the development of the "lady" poem toward the idyl, but much of it had already occurred in the text of 1832. *Mariana in the South* has its own virtues, but it is

less a variation on a theme than quite a different poem with a
similar title.

Mariana was pure image, but with *The Lady of Shalott* an element
of conscious symbolism has entered in, the key to which, according to Hallam Tennyson, is to be found in the lines, " 'I am half
sick of shadows,' said / The Lady of Shalott." To which Tennyson
is supposed to have added, "The new-born love for something,
for some one in the wide world from which she has been so long
secluded, takes her out of the region of shadows into that of
realities."[19] The authority for this statement is Canon Ainger in
his *Tennyson for the Young* (1891), but for those of us who are older
it may be difficult to believe that Lancelot and Camelot are to be
equated with reality, the isle and castle of Shalott with some
ivory-tower existence, and that there is any meaning in a curse
which would destroy the Lady for her (apparently commendable)
desire to clasp reality. Actually, when one turns to Canon Ainger's
volume, one finds that both the remark which Hallam makes on
his own and that which he attributes to his father are given by
Ainger without any indication that they come from Tennyson.[20]
Moreover, the former statement is qualified by a "perhaps" which
Hallam retained in the *Materials for the Life of A.T.*[21] but eliminated
in the *Memoir* itself, and the latter is followed by two sentences
(also retained in the *Materials*) which make the whole interpretation too palpably absurd: "The curse is the anguish of unrequited
love. The shock of her disappointment kills her."[22] Ainger was a
guest at Aldworth in 1886, but it seems unlikely that this interpretation could have come from Tennyson in this form. It is better to
leave this fine example of the intentional fallacy and look at the
poem itself.

It is apparent that the story is a version of the legend about a
fairy who falls in love with a mortal and who, in claiming him for
her own, dies. The Lady of Shalott is a "fairy" creature who lives
in a supernatural world of "magic" mirrors and "magic" webs and
whose life is governed by a mysterious "curse" conveyed to her by
a "whisper." She lives apart from the world, and her songs are
heard only by those closely associated with nature (the reapers)
and by them only at early dawn and by moonlight. She is an
elusive, secret spirit of nature, comparable to Arnold's Scholar-
Gipsy, or Lucy Gray, or Shelley's Witch of Atlas.

Lancelot, on the other hand, is presented in terms of dazzling
light and loud, clangorous noise. The sun flames upon his brazen

greaves, his shield sparkles, his gemmy bridle glitters like stars, his armor clashes as he rides, and his brow glows in the sunlight. Mythologically, he is the sun god, as the Lady is the moon goddess; he is the *vita attiva,* as she is the *vita contemplativa;* he is masculine and aggressive, riding boldly through the landscape, as she is feminine and recessive, enclosed within her tower. It would seem as if he were utterly alien from her world of silence and shadow, and this is suggested formally in the poem by the fact that the middle refrain-line of each stanza has hitherto been reserved for him and Camelot, as the last line is reserved for the Lady and her isle. But there is one image of powerful sexuality, an image which seems to be causally operative since it is repeated after the crisis,

> The helmet and the helmet-feather
> Burn'd like one burning flame together,

which suggests that, like the human lovers, union for them is possible. And so, with Lancelot compared to a "bearded meteor" flaming across the heavens,

> He flash'd into the crystal mirror,
> "Tirra lirra," by the river
> Sang Sir Lancelot,

thus intruding into her refrain as he had into her world. And in the next stanza she intrudes into his. Leaving her web and loom to look out directly upon the world, "she saw the water-lily"—image of her own recessive nature—"bloom,"

> She saw the helmet and the plume,
> *She* look'd down to Camelot.

This brings about the catastrophe:

> Out flew the web and floated wide;
> The mirror crack'd from side to side;
> "The curse is come upon me," cried
> The Lady of Shalott.

So far the story, the bare skeleton of which Tennyson derived from an Italian novella, could deal with any aspect of these two incompatible worlds. But by adding the device of the mirror, the web, and the curse, which are Tennyson's own invention, he has

made the story into a myth of the poetic imagination. The poet
cannot participate directly in reality but must view it through the
mirror of the imagination and weave it into the tapestry of his art.
The "curse" under which he lives is simply the inescapable conditions of the poet's art. It is natural that he should fret against it at
times and feel that, as in Plato's parable of the cave, he is living in a
world of shadows. But unless he wishes also to accept Plato's
theory of art, which holds that the work of art is but a copy of a
copy of reality, he will not ultimately conclude that this is true.
And indeed this is not the final conclusion of the poem. For by
violating the conditions of her art the Lady does not free herself
from shadows but rather becomes subject to the shadow of death.
And in harmony with this, part IV, which has now moved from
summer into late autumn, is conducted entirely in terms of the
grays, the pale yellows, the minor chords of that season. Neither
by turning away from her mirror and looking down at Camelot
does she see reality. Rather, with an ironic introversion, she becomes

> Like some bold seër in a trance,
> Seeing all his own mischance—
> With a glassy countenance. . . .

And finally, Lancelot's response is hardly what she would have
desired. He was evidently given pause—he "mused a little
space"—but his compliment to her beauty, "She has a lovely face,"
would have seemed trivial and misplaced to the reapers who had
heard her sing.

On the other hand, when one turns back to parts I and II and
realizes that all he has seen there he has seen through the consciousness of the Lady of Shalott—mirrored upon her mirror and
woven in her web—he realizes that, far from being a world of
shadows, this world is full of movement and variety, color and life.
Her vision, like that of the gods in Arnold's *The Strayed Reveller*, is
universal in extent. From her "four gray walls, and four gray
towers" she looks out "on either side" at the world of nature and
"up and down" the road to Camelot. Had she lived in reality she
would have been confined to one single existence, but living
vicariously in her imagination she can participate in all forms and
conditions of life. She can see heavy barges trailed by slow horses
and light shallops flitting under silken sails. As to the people, a
veritable Canterbury pilgrimage passes before her, an abbot on
his ambling pad, knights two by two, a long-haired page, damsels

glad, a curly-headed shepherd, the surly village churls, and the red cloaks of market girls. She sees a marriage and a funeral, and she sees these things at all seasons of the year. True, they may be called "shadows of the world" in the sense of being images or idealities of it, but they are not lacking in color, for they are described as crimson and red and the Lady weaves them in "colours gay." No wonder, then, that "in her web she still delights / To weave the mirror's magic sights," for we share that delight with her. "Well I remember," writes FitzGerald, "this Poem being read to me—before I knew the author—at Cambridge, one night in May 1832 or 3; and it's [sic] Images passing across my Mind, as across the Magic Mirrour, while half asleep on the Mail coach to London in the 'creeping Dawn' that followed."[23]

As the Lady of Shalott floats down the river "singing her last song," she becomes a kind of dying swan, and in the first version of the poem this image was actually used. It was a favorite with Tennyson, which he later employed of the barge carrying Arthur and the weeping queens to their home in the Great Deep and which he developed more fully in the lyric *The Dying Swan*. The value of this image is that it expresses, in its starkest form, the antithesis between art and life which is implicit in *The Lady of Shalott*. The swan sings so beautifully in death because it is pouring its whole life forces into song. Claribel, Mariana, Œnone make a song out of their sorrow, but here sorrow is the very price and condition of song. Or at least of this particular song. For, as James L. Hill has pointed out,[24] the Lady of Shalott sings two songs and so presumably represents two kinds of art. On the one hand, there is the song she sang to the reapers, which must be essentially that we hear in the first two sections of the poem. It is an art which is mimetic, pictorial, and very lovely, but, as Arnold said, it "dawdles with the painted shell." Hill calls it Apollonian in that, while beautifully ordered, it is essentially illusory, arresting life in a moment of time, not seizing on its vital process. Lancelot represents that vital process. His own song, "Tirra lirra," is a meaningless expression of pure vital energy. In response to that the Lady of Shalott grasps life but grasps death along with it, and her last song, a "carol, mournful, holy, / Chanted loudly, chanted lowly," though lacking the bright objective pictures of her former song, does express her true tragic condition. We cannot say that either song is better than the other, but they are profoundly different.

They are the same two kinds of song that Arnold speaks of in *The Strayed Reveller*, the comparable poem which stands at the forefront of his career. The Reveller, it will be recalled, distinguishes between the Apollonian poetry of the gods, serene, objective, detached, and the more inward and tormented poetry which alone is open to man. Modern man, in Arnold's view, can only deal with the tragic condition of life, but in order to do this he must enter imaginatively into his subject and suffer with it—"such a price / The Gods exact for song: / To become what we sing." Arnold's problem is how to combine the inward tragic vision of the Romantic poet with the serene objectivity of the classics, and he does this by adopting a quasi-dandaical, quasi-stoical stance which is essentially that of the Parnassians.[25] Tennyson, however, is not looking in this direction. For Tennyson the serene poetry of the gods is possible so long as one does not look down to Camelot, and, on the other hand, the tormented poetry of the moderns is necessary only after one has. The question is, of course, what it means to look down to Camelot and whether this is inevitable. Arnold, writing in 1849, assumes that it is; Tennyson prior to 1832 hopes that it is not. Tennyson does not wish to participate directly in human life but to participate indirectly in it by means of his poetry. And this he seems to be denied—or so the reiterated image of the isolated maiden suggests. But there is another element to this image and that is the auditor, the person who hears the song, for his reaction to it is essential to the meaning of the poem as a whole.

Lancelot, as we have already seen, "mused a little space." This, however, was in the second version of the poem, which is marked by much more dignity and awe than the first. In the first version the knights and minstrels who viewed the dead body of the Lady of Shalott were described as "the well-fed wits of Camelot," and they were "puzzled" rather than being afraid. But in 1842 all this was changed. The sound of revelry died upon their lips and they "cross'd themselves for fear." They clearly recognized that the Lady was a visitant from a world they did not understand—a world of the sacred, the divine, the magical. Lancelot's response is less adequate, but the poetic associations of "mused" suggest that he may have been affected more deeply than he knew. One imagines that he will hardly ride out again the very next day singing "Tirra lirra," and it is just possible that the seeds of some permanent change have been sown. On the other hand, the historical legend says not. At the time that Tennyson composed *The Lady of Shalott* he planned and partly composed a comic counterpart to it, in which Sir Lancelot would sing a loose song and be rebuked for it by Sir Galahad.[26] But he abandoned the plan, partly, perhaps, because it would have closed down the marvelous "open" ending of the revised version of *The Lady of Shalott*.

The situation is even more complicated in *The Hesperides*. The work is another myth of the poetic imagination, for the golden apples, which are "the treasure / Of the wisdom of the West," "the ancient secret," represent an arcane poetic knowledge that is guarded by Hesperus, the dragon, and the three Hesperides. The function of Hesperus is to watch, the function of the dragon is to guard, and the function of the Hesperides is to sing and keep the dragon awake, for "he is older than the world" and "his ancient heart is drunk with overwatchings." Thus, taken together, they constitute a golden chain of five links. "Five and three / (Let it not be preached abroad) make an awful mystery," for the chain extends from the heavens to the redcombed dragon, who, without being evil, is clearly associated with the old serpent. But in this instance the middle links of poesy are the most important, for it is through their "threefold music," corresponding to the blossom, bole, and root of the tree, that the sap will be drawn up from its dark sources in the root till it issues, honey sweet and liquid gold, in the blossom and fruit. And what is more, it is by their singing that the apples will be saved.

> If ye sing not, if ye make false measure,
> We shall lose eternal pleasure,
> Worth eternal want of rest.

Thus, the song which they are actually singing is a mystic incantation designed at once to bring poetic knowledge into being and to protect it against the profane ones who would destroy it.

Among these is "one from the East" who is coming to take the apples away. It is, of course, Hercules, who, according to one version of the myth, is to accomplish this labor by slaying the dragon and, according to another, by outwitting Atlas. But the point here is that he comes from the East, for in this poem the East-West dichotomy, reversing the usual values associated with Eastern and Western civilization, represents the antagonism between the active and the contemplative life. The warm sea breeze and the yellow light of the setting sun will ripen the apples, but the cold light of the dawn and the land wind would blight them. "Hesper hateth Phosphor, evening hateth morn." Tennyson has set his island off the west coast of Africa in tropical latitudes, and it constitutes a terrestrial paradise which loves secrecy and isolation, quietude and rest. Its enemy is struggle and conflict, the rise and fall of empires ("old Himala weakens, Caucasus is bold and strong"), and the eternal wandering over land and sea that Hercules represents.

This thematic conflict has been well analyzed by several critics, but the question that has not been clearly faced is why the Hesperides, those lovely representatives of an arcane poetic knowledge, are allowed to assume without censure an attitude which we condemn in the inhabitant of the Palace of Art. "All good things are in the west," they say, and "Hoarded wisdom brings delight." The "ancient secret" must not be revealed, for if it were, "the old wound of the world" would be healed. Why the old wound of the world should not be healed we are inclined to wonder, for as it is, "the world is wasted with fire and sword." But the answer is, "If the golden apple be taken, / The world will be overwise." It will, in other words, become one with the gods, for the original meaning of this myth, as H. J. Rose tells us,[27] is that the apples are the fruit of the Tree of Life, which confers immortality. Indeed, according to Apollodorus, after Hercules gave the apples to Eurystheus, he gave them back to Hercules, "from whom Athena got them and conveyed them back again [to the Hesperides]; for it was not lawful that they should be laid down anywhere."[28] They were too sacred for human disposition, for they were an esoteric wisdom appropriate to the gods. If man were ever to acquire such wisdom, he could transform his world into an island paradise and live without suffering and toil. But then he would not be man—he could not participate in the restless, striving existence which is typified by Hercules and is all we know on this earth.

Doubtless in some sense the apples are meant to be stolen and their virtue communicated to man. But how this can be done without destroying the apples and without man's becoming one with the gods—that is the question. An answer is perhaps provided by another heroic wanderer, Hanno the Carthaginian, who is also coming from the East and who corresponds more nearly than Hercules to the Lancelot-figure of the poem. For Tennyson makes Hanno the auditor of the Hesperides' song and places him in a brief blank-verse introduction, or frame, which, in its even measure and long, suspended periods, contrasts sharply with the irregularly cadenced, intricately rhymed lines of the "song." It is to this lyrical medium as prose to poetry, history to myth, or reality to art. It consists of a single long sentence which, by its syntactical structure, emphasizes the heroic intrepidity of one who sailed *beyond* Soloë, *past* Thymiaterion, *between* the Horns, "till he reached the outer sea." Also, he did not hear the natural music of the nightingale or the artificial tones of the Lybian lotos flute, but

> Beneath a highland leaning down a weight
> Of cliffs, and zoned below with cedar shade
> Came voices, like the voices in a dream,
> Continuous, till he reached the outer sea.

His reaction is as enigmatic as Lancelot's. Whether the voices moved him much or little we cannot say. All we can say is that he heard them, lived in them a little, and then sailed on. It will be apparent that by this oblique poetic device Tennyson is attempting something that was accomplished in a very different way by the Romantic poets. They too were concerned with the kind of visionary experience which is the arcane knowledge of the Hesperides, but they explored it through a meditative poem in which the unifying imagination of the poet mediated between the visionary and the phenomenal realm. At first sight Tennyson has radically disjoined these, moving toward symbolism by placing song in the objective symbolic figures of the Hesperides and isolating them from the experiential world of Hanno. But Hanno heard the song. Coming to him "like voices in a dream," it evidently corresponded to something in his dream. Indeed, one could speculate that he had dreamed the whole, and that he and not the Hesperides is the poet in the poem. This is the fascination of the device; we do not know. In this and other poems Tennyson has developed a method for mediating between history and myth, the visionary and the real, but it is not the unitary method of the swift imaginative leap. It is rather the much more problematic one of the power of song to operate upon the hearer and absorb him into its world.

One may see the transition to this method if one compares the companion poems *The Merman* and *The Mermaid* with *The Sea-Fairies*. Both are closely related to *The Hesperides* in that they present a vision of the joyous supernatural life of creatures of the sea, and both have some kind of introduction. That of *The Sea-Fairies* is very close in form and mood to the narrative of Hanno. It is in blank verse and emphasizes the weariness of the mariners—"Slow sailed the weary mariners"—and also the erotic beauty of the Sea-Fairies, with "rounded arms, and bosoms prest / To little harps of gold." From them the mariners heard "Shrill music . . . on the middle sea," and their reaction was exactly that of Lancelot and his companions: "They mused, / Whispering to each other half in fear." Of course, the "Song" of the Sea-Fairies, in rhymed, anapestic lines of varying length, is very different in content from that of the Hesperides or the songs of the Lady of Shalott. It invites the mariners to furl their sails and live with them in "the high green field, and the happy blossoming shore." But once again there is no indication whether they did. There is only the statement that weary mariners, toiling over the middle sea, heard a song of strange, disturbing power, but how they acted or how one ought to act we are not told.

In *The Merman* and *The Mermaid* the situation is a little different. True, both poems are again given up to a vision of the joyous undersea life of these legendary creatures. The Merman sees himself as frolicking with the mermaids and kissing them merrily, while the Mermaid, a little more skittish, sees herself as frolicking indeed, but not being kissed by all the mermen and marrying only the king of the sea. Because the poems are in the first person and are in a lyrical form comparable to the Songs of the Sea-Fairies and the Hesperides and the Chorus of the Lotos-Eaters, the average reader probably has a vague impression that they are spoken by the Merman and Mermaid themselves. But it is not so. They are spoken by someone who "would be" a merman or a mermaid. The entire poems are in the optative mood and are in answer to questions asked in the introductory stanzas, which again are in sharply contrasting meter. "Who would be / A merman bold [or 'mermaid fair']," is the question, to which the answer comes, "I would be / A merman bold," and so on into the description until we are almost convinced that it is the Merman or Mermaid speaking. But all is fantasy, all is unreal. Indeed, the poems have the aspect of the kind of literary parlor game which the Tennyson children might have played at Somersby, in which it would be the task of one person to ask the question, Who would be a pirate bold, or knight at arms, or some other romantic figure, and it would then be the task of another person to describe these figures as imaginatively as he could. Whether or not this is the origin of the poems, the situation is purely imaginary, and yet, unlike the romantic ode, the ascent into imaginative experience is by means of dialogue, not monologue, leading from the real world of the parlor into the imaginative realm of the sea. So

Hanno and the weary mariners might have asked themselves such
questions and received such answers. But with them imagination
has been objectified into myth. Nevertheless, in neither case is
there any attempt to minimize the fact that the response is art.
The "Songs" of the Sea-Fairies and the Hesperides and the
"Choric Song" of the Lotos-Eaters are formally so labeled, and the
fantasy of being a Merman or a Mermaid is distinguished as
fantasy by its own poetic structure. It is the more clearly so by
being repeated, once in the masculine and once in the feminine
gender, like Mariana in the North and South.

The structure of *The Lotos-Eaters* differs from that of *The Hesperides* and *The Sea-Fairies* in that the introduction is no longer so
sharply distinguished from the song that follows. Whereas in the
latter poems the introduction was in a heroic mode which contrasted with the highly lyrical measure of the song, the introduction of *The Lotos-Eaters* is in a Spenserian stanza which is quite as
lazy and indolent as the long, loping strophes that follow. The
reason for this is that the mariners are now both the singers and
the auditors of their song. The title *The Lotos-Eaters* is ambiguous.
They are the pale natives who swim out around the keel of the
vessel, bringing the enchanted fruit, but once the mariners receive and eat it, they become Lotos-Eaters too and so give voice to
the spirit of the isle. In the first line of their song they say, "There
is sweet music here," but it is notable that in the introduction the
only music they hear is that of their own beating hearts. They are,
indeed, temperamentally Lotos-Eaters when they first arrive, and
this is symbolized by the fact that they seem to approach the isle
from the West, not the East, and sit down between the full-faced
moon, which is the recessive but dominant body in this isle, and
the setting sun. Thus, the functions of introduction and song are
reversed in that the former is primarily concerned with the seduc-
tions of the isle and only the latter describes (unfavorably) the
rigors of the voyage. In other words, what we have here is visitors
from the West who do not sail sternly by or steal the apples, as
they do in *The Hesperides*, but settle down and eat the apples and
join with the natives in their song. The principle that the singers
should be feminine has not been breached because they have been
made effeminate by their act.

One may say that the isle of the Lotos-Eaters is a very different
place from that of the Hesperides, and it is true that we have
hitherto ignored the values attached to these isles and that that is a

complex and important question. I used to consider it a useful
exercise to ask my undergraduates to indicate how the condemnation of the life of the Lotos-Eaters (if such it is) is built into the
very language of the poem, and they used to point to the opening
word, "Courage!" which establishes the moral context within
which the action is to be judged, to the symbolic topography of the
isle, as it has already been described, to a certain element of excess
in the language of the poem which condemns itself, to a languor
and weariness in the rhythms and a too frequent use of the word
seems, to the slowly increasing length of the stanzas, as if one were
sinking lower and lower into lethargy, to the alternation of stanzas
about the sweetness of the isle with those on the harshness of the
world, so that both realms are kept fluctuating before us, to the
fact that ultimately it is Death rather than Life that the mariners
long for, and, most important of all, to the fact that they appeal to
the careless life of nature and the careless life of the gods but to no
human precedent. They wish to be vegetables or they wish to be
divine, they do not wish to be human, and this, of course, is what is
incorrect, if not morally wrong, about their position. This, I say, is
how my undergraduates used to reply, but in recent years so
many of them have themselves eaten of the enchanted fruit and
opted for the life of the Lotos-Eaters that, though I still consider
this to be the right "human" reading of the poem—the right
reading in terms of the values of Western (in the usual sense)
civilization—these values have so strenuously been called in question that I cannot be quite certain that that is the only reading of
the poem or even that Tennyson would, at all moments of his life,
have so read it. For one notices, first of all, that the long passage
about the Epicurean gods, which, with its stock unfavorable associations, is the "giveaway" of the poem, was not present in the
1832 version. In that version, too, as Alan Grob has pointed out,[29]
the lotos flower grows not only in the valley but also on "the
ancient heights divine," which are described in language remark-
ably close to that used of the source of poetic inspiration in *The
Poet's Mind.* It is clear that here at least the lotos is a sacred plant,
as sacred as the apples of the Hesperides, and, on the other hand,
the Hesperides have the same air of afternoon indolence as the
island of the Lotos-Eaters. Moreover, the "mild-minded Melancholy" that Tennyson attributes to the Lotos-Eaters he also attributes, in a contemporary sonnet,[30] to the valley where "first I told
my love," which is not at all a Bower of Bliss but a pure Garden of
Adonis.

Furthermore, we know that in his own life Tennyson was powerfully drawn to tropical vegetation. He was quite annoyed with Sir John Simeon for not having told him in time that he was going to winter in Madeira, so that he could have gone with him;[31] and when Thomas Woolner, the sculptor, emigrated to Australia, Rossetti said that "the great Alfred even declares that were it not for Mrs. T. he should go himself."[32] "In my old age," Tennyson told Carlyle, "I should like to get away from all this tumult and turmoil of civilization and live on the top of a tropical mountain! I should at least like to see the splendours of the Brazilian forests before I die."[33] He did see them in his imagination. Once when he was so injudicious as to follow FitzGerald into a vegetarian diet and finally broke it with a mutton chop, "I never," he says, "felt such joy in the blood. When I went to sleep, I dreamt that I saw the vines of the South with huge Eschol branches trailing over the glaciers of the North."[34] On the other hand, his attempt to stimulate the imagination of the aging Wordsworth was unsuccessful. On a visit in 1842, feeling the coldness of the old poet, he told him of "a tropical island where the trees, when they first came into leaf, were a vivid scarlet;—'Every one of them,' I told him, 'one flush all over the island, the colour of blood!' It would not do, I could not inflame his imagination in the least!"[35]

There is no question, then, but that tropical vegetation was associated by Tennyson with a luxuriant imagination, and if it does not have a perfectly constant value in all of Tennyson's poems, it is partly because rugged seafarers like Odysseus have no business pausing there too long. It is not equally good for all types of people. Moreover, categories like "good" and "bad" simply do not apply to the sacred, which is both demonic and divine. One may see this in the delightful, if somewhat topsy-turvy, poem, *The Kraken*. It is clear that this wondrous sea monster, who lives a silent, vegetative life "far, far beneath in the abysmal sea," is connected with the old serpent, for when

> the latter fire shall heat the deep;
> Then once by man and angels to be seen,
> In roaring he shall rise and on the surface die.

But we are so attracted by the faint sunlight playing along his shadowy sides, by the enormous polypi and "huge sponges of millennial growth" with which he lives, that when the fires disturb his "ancient, dreamless, uninvaded sleep," we think it an impertinence. Who are these men and angels in their narrow religiosity to flush out so kindly a monster from his home beneath the sea? Clearly, as he goes roaring to the surface he is a kind of subaqueous dying swan, and one may be sure that those who hear him, though touched perhaps with awe, are no more impressed than Lancelot and the well-fed wits of Camelot. It is great testimony to the power of poetic structures that Tennyson can take apocalyptic materials, which five years before he would have used conventionally, and reverse them so that the Kraken becomes an analogue of the Lady of Shalott.

Perhaps the least ambiguous of all these poems is *Anacaona,* a poem which Tennyson's Cambridge friends all admired but which he did not publish because he was not sure of the vegetation. He had never seen Haiti but had merely read about it in Washington Irving's *Life of Columbus* (1828). There he learned of a dark Indian maiden, the queen of Xaragua, whom he could use as a symbol of the poet not only because she danced and sang the traditional areytos, or ballads, of her people but also because her name and that of her country were so melodious that Tennyson, weaving them into his rhymes, could make it seem as if she and her island were of music all compact. To the Spaniards, too, Irving said, the island "seemed to realise their ideas of a terrestrial paradise."[36] The natives, who were without clothing, hardly gave themselves the trouble to cultivate the yucca root, the maize, and the sweet potato, which formed their main articles of food, and they loitered their time away under the shade of their trees, dancing and singing. "In fact," says Irving,

> they were destitute of all powerful motives to toil, being free from most of those wants which doom mankind, in civilized life, and in less genial climes, to incessant labour. In the soft region of the vega, the circling seasons brought each its store of fruits, and while some were gathered in full maturity, others were ripening on the boughs, and buds and blossoms gave promise of still succeeding abundance. What need was there of garnering up and anxiously providing for coming days, to men who lived amid a perpetual harvest? What need, too, of toilfully spinning or labouring at the loom, where a genial temperature prevailed throughout the year, and neither nature nor custom prescribed the necessity of clothing?[37]

The questions, and indeed the very accents, are those of the Lotos-Eaters, but the only misfortune here is that it cannot last. Tragically, the Spaniards killed Anacaona and subjugated her people.

> The pleasant life of the island was at an end;—the dream in the shade by day; the slumber, during the sultry noontide heat, by the fountain or the stream, or under the spreading palm tree; and the song, the dance, and the game in the mellow evening, when summoned to their simple amusements by the rude Indian drum. Or, if they occasionally indulged in a national dance, after a day of painful toil, the ballads to which they kept time were of a melancholy and plaintive character. They spoke of the times that were past, before the white men had introduced sorrow, and slavery, and weary labour among them.[38]

"What an example of human and civilized depravity is the ruin and desolation of these lovely spots by the Spaniards!" exclaimed Henry Alford, Tennyson's friend and fellow Apostle, who was reading Irving's work at the same time as Tennyson.[39] Timbuctoo had evaporated before keen Discovery because it never was more than a legend, but here was a genuine paradise, the very haunt of music and poetry, which was crushed by a cruel and oppressive civilization.

If one were to range the auditors of song on some kind of scale according to their response, the lowest would certainly be the Spaniards. How Claribel died and by whose hand we do not know, but the harsh and puritanical Angelo, the abandoner of Mariana, would be next, or perhaps his fellows in heaven who stoked the fires for the Kraken. Then would come the faithless Paris, the betrayer of Œnone, and after him Lancelot, who simply did not listen, did not think. Next would be the mariners who "mused / Whispering to each other half in fear," and after them Hanno, who listened though he could not linger. With the Lotos-Eaters it is doubtful if they were right to linger, but it is better to linger a little than never to have gone ashore. Only in *The Dying Swan* does poetry get a favorable response, and even there it is curiously ambiguous, for it is only by way of metaphor.

The dying swan, in the poem of that name, did not live in a tropical bower but in a northern waste. Nevertheless, when she poured out her life forces in song, her "death-hymn took the

soul / Of that waste place with joy / Hidden in sorrow." It began
low,

> But anon her awful jubilant voice,
> With a music strange and manifold,
> Flow'd forth on a carol free and bold;
> As when—

and now comes the metaphor;

> As when a mighty people rejoice
> With shawms, and with cymbals, and harps of gold,
> And the tumult of their acclaim is roll'd
> Thro' the open gates of the city afar,
> To the shepherd who watcheth the evening star.

If the poem stopped here, it would be clear that the preceding
lines were simply an image describing the swan's song. But they
continue by saying that the creeping mosses and weeds, the willow
branches hoar and dank, the soughing reeds, and indeed all the
desolate scene that has been described in the opening two stanzas
of the poem "Were flooded over with eddying song." Was it the
song of the rejoicing people which rolled out through the open
gates, or was it the song of the swan? In truth, it was both, for the
swan by its song transformed the waste into a rejoicing city, and
this is what Tennyson and the Apostles wanted poetry to do.

4

"O Civic Muse"

We held debate, a band
Of youthful friends, on mind and art,
And labour, and the changing mart,
And all the framework of the land.
In Memoriam

The Apostles, or to give them their full name, the Cambridge
Conversazione Society, was founded in 1820 by a group of undergraduates who deplored the narrowness of the university curriculum and determined to explore for themselves the wealth of
contemporary literature, philosophy, politics, and theology. They
met every Saturday evening in the rooms of one of the members
and took turns reading essays on subjects of their own choosing.
"Have Shelley's poems an immoral tendency?" "Is an intelligible
First Cause deducible from the phenomena of the Universe?" "Is
there any rule of moral action beyond general expediency?" A
lively discussion followed—wise, eloquent, or preposterous, as the
case might be—and then there was a vote. (Tennyson voted No on
the first two, Yes on the third.)[1] No subjects were debarred from
discussion, and absolute freedom of speech was the rule. Though
some members were pietistic and others facetious, the prevailing
mood was that of a serene and high-minded idealism established
by their spiritual founders, Frederick Denison Maurice and John
Sterling. Ultimately, their patron saint was Coleridge. As with
Coleridge, it is difficult to say whether they were radical or
conservative—conservative where spiritual values were concerned
but often radical as to moribund political institutions. They would
have purified religion of its outworn creeds, but only to add
fervor and depth to religious feeling. They were in favor of the
Anti-Slavery Convention and generally, though somewhat hesi-
tantly, of parliamentary reform. They were rather more receptive
to revolutions abroad than to those at home. Indeed, during the
disturbances of 1830 they found themselves in the painful position of deeply sympathizing with the plight of the poor but not
knowing quite what to do about it.[2] They decisively rejected the

method of Bentham and the elder Mill, they drew back with loathing from Paine and the Saint-Simonians, and yet they could not stomach the cold apologetic of Paley. They were thus thrown back upon poetry, which, in their view, was to be the chief instrument of moral good. For this they made exalted claims. Indeed, their name, the Apostles, was given them in banter, partly because they were usually about twelve in number but also because they acknowledged a mission, as Merivale put it, "to interpret the oracles of transcendental wisdom to the world of Philistines or Stumpfs."[3] Among these oracles were Niebuhr, the Roman historian, "who for a lengthy period formed all their sentiments";[4] Plato and Bacon; Dante, Shakespeare, and Calderón; and all the English Romantic poets except Byron. Coleridge's *Aids to Reflection* was perhaps their Bible, but in the period 1829–30 it was Shelley who spoke to them most immediately and directly.

There are two passages in Shelley that may be taken to represent the two conceptions of the poet which are dominant in Tennyson's verse at this time.[5] On the one hand, the lines from *To a Skylark:*

> Like a Poet hidden
>   In the light of thought,
> Singing hymns unbidden,
>   Till the world is wrought
> To sympathy with hopes and fears it heeded not:
>
> Like a high-born maiden
>   In a palace-tower,
> Soothing her love-laden
>   Soul in secret hour
> With music sweet as love, which overflows her bower.

This is the conception which has been developed in the last chapter. On the other hand, in the *Ode to the West Wind* we read:

> Be thou, Spirit fierce,
> My spirit! Be thou me, impetuous one!
>
> Drive my dead thoughts over the universe
> Like withered leaves to quicken a new birth!
> And, by the incantation of this verse,

> Scatter, as from an unextinguished hearth
> Ashes and sparks, my words among mankind!
> Be through my lips to unawakened earth
>
> The trumpet of a prophecy! O, Wind,
> If Winter comes, can Spring be far behind?

So Tennyson and his friends, when they too felt chained by "the heavy weight of hours" and felt that a poet singing hymns unbidden never would win the sympathy of the world, were sometimes drawn to this second conception of the poet, not as a feminine figure immured within her bower but as a masculine figure acting upon the world. Where the image of *To a Skylark* is circumscribed and enclosed, that of the *Ode to the West Wind* is linear and open, moving through the world with the boldness, the energy, the vital power of Lancelot himself. "The present race of monstrous opinions and feelings," wrote J. W. Blakesley, one of the Apostles, to Tennyson in 1830, ". . . require the arm of a strong Iconoclast. A volume of poetry written in a proper spirit, a spirit like that which a vigorous mind indues by the study of Wordsworth and Shelley, would be, at the present juncture, the greatest benefit the world would receive."[6] Already in 1828 Tennyson had written two poems in this spirit, in one of which, entitled *To Poesy,* Mind's "trumpet-tongued, aërial melody" was to blow alarum and "startle the dull ears of human kind," so that Poesy might "bind / Falsehood beneath the altar of great Truth." In the other, identical in title and written in collaboration with Hallam, Religion was to be the sword of Poesy and the poet himself was to be her arrow, which like Shelley's words was to be "not of viewless flight, but trailing flame," so that Poesy might go forth and possess the land. Turgid as these sonnets are, they are not so grotesque as the much more famous and frequently anthologized piece, *The Poet,* published in 1830.

The poet of this work might easily be mistaken for one of the apocalyptic figures of *Armageddon* or *Timbuctoo,* for he too in a golden clime was born and saw through life and death and his own soul. Apparently, he even stood on Mt. Calpe. But whereas his predecessors simply saw and spoke, he shot arrows—and to trace the course of these arrows is not easy. Initially they are the "viewless arrows of his thoughts," though paradoxically headed and winged with flame, but then they are compared to Indian reeds shot from a blowgun, and these reeds, in turn, to the "arrow-seeds" of the dandelion. The seeds, taking root, then grow up into adult flowers and send forth further "winged shafts of truth" till all the world "like one great garden" glowed. One recognizes, of course, that Tennyson's associations with dandelions were not those of the modern American homeowner, but still the idea of the entire world being covered by this plant is not a pleasant one. Fortunately, the dandelions so glow that they soon turn into a sunrise, and in the sunrise "Freedom rear'd . . . / Her beautiful bold brow." The beauty of that brow is not enhanced, however, by the fact that "round about the circles of . . . her keen eyes" the word WISDOM was traced in flame—as it also was on the hem of her garment. Finally, the most remarkable fact about her is that when she spoke, "as the lightning to the thunder / Which follows it, . . . / So was their meaning to her words"—that is, the meaning preceded the words. This may be what Tennyson meant, but so mixed are the metaphors that one hardly thinks he knew what he meant. He knew he wanted the world to be one garden, and apparently he momentarily believed that if people would not come into the garden in response to his singing, he would force it upon them by shooting arrows which would turn into dandelions.

The "arrows" which he chose took the form of sonnets, because this was the form that Wordsworth and Milton had used before him. Two he launched against the Russian czar, who had just savagely repressed the Polish people's bid for freedom, one against Bonaparte, one against the authorities at Cambridge, and two against the "brass-mouthed demagogues," O'Connell and Hume.[7] But in another sonnet he conceded that although "nothing is so swift as liberty / Linked to the thunderbolt of ruining thought,"[8] still some nations are so remote that the "lamps of song" have not yet risen among them. For them Love is available and will accomplish the same end as is achieved for the more civilized nations by poetry.

It appears that Tennyson was counseled not to despair by his friend James Spedding. Spedding, an Apostle whose stately "dome," as his bald cranium was affectionately called by his friends, was thought to be the repository of much wisdom, gave a Commemoration Day oration at Trinity in December 1830 which he later published as a pamphlet under the title, *Apology for the Moral and Literary Character of the XIXth Century*. The future editor of Bacon began by saying that we should not become unduly critical of our own age because it does not readily acknowledge its great poets and philosophers but should recognize that it takes time for originality to come into its own. This was true even in the great age of Elizabeth. Moreover, modern poetry, which is primarily a "poetry of reflection," is peculiarly difficult, and therefore it is not to be wondered at that original geniuses "are for a while strangers in their own country—for how should it be otherwise?—till at length some man is attracted, either by the peculiar insight of a congenial spirit, or, which is oftener the case, by accident, to a more careful and reverent examination." He may then come to appreciate genius more fully, but he may also forget how long it took him. So "when we hear one of the chosen spirits of this our day (whose light we have been so favoured as to see and comprehend) slighted or sneered at as a mystic [cf. Tennyson's *The Mystic*] or an enthusiast, we shall learn from this not to rail at the latterness of the times on which we have fallen; but rather to remember how that which is very high is not easily attained to."[9]

Tennyson endeavored to take this counsel to heart by using as the introductory sonnet of his new volume, *Poems* (1832), a work very different from *The Poet*. In *Mine be the strength of spirit, full and free,* he returned to his earlier image of the river rushing down from its fount on high and, as it flows into the "green salt sea," keeping its "blue waters fresh for many a mile." So its purity would be maintained among the critics. But then in the sestet he added:

> Mine be the power which ever to its sway
> Will win the wise at once, and by degrees
> May into uncongenial spirits flow;
> Even as the warm gulf-stream of Florida
> Floats far away into the Northern seas
> The lavish growths of southern Mexico.

Christopher Ricks has noted that Tennyson's image of the Gulf Stream carrying the tropical vegetation of the Caribbean into the North Atlantic probably comes from the same *Life of Columbus* which had furnished Tennyson with the materials of *Anacaona*. Thus, instead of imposing a garden upon the world by shooting his readers with flame-tipped arrows, Tennyson now steals insensibly into their hearts, warming, thawing, relaxing—hoping to win them to beauty. It is a process he illustrates at length in a contemporaneous and very lovely poem, *The Progress of Spring*.

"Fair Spring," like the Gulf Stream, "slides hither o'er the Southern sea." Speaking of her own life, she breathes, "On a tropic mountain was I born." However, rather than linger there alone, she "drank the dews and drizzle of the North, / That I might mix with men." The poem, describing her slow progress across the zones of earth, thinning the icicle, plumping the bud, stealing across hamlet and field, is a beautiful illustration of its own message. But the poet would have this message learned of man. "A simpler, saner lesson might he learn / Who reads thy gradual progress, Holy Spring," that of abandoning the clash of warring wills for the slow, gradual realization of Life itself.

But we are getting ahead of our story, for the Apostles are not ready yet for that wise and temperate gradualism which was to flower in Tennyson's political poems of 1831–34. They have yet the Spanish revolutionists to free from their masters the Bourbons, and Tennyson has *The Palace of Art* and *Œnone* to write.

"Tennyson, we cannot live in art." Such was the remark which Richard Chenevix Trench, later archbishop of Dublin, made to Tennyson when they were at Trinity together and which, according to the poet, was the inspiration of *The Palace of Art*.[10] It is usually assumed that Trench intended the remark as a kind of rebuke to Tennyson for the presumed aestheticism of his 1830 volume and that Tennyson, accepting the rebuke, sharply changed his course and wrote *The Palace of Art*. By this interpretation *The Palace of Art* is in some degree a palinode or recantation. If one asks, however, under what circumstances the remark was originally made, one finds that Trench had himself in mind much more than Tennyson, whose poems he had probably never read at the time, and that Tennyson would have been surprised to discover that he had written a palinode.

For it so happens that Trench was himself something of an aesthete in his undergraduate years. Introduced into the Apostles by Maurice and Sterling, he found his life primarily among the members of that group and derived little benefit from the regular studies of the place. He was interested chiefly in poetry, especially Spanish poetry, which he hoped to translate into English. Leaving Cambridge in February 1829, he traveled to Spain, where he hoped to pursue his literary studies, but he soon found himself caught up in the political situation. Six years before, the Bourbon monarch, Ferdinand VII, had been restored to absolute power by the French army and after a period of indecision had come down more and more on the side of repression. A group of liberals, about two hundred in number, had tried to secure from the king acceptance of a constitution, but they had ultimately been denied and forced to leave the country. These "Constitutionals," as they were called, came to England as political exiles and there attracted a great deal of attention.[11] Maurice and Sterling campaigned in their behalf in the *Athenaeum,* and Trench contributed two sonnets to their support. Now, witnessing the situation at first hand, he gradually lost faith in his literary projects and, sick at heart at the misery of the Spanish people, went to Italy to join his father and brother.[12] There, sometime in the winter or early spring of 1830 he suffered his version of the Victorian spiritual crisis.

To understand it we must go back a little and explore some of the other matters that had been occupying Trench's mind. Though as an undergraduate his interests had been primarily literary, he was not unaware of the dangers of relativism and solipsism in a purely philosophical culture. Sterling, for instance, had come back from a trip to France alarmed at the miserable condition of religion and the arts in that country. "The most melancholy circumstance of all," he wrote to Trench on November 21, 1828, "is that the best school of French thinkers . . . are not at all inclined to do more than treat Christianity as a highly respectable form of the 'religious idea,' without having in general a notion that it should be made a matter of personal concern to every man. The continental philosophy of the eighteenth century undervalued Christianity because it looked at all religions with equal contempt. The continental philosophy of the nineteenth century undervalues it because it looks at all with equal respect, and is as far in the one case as in the other from comprehending rightly the wants of the individual mind. Cousin makes it the peculiar glory of our epoch that it endeavours to comprehend the mind of all other ages. And I fear it must be the tendency of his philosophy, while it examines what all other philosophies were, to prevent us being anything outselves."[13] The following July, writing to Trench in Spain, he added, "I am more and more convinced that Goethe rescues the individual from contending passions, not to animate it with new life, but to bury it amid the pomps and beneath the mausoleum of art."[14] Trench was so impressed by Sterling's remarks that, more than a year later, when he writing to Kemble from Florence and inquiring about his plans to go to Germany to study, he asked, "Is German literature good for the inner man? You are not cosmopolitizing, I am sure; if as Englishmen we include anything, we must exclude much more. They seem rather to look on Christianity as the best form of the religious idea, than as having anything to do with the individual's wants. They would receive Christianity somewhat after the fashion that the Roman emperor proposed to receive the statue of its founder—as one among the gods of a peopled Pantheon."[15] We recall that in *The Palace of Art* Christianity was simply one among the "legends fair" that adorned the Palace, and that the inhabitant of the Palace dwelt apart, "holding no form of creed, / But contemplating all." In this same letter Trench alludes to his own crisis: "For myself, I have been but a recreant knight from Poesy and all good. Ill health, and low spirits, partly its consequence and partly that of solitude, were strong against me during much of my residence in Spain. However, when I had been almost driven to the extreme edge, I took heart, and turning on my pursuers, stood at bay, and they fled directly; 'and I again am strong,' and, almost for the first time in my life, earnest."[16] The importance of being earnest Trench had learned, but not yet what to be earnest about. This he would learn in Rome, whither he now proceeded with his brother and father.

In Rome he met Joseph Severn, the friend of Keats, who told him that Keats had died a terrible death, deprived of his belief in Christianity by Hunt and Shelley. He then fell in with a group of artists whose views he found intensely interesting but whose morality, especially with regard to sex, was far from satisfactory. He wrote a sonnet on the subject, beginning, "What is thy worship but a vain pretence, / Spirit of Beauty," if those who tend thy altars remain selfish and find in their ministrations no defense from "Life's sordid stain." He is "Vexed that my soul should ever moved have been / By that which has such feigning at the heart."[17]

As a result, though living in the very city of art, he had no appetite for its treasures, and he tells us that he either wandered alone through its ruins or sat up late at night debating with his artist friends the evil of the world. Like the Soul in *The Palace of Art,* on whom "Full oft the riddle of the painful earth / Flash'd . . . as she sat alone," Trench at this time was deeply impressed with the parable of the Sphinx—one must either solve the riddle of life or be destroyed by its propounder. Ultimately, the riddle was solved for him in a dramatic conversion that he experienced as he traveled south, probably at Paestum or at Agrigentum on the south coast of Sicily.[18] For in *The Story of Justin Martyr*, Trench's first published poem, he tells us that he wandered forth one morning amid a ruin where two solitary pillars stood on a hillside. A little distance away another was fallen. In deep despair he thought, this pillar the hand of man might raise again but who will raise the fallen spirit? At that moment he heard a voice and, looking up, saw an old man, the counterpart of Wordsworth's Leech-gatherer, to whom he told his story. He said that in his youth he had pursued beauty exclusively and wished "to dwell alone, / My spirit on its lordly throne,"[19] but now beauty had failed him. The old man replied that he had not erred in seeking a higher life than that of most men but only in thinking to find the root of good in his own heart. It was to be found only in God. As the youth returned home through the evening, his heart filled with the promise of the Christian faith, it seemed to him as if the fallen temple had been raised and stood all perfect as before— nay, was transfigured by the setting sun into the very image of the Heavenly City.

Trench's illness, his desolation, and his travels in Italy and Sicily remind us very much of Newman's Sicilian experience just three years later, and just as Newman was very eager to get home because, as he cried out in his illness, "I have a work to do," so too was Trench. He had been receiving letters from his friends at home telling him about the flourishing state of the Apostles. On January 24, 1830, J. W. Blakesley had written:

> You ought to come home. . . . We have a handful of men in Cambridge who will continue the race of the Maurices and Sterlings, and cherish an untiring faith in the undefeated energies of man. The majority of the Apostolics are decidedly of the proper way of thinking, and the society is in a flourishing state. We are now twelve in number, and those whom we shall lose this Christmas are by no means the best. I think that we are now in a better state, and that the tone of our debates is higher than it ever has been since the giants were on the earth.[20]

A little later in the same letter he adds, "The Society has received a great addition in Hallam and in Alfred Tennyson, the author of the last prize poem, 'Timbuctoo' (of which Landor, whom, I dare say, you will see at Rome, will give you an account)—truly one of the mighty of the earth. You will be delighted with him when you see him." On April 1 Kemble wrote, "Hallam you already know, and, I hope, like. He is an excellent man, full of high and noble qualities, and is young enough to become a greater and better man even than he is. But you do not know either Charles or Alfred Tennyson, both of whom are dying to know you. The first opportunity, therefore, that you have of making their acquaintance, neglect it not. They are poets of the highest class. In Alfred's mind the materials of the very greatest works are heaped in an abundance which is almost confusion. Charles has just published a small volume of superb sonnets; and his brother and Hallam are about to edit their poems conjointly. One day these men will be great indeed."[21] This would obviously have whetted Trench's appetite to meet Tennyson, and the thought that all his friends were taking orders, winning fellowships, and otherwise finding their niche in life made him very eager to return. By May 7 he was back in Milan and "thirsting for England." He hoped to arrive before the end of May. "If I am in time I shall pay a visit to Cambridge immediately." There is no information as to the exact date of his return, but it must have been late May or early June, and therefore it was between that date and July 2, when Tennyson and Hallam left for the Pyrenees, that Trench must have made his famous remark.[22] For on July 11 he too left again for Spain and did not see Tennyson again for nearly a year, by which time his mind was on other things.

Though the specific bearing of Trench's remark was primarily on himself, his conversion was a paradigm of what all the Apostles were experiencing, and his view of the intellectual and spiritual condition of Europe was to some degree shared by them all. It is, indeed, very likely that Trench's letters to Blakesley, Kemble, and Donne were read aloud to the whole group of the Apostles, and Trench probably poured out his whole experience to them upon his return. Sterling's thought would also have been available to Tennyson, for the alumni of the Society did not cease to be active on leaving Cambridge. They returned to meetings with the younger set and provided them with a base in London. In any case, in the spring and summer of 1830 Tennyson would have been seeing quite a bit of his friends, for they were engaged in a fantastic scheme to do nothing less than overthrow the Spanish monarchy.

Sterling was the leader of this project. He had become intimate with General Torrijos, the leader of the Constitutional exiles, and had persuaded himself that if a small band of patriots, well armed and resolute, were to land on the Spanish coast the whole country would rise in sympathy and the monarchy be toppled. He involved his friends and particularly his cousin, Robert Boyd, just back from service in the Indian army. Hallam and Tennyson were to take money to rebel leaders in the north, whose rising would effect a diversion. The rest were to embark in an armed brig which Sterling and Maurice had purchased and make a simultaneous landing on the south coast. Unfortunately, the English government got wind of the scheme and seized the brig, but the adventurers, nothing daunted, arranged for alternative passage. Hallam and Tennyson left on July 2, Kemble on July 7, Trench with the main body of exiles on the eleventh. Sterling did not go. His health was not good, and at the last moment his fiancée persuaded him to stay home and get married.

The sequel of the story is well known. Hallam and Tennyson delivered their money and returned without any difficulty. But the risings in the south did not occur, the sympathizers in the north never materialized. Cooped up in Gibraltar, bored and inactive, the exiles were unable even to land in Spain because they were watched by the Spanish gunboats. Trench finally returned home in March 1831, and Kemble in May. The rest lingered on until December, when they were finally told by the British authorities, whose patience was naturally exhausted by the presence of a group planning a hostile act against a country with which England was ostensibly at peace, that they would have to leave. Their ship was run aground by the Spanish boats at Málaga, and all, including Boyd, were executed. So ended this Victorian version of the Bay of Pigs.

For the Apostles this was a traumatic experience, and it is remarkable how soon they all ceased being revolutionaries and became clergymen. Sterling took orders in 1831 to the surprise of his friends. As for Trench, Spedding wrote to Donne in October 1831, "Trench is here [Trinity College], attending Divinity Lectures and groaning over the prospects of mankind; he has cast down the magnificent temple of Shelleian religion, and his only hope is in a speedy millennium, of which he hails the newly given gift of unknown tongues as a forerunner and assurance."[23] And to the same correspondent the following April, "You speak of

Trench's metamorphosis; ay marry! but what could you expect of a man who used to believe in Shelley? Did I not tell you that people would come round to my opinions concerning that great warrer against Customs and Rights and Forms and 'the crust of outworn opinions on which established superstitions depend?' Blakesley never admits that he has changed an opinion, but he, too, is full of the inviolable sanctity of conventionalities."[24]

Tennyson, who had gone along on the Spanish expedition more or less as a tourist, was probably less affected than the others. "A wild, bustling time we had of it," wrote Hallam. "I played my part as conspirator in a small way, and made friends with two or three gallant men, who have been since trying their luck with Valdes."[25] As they came back by steamboat, Paris was in an uproar, the royal standard had been pulled down and trampled upon, and when they arrived home, ricks were burning all over the south of England. It was, indeed, the reign of "Captain Swing," whose name, chalked on wall and gatepost, inspired terror in the hearts of the gentry. "The country is in a more awful state than you can well conceive," wrote Hallam on December 2, 1830. "While I write, Maddingley, or some adjoining village, is in a state of conflagration, and the sky above is coloured flame-red. . . . The laws are almost suspended; the money of foreign factions is at work with a population exasperated into reckless fury. I do not, however, apprehend a revolution, as the intelligent part of the community are tolerably united, and the present ministers seem prepared to meet the emergency."[26] The fire was actually at Coton, a village a little over a mile from Cambridge, for Henry Alford, Tennyson's friend, tells us that he "went there and worked engines." So too in all likelihood did Tennyson, for in the poem *To Mary Boyle* he recalls participating in a bucket brigade to put out a blazing homestead. "Peacock," continues Alford, "assembled the men in the cloisters and organized us in bodies of ten or eleven, in case of an attack on Cambridge which is meditated."[27]

It was not idly, then, that Tennyson said at the conclusion of *The Palace of Art,*

> 'Yet pull not down my palace towers, that are
> So lightly, beautifully built:
> Perchance I may return with others there
> When I have purged my guilt.'

For there is no question but that Tennyson had Cambridge partly in mind when he wrote *The Palace of Art*. It is not merely that the four great courts, the fountains, and other architectural features duplicate those of Trinity College, but also that Tennyson's sonnet, *Lines on Cambridge of 1830*, makes the same contrast between the splendor of external equipment and the hollowness within. "There was no *love* in the system," he said.[28] The dons led a life of selfish leisure, leading to intellectual pride, and the hungry sheep looked up and were not fed. There was also one Sunderland, an undergraduate, unfortunately a member of the Apostles (the Judas of the group), who gave himself great airs and was accustomed to prate about the "rational intuition," which it seems that he alone could understand. He was a great trial to all his fellows, was satirized by Tennyson in *A Character*, and probably contributed as much as anyone to the ethical character of the Soul in *The Palace of Art*.[29]

Moreover, it is clear that the pantheon of wise men whose busts adorn the Palace of Art is virtually that of the Apostles themselves. Tennyson indicates that the description of "large-brow'd Verulam" was suggested by the bust of Bacon in the Trinity College Library, and he admits that Livy, who in the 1832 version was grouped along with Plato, Petrarch, and Raphael as one of the immortals, "looks queer. Our classical tutor at Trinity College used to call him such a great poet that I suppose he got into my palace thro' his recommendation."[30] Tennyson has evidently forgotten that the reason their tutor—presumably J. C. Hare, the translator of Niebuhr—called Livy a poet is that Niebuhr insists that the legends of early Rome were "lays"—as Macaulay in his *Lays of Ancient Rome* would later agree.[31] But Livy was also called a poet by Shelley, and it is remarkable that of the twenty names mentioned in the 1832 version of *The Palace of Art* (there were many fewer in 1842) all but four appear in the *Defence of Poetry*. "It exceeds all imagination," said Shelley, "to conceive what would have been the moral condition of the world if neither Dante, Petrarch, Boccaccio, Chaucer, Shakespeare, Calderón, Lord Bacon, nor Milton had ever existed; if Raphael and Michael Angelo had never been born; if the Hebrew poetry had never been translated; if a revival of the study of Greek literature had never taken place; if no monuments of ancient sculpture had been handed down to us; and if the poetry of the religion of the ancient world had been extinguished together with its belief."[32] All these figures, except for Boccaccio and Chaucer, appear in Tennyson's Palace of Art. The ancient sculpture he had intended to include but had not been able to represent to his satisfaction, and as for "the poetry" of the religion of the ancients, the whole point of one section of the poem is that modern religion, as well as ancient, is prized merely for its poetry.

With all these local thoughts, feelings, and associations *The Palace of Art* was peculiarly an "Apostolic" poem. "All [at Cambridge] were anxious for the 'Palace of Art,' etc.," wrote Hallam to Tennyson, "and fierce with me for not bringing more." "Only think of an 'Apostolic' dinner next Friday," wrote Spedding to Thompson. "Only think of the 'Palace of Art.' " Merivale says that it was customary for the poem to be "read successively to each man as he came up from the vacation," and by his reaction to it he was judged. "We talk out of the 'Palace of Art,' and the 'Legend of Fair Women,' "[33] wrote Spedding, and Spedding at least knew the whole of the poem by heart. It was, indeed, considered communal property, and since there was no fixed text but only an expandable or contractable body of stanzas, each man felt privileged to suggest that "Kriemhild" should be left out or "Tarpeia" included. Since it is notorious that poems cannot be written by a committee, it is very probable that *The Palace of Art* would have been a better poem had it been written by Tennyson alone.

But although *The Palace of Art* is in some respects a "Cambridge" or Apostolic poem, it also has reference to the great country houses of England. For we must remember that in the days before the National Gallery, when there was only the Dulwich Picture Gallery and the as yet unhoused Fitzwilliam collection, these were the great art palaces of England. Fonthill Abbey, Beckford's fantastic vanity, may have contributed to the poem both directly and through *Vathek*, but there were also others which Tennyson may have visited and which he had certainly read about in William Hazlitt's *Sketches of the Principal Picture-Galleries in England* (1824). Tennyson possessed a copy of this work (now at the Tennyson Research Centre), and we know that he read it, for it is the source of *The Lord of Burleigh*. It gives descriptions of eleven galleries, most of them private or semiprivate, and each description follows the pattern of Tennyson's poem in beginning with a tour of the building itself and then going on to describe its treasures. Moreover, it mingles a rather extravagant aestheticism with Hazlitt's well-known republican sentiments. Of Angerstein's collec-

tion: "Here is the mind's true home. The contemplation of truth
and beauty is the proper object for which we were created, which
calls forth the most intense desires of the soul, and of which it
never tires." Of Dulwich: "It is like a palace of thought—another
universe, built of air, of shadows, of colours." Of the marquis of
Stafford's: "Oh! thou, whoever thou art, that dost seek happiness
in thyself, independent on others . . . seek it (if thou art wise) in
books, in pictures, and the face of nature, for these alone we may
count upon as friends for life!"

On the other hand, Hazlitt is not without resentment against
the wealthy owners of these pictures. As he leaves Lord Gros-
venor's mansion he comments on the difficulty of returning to
humble scenes and tries to "abstract the idea of exclusive property" from his mind and concentrate on the beauty of the pictures.
"Fonthill-Abbey," he notes, "which was formerly hermetically
sealed against all intrusion, is at present open to the whole world;
and Wilton-House, and Longford-Castle, which were formerly
open to every one, are at present shut, except to *petitioners,* and a
favoured few. Why is this greater degree of strictness in the latter
instances resorted to? In proportion as the taste for works of art
becomes more general, do these Noble Persons wish to set bounds
to and disappoint public curiosity? Do they think that the admira-
tion bestowed on fine pictures or rare sculpture lessens their
value, or divides the property, as well as the pleasure with the
possessor?"[34] In the frame to *The Princess* Tennyson has Sir Walter Vivian, the type of a fine English gentleman, open up his park
one day a year to the Mechanics Institute, and he implies that it is
this English condescension which "keeps our Britain, whole within
herself," whereas the French overseas are constantly going to the
extremes of tyranny and revolution. "Why," he cries, "should not
these great sirs / Give up their parks some dozen times a year / To
let the people breathe?" Thus, whereas in the early apocalyptic
poems Nineveh and Babylon are destroyed in their pride, Tennyson hesitates to invoke this doom on England. That doom will
befall it if the great of the land do not take heed. In particular, it
will befall it if the Reform Bill is not passed. For *The Palace of Art*
was written precisely during the period, 1831–32, when the great
debates on this subject were taking place in the House of Com-
mons and the House of Lords. Macaulay, with his elaborate and
florid rhetoric, was using the argument from fear with great effect
in his celebrated series of orations on behalf of the bill. The

peroration of his speech of March 2, 1831, was delivered in a
frenzy of passion.

> Save the aristocracy [he cried], endangered by its own un-
> popular power. Save the greatest, and fairest, and most
> highly civilized community that ever existed, from calamities
> which may in a few days sweep away all the rich heritage of so
> many ages of wisdom and glory. The danger is terrible. The
> time is short. If this bill should be rejected, I pray to God that
> none of those who concur in rejecting it may ever remember
> their votes with unavailing remorse, amidst the wreck of laws,
> the confusion of ranks, the spoliation of property, and the
> dissolution of social order.[35]

Tennyson was not trying to save the aristocracy, but he was trying
to save the England he knew; and his highly rhetorical *Palace of
Art* is the poetic equivalent of Macaulay's florid orations delivered
during the spring and summer of 1831.

Ultimately, then, the poem is addressed to all of England, to all
of Europe. Its Palace is not any particular building but the
metaphorical palaces which, in the language of Tennyson's contemporaries, denoted the mind of Europe—Hazlitt's "palace of
thought," Spedding's "magnificent temple of Shelleian religion,"
Sterling's "mausoleum of [Goethean] art," and Trench's "Pantheon" of the religious idea. *The Palace of Art* is not directed against
the so-called Art for Art's Sake Movement, which at this date
hardly existed. It is directed, as Spedding notes, against the selfish
misuse of beauty by a privileged class and against its isolation from
other values. More generally, it is directed against the whole
tendency of modern European thought to make a religion out of
its own culture.

This is why Tennyson, especially in the stronger, more firmly
organized 1842 version of the poem, emphasizes the tendency of
the aesthetic attitude to result in the relativity of moral and religious judgments. In the series of seven rooms, for example, which
the speaker has fitted up "for every mood / And change of my
still soul," as if every mood were to be indulged equally, it is
apparent that the seventh, depicting an English home, presumably on Sunday, with "all things in order stored, / A haunt of
ancient Peace," from a moral point of view ought to be preferred.
And it is, of course, egregiously "philosophic" to group the
Madonna and Child and St. Cecilia along with the gods of the

Greek, Roman, Indian, and Mohammedan religions as merely one of the "legend[s] fair / Which the supreme Caucasian mind / Carved out of Nature for itself." This, too, is probably what led to Tennyson's picking Bacon and Plato out of the crowd and placing them opposite one another in a single stanza in 1842. For in 1837 Macaulay's famous essay on Bacon had appeared in which he emphasizes that they could not be reconciled—that one is either a Baconian or a Platonist—and it would be part of the Soul's relativism that she is both. Neither would this be inconsistent with some memory of the fact that Coleridge, in *The Friend* and elsewhere, had emphasized that they could be reconciled, for even Coleridge's philosophism was now slightly suspect. Probably the four ages of man represented in the mosaics of the Palace are those in the philosophy of history of the Saint-Simonians, which Tennyson, under the tutelage of Sterling and Hallam, had come to detest.[36] But the crowning fact is that the Soul, in its godlike isolation, cares not "what the sects may brawl. / I sit as God holding no form of creed, / But contemplating all." One notes that Sterling, after visiting the Saint-Simonians in France, had written Trench, "I would rather be a believing Jew or pagan than a man who sees through all religions, but looks not with the eyes of any."[37]

In all this one does not mean to say that Tennyson himself was absolutely free from the taint of modern aestheticism. Hallam, writing to him in July 1831, exclaimed, "You say pathetically, 'Alas for me! I have more of the Beautiful than the Good!' Remember to your comfort that God has given you to see the difference. Many a poet has gone on blindly in his artist pride."[38] Trench too thought that there was spiritual danger for Tennyson in the fact that the Apostles praised him so much. "No young man under any circumstances," he wrote sternly, "should believe that he *has* done anything, but still be forward looking."[39] Thus, though the inhabitant of the Palace of Art is primarily *not* Tennyson but the mind of England, the mind of Europe, still a delicate ambiguity is preserved by the separation between the speaker and his Soul. "I built my soul a lordly pleasure-house, / Wherein at ease for aye to dwell. / I said, 'O soul' . . . ," and so on until, at the end, the Soul is so tortured with guilt that she "howled aloud," and yet the "I" seems relatively undisturbed. This division in the persons corresponds to a division in the form, for on the one hand, the speaker is one with the apocalyptic poet who sees a vision of the doomed city, and on the other, the Soul is in the same enclosed situation as the immured maiden. Like these two figures, the speaker is apparently masculine and the Soul, except for one slip (the rhyme-word "King" in line 14), feminine. It is perfectly apparent, as we have already noted in chapter 2, that the Palace of Art is a version of the sinful city of Babylon, and when we come to the place where "Mene, mene" is written on the wall, the identification seems complete. On the other hand, it is not destroyed, merely democratized, for it is not evil in itself but merely in its use. And if the Soul is enclosed, it is not because she has been abandoned by any lover who is insensitive to her beauty. Rather, she is self-enclosed by pride. Indeed, she is not a creative artist at all but an art collector, and her fountain does not water the plains below but turns into an incense in tribute to herself. Because there is no Love in the Palace, everything in it that is naturally good is turned to the use of self-destructive Pride.[40]

In the introductory sonnet that accompanies *The Palace of Art* Tennyson says that "Beauty, Good, and Knowledge, are three sisters / That doat upon each other. . . . / And never can be sunder'd without tears," and that the fault of the Soul was that she "did love Beauty only . . . , / And Knowledge for its beauty; or if Good, / Good only for its beauty." This theme of the unity of the virtues is made even more explicit in the exactly contemporary *Œnone,* which is also a hybrid poem in that it combines the lament of Œnone with a more ethical Judgment of Paris. In his *Apology for the XIXth Century* Spedding had noted that Bacon, commenting on the shallow judgments of previous times, had included that "of Paris, that judged for beauty and love, against wisdom and power."[41] Power, wisdom, and love and beauty do seem to be the values that Tennyson attributes to Herè, Pallas, and Aphrodite, and although these are not exactly the three mentioned in the introductory sonnet to *The Palace of Art,* still, since Knowledge in contemporary thought leads to Power, and Wisdom conduces to the Good, they are at least roughly equivalent. The choice among them obviously involves the central question of ancient ethics, what is the *summum bonum* or supreme good of life.

It had also become the central question in modern ethics, for the three virtues correspond roughly to the three ways of life competing for supremacy in nineteenth-century England—the Utilitarian, the Christian Humanist, and the Romantic. Herè, in offering power as the only thing that can make Paris one with the gods, specifically associates her gift with the Epicurean philosophy which is the ancient equivalent of Utilitarianism. She says, moreover, that power is the end all men have in view in action, and she implies that through it the face of nature can be transformed. To this Pallas angrily replies,

> ' "Self-reverence, self-knowledge, self-control,
> These three alone lead life to sovereign power.
> Yet not for power (power of herself
> Would come uncall'd for) but to live by law,
> Acting the law we live by without fear;
> And, because right is right, to follow right
> Were wisdom in the scorn of consequence." '

Pallas has clearly seized upon the central issue between Utilitarianism and Christian Humanism by emphasizing that values are absolute, not relative, and that we follow the right because of its intrinsic character and not because of its consequences. Further, we achieve the good not by transforming nature but by transforming ourselves. It is through renunciation, the submission of the will to eternal law, that we achieve true power and true freedom, for the only freedom worth having is the freedom to do right and the only power worth having is the power of self-control. Hearing this, Œnone cries, "O Paris, / Give it to Pallas!" but Paris does exactly what Lancelot did—he "ponders." Meanwhile, Aphrodite, who has seen two ladies spend many words in vain, uses no argument at all. She simply sidles up to Paris, so that her naked beauty will have its full effect upon him, and, with a "subtle smile . . . , The herald of her triumph," half-whispers in his ear, " 'I promise thee / The fairest and most loving wife in Greece,' / She spoke and laughed." Aphrodite laughs not only because she knows the weakness of men but also because she foresees all the destruction of the Trojan War and she delights no less in eros than in violence. Her smile is "subtle" because she is the serpent in this garden, the insidious *femme fatale* who, in a long line of temptresses from Eve to Pater's Mona Lisa and the Salomé of Oscar Wilde, lures men to their destruction. Hence, whereas after Pallas's speech Paris "pondered," and after Here's he, by a kind of reflex action, held the fruit out at arm's length, now he simply dissolves in sexual desire. His will caves in and, as Tennyson says of a similar situation in *Merlin and Vivien*, "what should not have been had been."

The reader doubtless concurs in this judgment, for, initially at least, he feels no uncertainty at all as to which is the "right" choice within the context of the poem. Herè is not seriously in question, for she is supported neither by Paris nor Œnone and, being in first position, simply prepares the way for the real contest which follows. But Aphrodite is obviously "wrong" for the reasons already given. If she represents Love, it is the kind of carnal love that leads to Death, and if Beauty, it is the purely sensuous beauty that is divorced from spiritual values. On the other hand, Pallas is clearly the "right" choice, not only because she is approved by Œnone but also because her speech is so obviously the "moral" of the poem—the passage that generations of schoolboys will have to memorize. Still, if Pallas is morally right, she is aesthetically and even humanly wrong. As Chesterton said,

> Self-reverence, self-knowledge, self-control,
> These three alone would make a man a prig—

And Pallas does have a little of the prig in her. Even from the first she stood apart, and as she is described with "the brazen-headed spear / Upon her pearly shoulder leaning cold," "her snow-cold breast and angry cheek," she is anything but an attractively warm and human person. She has not a little of Cordelia in her in a similar judgment scene—something a bit churlish and ungracious, an unwillingness to combine with her undoubted spiritual qualities the grace and charm that would make her a totally admirable person. This is seen more especially in her style, which is stiff, abstract, didactic, and so opposed to the exotic, luxuriant beauty of the poem as a whole that she cannot be right unless the poem is wrong. Since the poem is Œnone's it is hard to see why Œnone, who, as a passionate woodland nymph, the playmate of pard and panthers, is more like Aphrodite than Pallas, would side with her. But that is the very reason—Pallas would complement Œnone more nearly than Aphrodite would, who is beauty as artifice, love as artifice, competing with the natural love and beauty of Œnone.

The true answer is, then, that, as in *The Palace of Art*, Power, Wisdom, and Beauty are three sisters that dote upon each other and never can be sundered without tears. This Discord has done by throwing the apple on the board, and Œnone recognizes this when, in a passage added in 1842, she yearns to seek out the Abominable (Discord) and tell her how she hates her. And Paris's error is that in choosing any one of the goddesses over another he has shown a lack of harmony and balance. This, indeed, is the traditional Renaissance interpretation of the myth, for in the Renaissance it became a fixed formula to compliment a prince on his universality by contrasting his judgment with the partial judgment of Paris. In Lyly's *Euphues and His England,* Peele's *Arraignment of Paris,* and Sabie's *Pan's Pipe* the compliment is extended to Queen Elizabeth, who, it is suggested, combines in herself the gifts which the three goddesses possess only separately.[42] That Tennyson was aware of this tradition is suggested by a passage, added in 1842, in which Paris recognizes that the inscription "For the fairest" would seem to award the fruit to Œnone, and certainly in his life with Œnone (who presumably represents Poetry) love and beauty, wisdom, and all the power they need were harmoniously mingled. Thus, the violation of Œnone is symbolized by the violation of nature when "they" came and cut away her tallest pines, destroying the haunt of eaglet and panther, the gathering place of mist and silver cloud. But in truth, the bower had already been violated when first the goddesses came, for Tennyson emphasizes by initial position and incremental repetition that "*Naked* they came to that smooth-swarded bower," and clearly, the bower was never again the same. Fire broke out among the crocuses, a wind arose, and even the ivy began to riot. The scene, as many critics have pointed out, has echoes of the temptation scenes in *Paradise Lost* and *Paradise Regained,* and, indeed, it is less a judgment scene than a temptation. It is a temptation *to* judge, as well as to judge wrong, for when Paris tells Œnone that if she hides behind the tuft of pine she may behold divinity unobserved and "see thy Paris judge of Gods" he has already committed hubris. His initial fall was through pride in thinking he should choose at all, his second was in choosing wrong.

Throughout the poem Œnone has been associated with the mist or vapor that seems a part of the soft beauty of the vale. This vapor, which "slopes athwart the glen, / Puts forth an arm, and creeps from pine to pine," is a source of the unity of the scene, where things blend into one another, as the language does by moving softly back and forth, in a self-reflexive mood, or in the refrain. "The lizard, with his shadow on the stone, / Rests like a shadow." "Yonder walls / Rose slowly to a music slowly breathed." "Behold them unbeheld, unheard / Hear all." "My heart / Went forth to embrace him coming ere he came." "He heard me not, / Or hearing would not hear me." "Round her neck / Floated

her hair or seem'd to float in rest." The silver cloud of Œnone is
not to be confused with the golden cloud into which Herè and her
peacock retire, for the point is that when the goddesses come, the
silvery cloud gets lost, the mist of poetic indistinctness is dis-
persed, and all is subjected to the harsh light of analysis. But at
this point something happens to Œnone that has not happened to
any of her predecessors. Though she says with Mariana, "I am all
aweary of my life," she does not die but issues forth from her vale
to pronounce doom and vengeance on the sinful city of Troy. The
silver cloud darkens into the "ever-floating cloud" of Death, but it
will not shadow her alone. Just as the city "rose slowly to a music
slowly breathed, / A cloud that gathered shape," so now "fiery
thoughts / Do shape themselves within me, more and more," moving the poem from the swimming vapor in which it began to the
destructive fire with which it ends.

> I will rise and go
> Down into Troy, and ere the stars come forth
> Talk with the wild Cassandra, for she says
> A fire dances before her, and a sound
> Rings ever in her ears of armèd men.

Through her own rising fury and wild passion Œnone has to all
intents and purposes become Cassandra, thus transforming herself from the immured maiden who "built up all / My sorrow with
my song," to the apocalyptic poet who denounces judgment upon
the city of discord. Just as the speaker in *The Palace of Art* was
distinguished from his Soul, so Œnone is given an active as well as
a passive function. It is clear that Tennyson, in combining forms
and multiplying persons, is searching out a more complicated
structure for a more complicated point of view. And it is equally
clear that the problem now is not merely a generation that is too
dull to hear but one that listens to the false siren voices of sensual-
ity and pride.

Tennyson began the composition of *Œnone* in the Cinque de
Gavarnie in the French Pyrenees. It is perhaps the most beautiful
of all the valleys of that region, a vast amphitheater two miles wide
with steep walls in places reaching to 5,600 feet, over which the
gave, or mountain torrent, flows in a spectacular waterfall 1,400
feet high, "slow-dropping veils of thinnest lawn." It may be that as
he sat there something like the choice of Paris presented itself to
him. In Bayonne a black-eyed Aphrodite had looked at him from

a latticed window so that he was "confused / And dazzled to the heart with glorious pain."[43] She even had dimples, as did the 1832 Aphrodite in *Œnone*. Beyond the mountains in Spain lay the world of power, and doubtless Cambridge, for want of a better, might represent wisdom. Meanwhile, here in this beautiful valley, the original of Ida though far more lush than any Greek valley, was the very haunt of poetry. How did he proceed? how did the rest of the world respond to the brook falling down "in cataract after cataract to the sea?" Not until he got home and experienced the fears of the late autumn, the shock of Boyd's death in December, and the violence of the reform movement over the next three years would he know. When he did, he evolved a more temperate and balanced philosophy which he expressed in a group of political poems written between 1831–34. Significantly, for these poems he found a new form, not the sonnet, which had been the "arrows" of his revolutionary ardor, but a four-line stanza which he probably would have described as Alcaic. Only fragments of Alcaeus, the seventh-sixth century B.C. lyric poet, have come down to us, but they are enough to show that in his day too the ship of state was making heavy weather and that he fiercely hated all democrats and their leaders, the tyrants to be. He also invented or adapted a four-line stanza, very similar to the Sapphic, which was later made more widely known by Horace. Either the *a b a b* stanza or the *In Memoriam* stanza (*a b b a*), both used in these political poems, Tennyson might have thought an approximation of these forms. In any case, writing to Spedding in 1834, he said, "You ask me what I have been doing: I have written several things since I saw you, some emulative of the 'ἡδὺ καὶ βραχὺ καὶ μεγαλοπρεπές' [sweetness, brevity, and high-mindedness] of Alcaeus, others of the 'ἐκλογὴ τῶν ὀνομάτων καὶ τῆς συνθέσεως ἀκρίβεια' [choice diction and concern for accurate composition] of Simonides, one or two epical, but you can scarcely expect me to write them out for you: for I can scarcely bring myself to write them out for myself."[44] On second thought he did copy out for Spedding *Love thou thy land,* which is one of the political poems referred to above. The most important of the others are *Hail Briton! You ask me, why, though ill at ease,* and *Of old sat Freedom on the heights.* The first of these, though never published by Tennyson, gives the fullest view of his political philosophy at this time. It is a slightly liberalized version of the thought of Burke, recognizing change as necessary, seeing in the Glorious Revolution the foundation of English liberties, but fearful now that change will proceed too fast, not growing organically out of the past and with a clear vision of the future but hastily imposed by factions and self-interested demagogues. Tennyson's failure to publish this work does not mean that he ceased to believe it. On the contrary, it remained his political creed for the rest of his life, and he did not publish it only because he quarried it for other poems for the next fifty years. But more interesting for our purposes are two poems which show Tennyson arriving at this view from positions adopted in the past.

In *Of old sat Freedom on the heights* the imagery shows him abandoning the apocalyptic conception of Freedom enunciated in *The Poet*. Whereas of old Freedom sat on the heights, the starry lights and thunders all about her, "Self-gather'd in her prophet-mind," with only fragments of her "mighty voice" coming to mankind, now she has "stept . . . down thro' town and field / To mingle with the human race." In this she is like Spring who, in her progress poem, stepped down from her tropical mountain "that I might mix with men." And whereas in *The Poet* Freedom's eyes had burned with a flame to shake all dreams of evil power, now "the wisdom of a thousand years / Is in them," and, far from riving the spirit of man with thunderbolts, she turns to scorn "the falsehood of extremes." She is, as one of the other poems says, "sober-suited," a thoroughly domesticated, bourgeois goddess who believes that only minor adjustments are needed in the social machine.

But what about the tropical garden? According to Hallam Tennyson, about 1832–33 Tennyson "fancied that England was an unsympathetic atmosphere, and half resolved to live abroad in Jersey, in the south of France, or in Italy."[45] Apparently, it was to someone (probably Spedding) who asked him why, if he felt so, he did not go abroad, that he addressed the poem beginning,

> You ask me, why, though ill at ease,
>   Within this region I subsist,
>   Whose spirits falter in the mist,
> And languish for the purple seas.

His answer is that England is the land of freedom, where "a man may speak the thing he will." It is, moreover, a "land of settled government,"

> Where Freedom slowly broadens down
> From precedent to precedent,

where the strength of some "diffusive thought" seldom gathers
head in faction but "by degrees to fulness wrought . . . / Hath
time and space to work and spread." If ever this should cease to be
true, then he will have the wind waft him from the harbor mouth,

> And I will see before I die
> The palms and temples of the South.

Thus, Tennyson is essentially able to say, "Love thou thy land,"
because Freedom has descended from the heights and Poetry has
come up from its tropical isle and they have met in England and
shaken hands. With this reconciliation there has been a change in
his conception of himself as poet. No longer a seer on a mountain-
top or an isolated maiden, he is a man speaking to men. Using
essentially the middle style, he addresses his hearer as "you,"
"thou," "Hail Briton!" In the latter poem he complains that amid
civil broil "the Arts / Hush all their many-varied songs"; but by the
end of the poem, when he paints a picture of the true patriot who
leads his country slowly forward by "seasonable changes fair," he
sees the possibility of a new kind of poetry.

> O civic Muse, for such a name,
>   Deep-minded Muse, for ages long
>   Preserve a broad approach of song
> And ringing avenues of fame.

It is this kind of poetry that he has just been practicing, and
although it had its precedent in Alcaeus and Horace and in
seventeenth-century England, it was a new note in Tennyson's
day. It was by these poems that Wordsworth was first led to
concede that Tennyson was a rising star. "Very solid and noble in
thought," he said. "Their diction also seems singularly stately."[46]
And Arthur Sidgwick commented, "It is easy to idealize freedom,
revolution, or war: and the ancients found it easy to compose
lyrics on kings, athletes, warriors, or other powerful persons. . . .
But the praise of ordered liberty, of settled government, of political moderation, is far harder to idealize in poetry."[47]

5

From Ulysses to Sir Bedivere

"And I, the last, go forth companionless."
Morte d'Arthur

Arthur Hallam died in Vienna on September 15, 1833, and Tennyson immediately felt like an old man. At least in the coming months he wrote three poems in which he spoke with the voice of an aged seer, of a quester setting out again in the sunset of life, and of a mortal cursed with immortality. *Ulysses* was written on October 20, less than three weeks after Tennyson received the news of Hallam's death, and, as Tennyson said, it "is more about myself" and "was more written with the feeling of his loss upon me than many of the poems in *In Memoriam*."[1] *Tithonus*, which was "originally a pendent"[2] to *Ulysses*, was written at the same time, and *Tiresias*, though not completed and published till many years later, was also "begun about the *Ulysses* period."[3] Of course, these were not Tennyson's only response to Hallam's death. On October 6 he had written, in the language and stanza which he had employed for *Hail Briton!* and *You ask me, why*, the first of the sections which, gathered together, were later to constitute *In Memoriam*.

> Fair ship, that from the Italian shore
>   Sailest the placid ocean-plains
>   With my lost Arthur's loved remains,
> Spread thy full wings, and waft him o'er.

Into this mold Tennyson was to pour all the thoughts and feelings that he felt could legitimately be presented to a wider public. In the realm of consolation it would present the same via media that *Hail Briton!* did in the political realm. For *In Memoriam*, as Tennyson was later to say, is "both a very personal and an impersonal poem." " 'I' is not always the author speaking of himself, but the voice of the human race speaking thro' him."[4] In *Tiresias, Tithonus*, and *Ulysses*, on the other hand, despite the classical persona, "I" is the author speaking of himself. For in these poems Tennyson is less concerned with the great universal problems raised by Hallam's death than with its meaning for him as a poet. As a result, he used, not the quatrain which he had devised for the public poems, but the more meditative medium of blank verse and the form of the dramatic monologue.

For these poems are the first great Victorian examples of that form. *St. Simeon Stylites,* which may have preceded them by a few months, is rather a special case, and Browning's earliest efforts were still two years away. Robert Langbaum has said that the dramatic monologue originated when the post-Romantic poet took the lyric of experience and fathered it upon another person.[5] Certainly it is true that what Wordsworth did in *Tintern Abbey* and Coleridge in *Dejection: An Ode* is being done by Tennyson for himself in these poems. On the other hand, one must remember that Tennyson had never heard the term *dramatic monologue,* which did not come into wide use until the very end of the century, and that he had already been writing dramatic monologues under another name for many years. The name that he would have used was, in all likelihood, *prosopopoeia* or perhaps *monodrama.*[6] Monodrama we will speak of later in connection with *Maud,* but of prosopopoeia, or impersonation, one may say that it was an ancient rhetorical form in which the poet or orator imagined what a particular historical or literary character might have said in a certain situation and then presented that character as actually speaking. Thus, one could imagine what it was that Antigone said to Eteocles in begging him to make peace with Polynices, or how Sulla addressed the people on resigning the dictatorship. The form soon became an important exercise in the literary education of youth, for it was of value to the schoolboy in helping him realize the situation in his Greek and Latin classics. It also taught him invention in finding arguments and sentiments for his various speakers, and decorum in selecting words that would be appropriate to their age and character. It was also valuable in the study of letter writing (for the epistle is merely a prosopopoeia committed to paper), and it was so used, in textbooks by Erasmus and others, right up through the Renaissance and into the nineteenth century.[7] That Tennyson wrote such exercises as a schoolboy there can be no doubt, for in his *Poems by Two Brothers* there are half a dozen pieces of this character: *Anthony to Cleopatra, Written by an Exile of Bassorah, Mithridates Presenting Berenice with the Cup of Poison,* and *The High Priest to*

Alexander. These pieces are not dramatic monologues in the sense in which we now use the term, for there is no revelation of character and no irony. Yet they are not fundamentally different in form from the poems that Tennyson will begin writing five or six years later—*Œnone, Tithonus, Tiresias*, and *Ulysses*. *Œnone* is actually modeled upon one of the prosopopoeiae that make up the *Heroides* of Ovid—that collection of letters from abandoned maidens which is the great source of the feminine image. But in the other poems the impulse that transformed the stiff rhetorical exercise into a moving dramatic monologue is the experience of Hallam's death as mediated by the poetry of Wordsworth and Coleridge.

For what is Tennyson saying in these poems? The striking thing is that their protagonists are all poet figures—a seer, a quester, a consort of the Dawn—all persons who are an incongruous mixture of the human and the divine. Like the Lady of Shalott, both Tithonus and Tiresias have received a gift from the gods, but subject to a crippling condition which constitutes just the human predicament. Tiresias, yearning in youth "for larger glimpses of that more than man / Which rolls the heavens," wandered among the mountain peaks, ever scaling "the highest of the heights / With some strange hope to see the nearer God." One day his efforts were rewarded.

> There in a secret olive-glade I saw
> Pallas Athene climbing from the bath
> In anger.

Immediately he was stricken blind, yet in his heart he still carries the divine image: "In the hidden world of sight that lives / Behind this darkness, I behold her still," and this image is the source of his prophetic power.

> Ineffable beauty, out of whom, at a glance,
> And as it were, perforce, upon me flash'd
> The power of prophesying.

The power was of no avail to him, however, for with it was coupled the "curse" that his prophecies should never be believed, and thus though he carries in his soul the vision of divine truth and beauty, he can never translate this vision into reality or persuade others to accept it. He is as mocked by the people of Thebes as the Lady of Shalott was by the well-fed wits of Camelot.

Tithonus, too, is the victim of a divine gift—immortality—which a careless deity failed to couple with immortal youth so that, withered in age, his marriage to Aurora is not a boon to him but a burden. It should not be thought that this poem is about Tennyson's love for Hallam, or about immortality, or about the desire for death. It is about a poet who feels his poetic powers failing. It is a myth of one who, feeling his brow kissed by the dawn and remembering how rapturously in youth his heart had bounded to meet it, laments that he can no more.

> Ay me! ay me! with what another heart
> In days far-off, and with what other eyes
> I used to watch—if I be he that watch'd—
> The lucid outline forming round thee; saw
> The dim curls kindle into sunny rings;
> Changed with thy mystic changes, and felt my blood
> Glow with the glow that slowly crimson'd all
> Thy presence and thy portals.

So Coleridge, gazing upon the western sky with its peculiar tint of yellow green, exclaimed, "I see them all so excellently fair, / I see, not feel, how beautiful they are." Neither can Tithonus now find within himself the fervor to respond.

> Coldly thy rosy shadows bathe me, cold
> Are all thy lights, and cold my wrinkled feet
> Upon thy glimmering thresholds.

For *Tithonus* is Tennyson's *Dejection: An Ode;* it is the negative part of his *Resolution and Independence,* of his *Tintern Abbey* or *Immortality Ode.* With the death of Hallam he had lost Joy, that active, sacred power by which the poet creates worlds about him, by which he glorifies the earth. To the poet the loss of Joy is the loss of imagination, and that that is what he meant Tennyson makes clear in the lines that follow. While Tithonus in youth was being kissed by the dawn, he

> could hear the lips that kiss'd
> Whispering I knew not what of wild and sweet,
> Like that strange song I heard Apollo sing,
> While Ilion like a mist rose into towers.

Just as Tiresias saw in the naked goddess the divine beauty which was the source of his prophetic power, so in the song breathed by the lips of Aurora did Tithonus find his inspiration. At that moment he felt himself a god—one

> So glorious in his beauty and thy choice,
> Who madest him thy chosen, that he seem'd
> To his great heart none other than a God!

"By our own spirits are we deified," says Wordsworth, and Coleridge adds, "Ah! from the soul itself must issue forth / A light, a glory, a fair luminous cloud / Enveloping the Earth." Tithonus's marriage to the Dawn is simply the conviction of every great poet in his youth that he is immortal and cannot die. But alas! it is not so. "We Poets in our youth begin in gladness; / But thereof come in the end despondency and madness." So says the poet in *Resolution and Independence,* and Tithonus perforce agrees. "How can my nature longer mix with thine?" And so what he asks is not to be released into death, which would be to take the metaphor literally, but to be relieved of the burden of his divine gift—to be released into ordinary mortality again. The main change that Tennyson made in the later revision of the poem was to omit Tithonus's threat to introduce Death into the halls of Aurora. For he knows by this time that the goddess's gift cannot be withdrawn: the immortal element in man is ineluctably his—his fate will be to continue forever, an incongruous mixture of the human and divine.

Tiresias's problem is not that of failing poetic powers but of powers that work no good to the state. It should be noted that the condition that Tiresias's prophecies shall not be believed was not a part of any classical version of the myth but was added by Tennyson, presumably from the story of Cassandra. It is obvious that Tennyson wants to make this point the central theme of the poem, for it is further emphasized by being connected with the story of Menœceus. In Euripides' *Phoenician Women,* which is Tennyson's main source for this part of the story, Tiresias is brought very reluctantly to tell Creon that the one means by which the city of Thebes can be saved is the sacrifice of his own son, Menœceus— only so can Ares be appeased for the slaying of the dragon by Cadmus. But Tennyson has Tiresias approach Menœceus directly. By so doing he makes his prophet a considerably less sympathetic character than he was in Euripides, and that Tennyson was willing to run this risk is but a further indication of the importance to him of his theme. For to him Menœceus is not only

the means of the salvation of the city but also the means of the
fulfillment of the prophet. It is the torment of Tiresias that when
he has warned the people of Thebes of natural disasters or
preached against war or civil outbreak, they have not heeded him.
If the yearning to do good were sufficient in itself, he would be
happy; but "virtue must shape itself in deed"—the vision of the
prophet must realize itself in the world. The "song-built towers"
of Thebes were orginally built to the music of Amphion's lyre.
Now they are about to be destroyed by the discord of fratricidal
strife. Of itself the music of Tiresias's divine vision cannot preserve these towers unless he have some mediator or deputy to act
for him. It is at this point that the figure in Tennyson's poems
whom we have hitherto called the Auditor—sympathetic or
unsympathetic—adds to his role that of Enactor. For Menœceus,
by what means we know not, believes Tiresias's warning and,
serving as his eyes and hand, acts for him, turning his purpose
into deed. In so doing he creates a new music, greater even than
that of Tiresias, greater perhaps than that of Amphion himself,
the music of his own name and fame. For just as the "Civic Muse"
of *Hail Briton!* was to preserve for the name of the True Patriot "a
broad approach of song / And ringing avenues of fame," so here
Menœceus is told,

> No sound is breathed so potent to coerce
> And to conciliate, as their names who dare
> For that sweet mother land which gave them birth
> Nobly to do, nobly to die. Their names,
> Graven on memorial columns, are a song
> Heard in the future.

The passage continues in language which, as Christopher Ricks
has noted, clearly echoes that of *Hail Briton!* and shows how
closely the plight of the unattended prophet reflected Tennyson's
feeling about himself in the England of 1833. Only a few years
before he was telling the profane multitude to keep its distance.
Now he acknowledges that there is no music like the name of a
True Patriot, no light like that shed upon the ways of men by "one
great deed." It is strange to hear a poet cry, "This useless hand!"

After this, is it possible to accept the interpretation of some
modern critics that Ulysses is condescending toward Telemachus?
For it is clear that Telemachus occupies the same position toward
Ulysses that Menœceus does toward Tiresias. True, he did not

give his life for rockbound Ithaca, and so presumably his name does not make quite the music that Menœceus's did. Still, he is the one who enacts for Ulysses what Ulysses cannot or will not do for himself, and given the very high place which Tennyson, in a precisely contemporary and substantially parallel poem, gives to action in relation to contemplation, it is hard to believe that he is contemptuously treated. But perhaps we had better go back and place the whole matter in context.

When Tennyson wrote to Spedding in 1834 about the poems emulative of Alcaeus that he had been writing, he added that he had also written "one or two epical, but you can scarcely expect me to write them out for you; for I can scarcely bring myself to write them out for myself."[8] One wonders what these "epical" poems were, for nothing has survived from the period that would obviously fit the description. If one were to take literally the assertion in *The Epic* that Everard Hall had written twelve books on King Arthur, and if one believed that Tennyson was the original of Hall, then these would be the pieces. But otherwise it might well be that Tennyson was thinking of *Tithonus, Tiresias,* and *Ulysses,* for these are "epical" in subject matter and by this time Tennyson was certainly thinking in terms of the brief epic. Speaking of his literary ideals in the mid-1830s, Tennyson said, "I felt certain of one point then; if I meant to make any mark at all, it must be by shortness, for the men before me had been so diffuse, and most of the big things except 'King Arthur' had been done."[9]

In this statement Tennyson was declaring himself a Victorian Alexandrian, for the learned and sophisticated poets of the third century B.C. also considered that the large epic and tragic subjects were played out and that they should make their name by the short but highly wrought poem. Hence, poets like Callimachus and Theocritus turned their attention to the elegy, the idyll, the pastoral, and the "little epic," or, if to the long poem at all, to the composite or discontinuous epic that consisted of a number of short poems united by a narrative thread. They also took a new approach to myth. Writing for a highly cultivated audience in the great research center of Alexandria, they were little inclined simply to tell over again the stories that had already been told by Homer and the Greek dramatists. If they could not find new stories, they would at least seek out little-known aspects of the old stories and would tell them from a novel point of view. If they treated the myth of Tiresias, for example, they would not focus on the blinding as such but on Pallas Athene's defense of her action and on the grieving mother. The story of Theseus they would tell not from the point of view of the hero but from that of Ariadne, who was left behind. Partly, perhaps, because the dominant point of view had hitherto been masculine, they affected a feminine point of view and dwelt upon the feeling behind the event rather than upon the event itself. In thus focusing upon one little portion of the story with the rest sketched in briefly or by cryptic allusion, they naturally produced what, from a traditional point of view, was a one-sided or asymmetrical treatment of the myth. This they often intensified by odd forms, by the digression or the poem-within-the-poem, with the result that what was formally a subordinate part of the story became thematically the most important. For they were primarily interested in using the old myths as the materials for art—in creating out of narratives that a previous generation had taken rather seriously something that would be shapely, intense, learned, and graceful. This was the serious "modern" poetry of the Alexandrian age.

The ideals of Callimachus and Theocritus were transmitted to a group of Roman poets called the Neoterics—Cinna, Catullus, Calvus, and Valerius Cato—who were also wearied by the inflated, long-winded epics of the followers of Ennius.[10] They in turn influenced the work of Propertius, Tibullus, Ovid, and the young Virgil, and although the epyllion, or brief epic, is now considered to be a ghost form which never properly existed, still there was a general literary movement with comparable forms that deeply influenced the Victorians.[11] They saw an analogy between that exhausted period—so rich in science and criticism but so lacking in true creative impulse—and their own day. Arnold prefixed to both the first and the third volumes of his verse a motto from Choerilus of Samos which indicated that "everything had been done," and novelists like Kingsley, Newman, Bulwer-Lytton, and Pater set the scenes of their novels in ancient Alexandria, or North Africa, or the Roman Empire in the period of its decadence. William Morris, that "idle singer of an empty day," was perhaps the prime example of a Victorian Alexandrian, not only because he wrote a composite epic in *The Earthly Paradise* and modeled his *Life and Death of Jason* upon the *Argonautica* of Apollonius of Rhodes, but also because in *The Defence of Guenevere* he elected to examine the other side of the question—not to narrate the epic battles of Arthur but to see what could be said in behalf of

Guenevere. *Œnone* is also an Alexandrian poem in the sense that
it is a retelling of the Judgment of Paris not from the point of view
of Paris or the gods, or even of the Trojan War, but from the
point of view of the woman who was crushed and bypassed by this
process. So too with the dramatic monologues. Whereas Tennyson as a boy at Somersby had written "in Greek hexameters an
Homeric book on the Seven against Thebes,"[12] now, confronted
by the same material, he elected to go inside Tiresias and see what
it felt like to be an aged and neglected prophet.

Part of the Callimachean ideal was that myth should be modernized, and this too was Tennyson's view. "It is no use," he said,
"giving a mere *réchaufé* of old legends."[13] Hence, in defiance of all
classical texts he made Tiresias into a nineteenth-century liberal
theologian who was shocked by the primitive vengefulness of Ares
and tried to gain a higher and better conception of divinity. One
wonders whether his being blasted by Athene is Tennyson's indication that any such inquirer will not be believed in the conventionally religious Thebes of his own day.

Against this background it is not difficult to see that *Ulysses* also
affords almost the perfect instance of an Alexandrian subject.
Avoiding the regular adventures of Odysseus as having been
reasonably well told by Homer, Tennyson takes up a little-known,
in fact, virtually unknown, part of the myth and tells that. And he
tells it from the point of view of Ulysses. That he was not being
completely out of order in so doing is indicated by the fact that
even in antiquity questions of this sort had arisen. Homer, indeed,
had opened the way for them by having Tiresias prophesy, in
book XI, that Odysseus would not remain in Ithaca after his
return but would have further adventures and that "an ever so
mild death" would come to him "off the sea." Speculations naturally arose as to how this would come about. Sextus Empiricus
reports a tradition that Odysseus "breathed his last when a sea-
gull dropped on his head the sting of a ray-fish." Plutarch says
that after slaying the suitors he was banished to Italy by Neop-
tolemus, to whom the kinsmen of the suitors had appealed for
justice. Theopompus, a writer of less repute, says that he went to
Etruria and died there quietly in old age. But the story most
commonly told is that Odysseus sent Penelope back to her father
because of her infidelity with the suitors and then went himself
among the Thesprotians, where he married Callidice, their
queen. After her death he returned to Ithaca but, fearful of an

oracle that predicted his own death at the hands of his son, banished Telemachus to Cephallenia, only to be accidentally slain by Telegonus, his son by Circe. Telegonus then took the body of his father, along with Telemachus and Penelope, to Circe's isle, where he married Penelope and Telemachus married Circe. This astonishing tale formed the basis of the sixth-century epic *Telegonia*, written by an African Greek, Eugammon of Cyrene.[14]

As a result of all these speculations one of the great medieval literary questions was, What happened to Ulysses after his return? and this is the reason why Dante was so eager to speak to Ulysses when he met him in the eighth pouch of Malebolge. Dante, of course, had never read Homer and so could not know that the *Odyssey* is a centripetal poem—that Odysseus's entire effort, despite his marvelous adventures, is to get home. And so, without even taking him home, Dante has him go straight from Circe's palace through the Strait of Gibraltar and makes him into a symbol of intellectual curiosity. What is not clear is whether Dante also in part condemns him for it. To the medieval mind *curiositas*, the desire to go beyond the limits of what is ordinarily prescribed for man, is a sin, and the Pillars of Hercules were the *ne plus ultra* of the ancient world. To the Renaissance, however, they merely beckoned to a world unknown, and so when Pulci and Tasso repeated Dante's story they did not condemn Ulysses for his voyage but commended him as a precursor of Columbus.[15] Most interesting, however, is the comment of Bacon, for at the end of the first book of *The Advancement of Learning*, certainly one of the greatest defenses of pure inquiry ever written, Bacon lists a number of people who in antiquity had opposed these values. One of them was Paris, and we have noted that this passage, called to Tennyson's attention by Spedding, may have had some bearing on *Œnone*. Another was Ulysses, "*qui vetulam praetulit immortalitati* [that preferred an old woman to immortality], being a figure of those which prefer custom and habit before all excellency."[16] Bacon is referring, of course, not to Ulysses' later travels, which he clearly did not know about, but to his refusal of Calypso's offer of immortality if he would stay with her instead of going back to Penelope. Here, then, is another person who thought Ulysses would have done better to pursue knowledge rather than be "matched with an aged wife." By the Romantic period this view had triumphed. Goethe was so fascinated with Ulysses as the type of the romantic wanderer that he would have made him the subject of a major work if he had not been diverted into Faust. And Keats's sonnet *On First Looking into Chapman's Homer* is so imbued with the Renaissance spirit of exploration that one cannot but think that he has transferred to the author of the poem the spirit of its questing hero. Landor wrote a poem, *The Last of Ulysses,* in three parts, of which a Latin version was published in 1820, but it was based largely on the *Telegonia.* Tennyson's task it was to take the narrative of Dante and the spirit of the Renaissance and Romantic age and make Ulysses into a symbol of the eternally restless, the insatiable element in the mind of man.

As a result, Tennyson takes Ithaca as a symbol of limitation. "Refusal of limitation by the religious sentiment" is the way Arnold described his hero Empedocles. "Refusal of limitation by anything" might be the description of Ulysses. For it is not merely that Ithaca is presented as "idle," "still," "barren," and "savage," but also that it is denoted by a series of words that have a quantitative or delimiting idea: "matched," "profits," "mete," "dole," "unequal," and "hoard." Enclosed by its crags and isolated by the sea, Ithaca is a stagnant, sterile, subhuman place, and over against it are the infinitely open sea and the ringing plains of windy Troy. There one does not "feed" like an animal but roams forever with a "hungry heart." Though Ulysses can say, "I am a part of all that I have met," he is not satisfied. For

> all experience is an arch wherethro'
> Gleams that untravell'd world whose margin fades
> For ever and for ever when I move.

Using the same image of the Titans piling Pelion on Ossa that he had used in a sonnet a few years before, Tennyson finds that "Life piled on life / Were all too little,"

> And this gray spirit yearning in desire
> To follow knowledge like a sinking star,
> Beyond the utmost bound of human thought.

Not until the twentieth century did any critic suggest that Tennyson's Ulysses was not entirely admirable, and this apparently means that the line which began with Dante and continued through the Renaissance and Romantic period is now over. Indeed, it was nearing its end in Tennyson's day, for by 1833 the high Romanticism of Werther and René, of Childe Harold and Alastor, was past, and Tennyson's figure has not only lost any element of Satanism which they may have had, but also, before he launches out upon the deep, he pauses, makes his will, and arranges for the succession.

Had he not done so—had the poem ended with line 32— Auden's charge of irresponsibility would have been justified. But as it is, the poem is built upon a dialectic. In the first paragraph (1–5) there is the stay-at-home life on Ithaca, negative and finite; in the second (6–32) there is the infinitely open life of the Romantic wanderer; and now, with the introduction of Telemachus, there is a kind of synthesis as the circular image of the first part and the linear image of the second are combined into the spiral image of gradual political progress. For it is notable that we have here a reassessment of Ithaca by a more judicious and reasonable Ulysses. The characterization of his countrymen as a "savage race," which was spoken in frustration, is now modified into a "rugged people," as he acknowledges their capability for improvement. It is perhaps unfortunate that he did not have time to comment on how gracefully Penelope had grown old and search for the Attic equivalent of "senior citizen." But his thoughts were on politics at the moment, and it was the politics of reform. Hence we have the images of centrality appropriate to the island, but of movement within the center. Telemachus is "discerning to fulfill," he has "slow prudence," will work by "soft degrees," pay "meet adoration" to the household gods, and is himself "centred in the sphere / Of common duties." The Telemachean ideal is so little in favor today that it is difficult for readers, particularly young readers, to believe that Ulysses is not being condescending. Presumably everyone is to some degree condescending toward a way of life which he has not elected for himself, and yet Ulysses could hardly be more affectionate or more approving. Most of the terms which he employs carry connotations, now to some degree lost, of ancient political wisdom, of Greek and Roman discussions of justice and the state. "The useful and the good" is a major subject in Aristotle's *Ethics* and in all accounts of the Stoic and Epicurean philosophy. Prudence, reduced by Benjamin Franklin and others to a matter of self-interested calculation, was defined by Cicero as the knowledge of "what is good, what is bad, and what is neither good nor bad." It is one of the four cardinal virtues and is composed of memory, sagacity, and foresight. "Common duties" are not vulgar duties but those appropriate to all men, to the community; and "decent" (from Latin, *decens*) is that which is seemly, comely, or becoming, essentially the same idea as in "meet." "Offices" again brings to mind the great Latin treatise on social and political duties, Cicero's *De officiis*. All these words have suffered a deterioration in meaning, but it is virtually certain that Tennyson meant to employ them in their ancient and honorable sense.

It would be particularly odd if Ulysses were condescending toward Telemachus since Telemachus's political philosophy is Tennyson's philosophy. It is identical with the philosophy of gradualism expressed in *Hail Briton! You ask me, why, Love thou thy land,* and other poems of the years 1833–34. The England that Tennyson loves, like the Ithaca he envisons, is "A land of settled government . . . / Where Freedom slowly broadens down / From precedent to precedent"; where ideas, "by degrees to fulness wrought," have "time and space to work and spread." The true patriot is one who "with seasonable changes fair / And innovation grade by grade" shapes new usages to replace the old. In language that echoes Ulysses' image of the scabbard as well as those applied to Telemachus, Tennyson says,

> Meet is it changes should control
> Our being, lest we rust in ease.
> We all are changed by still degrees—

or, as another poem says, "by just degrees / With reason and with law." The task of Telemachus, then,

> by slow prudence to make mild
> A rugged people, and thro' soft degrees
> Subdue them to the useful and the good,

is one that Tennyson would thoroughly have approved, and we can only believe that when Ulysses says, "He works his work, I mine," both he and Tennyson mean just that—that there are two ways, the active and the contemplative, and that both are necessary. Tiresias thought so and had Menœceus to translate his vision into reality. Ulysses has Telemachus and would have been quite as helpless without him as Tiresias was without Menœceus. But so too would Telemachus have been helpless without Ulysses. For it was presumably Ulysses, whose experiences included "cities of men / And manners, climates, councils, governments," who brought to Telemachus his political ideal. Neither one could have done the other's work, and neither could effectively have done his own without the other.

Indeed, in the fourth section of the poem (44–70) Ulysses seems to have absorbed some of Telemachus's virtues. For just as Telemachus was a synthesis of the first section of the poem and the second, so now Ulysses is a synthesis of the second section and the third. He seems to be a more solid and responsible citizen than he was. For one thing, he is now seen among his companions and so is part of a community again, and there is more emphasis on organization, activity, and achievement. It is only by "sitting well in order" that they can do their task, and they must do it with "one equal temper" of heroic hearts. Indeed, Ulysses is now interested not only in striving and seeking but also in finding and not yielding. Those last two verbs are the Victorian addition to an otherwise Romantic poem, for whereas in the second paragraph the margin faded for ever and for ever, it now appears that at some point it will stop. Indeed, almost as if Carlyle had not merely admired the poem but had also written some part of it, there is emphasis upon doing "some *work* of noble note." There is more about "toil" than we had been led to expect from the travel posters of the second section, and one is almost afraid that Ulysses, having said, "He works his work, I mine," has taken this literally and forgotten that the proper "work" of a poet is to dream.

But it is not so. For the second major change in the final section is a change in mood. The landscape darkens, the lights come out, the wind arises, the deep "moans round with many voices." There is no use discussing, as some critics have, whether Greek sailors do or do not set out upon their voyages in the evening, for this is ineluctably a night voyage. It is a voyage into all that is obscure upon the map, all that is dark and mysterious in the human consciousness, all that is shadowy either in this world or the next. It is certainly a voyage into Death, for all Romantic heroes, from Werther on, have known that this is the ultimate experience. Those readers who find this element incompatible with the rest of Ulysses' quest seem to me to interpret that quest too narrowly, for it is not a real voyage but a visionary voyage, and, like Browning's *"Childe Roland to the Dark Tower Came,"* includes the "last curiosity" of death.

As Ulysses sails out over the western sea he will be following the course that Hanno will follow in later years, and one may presume that he too will hear the song of the Hesperides, be refreshed by it, and then sail on. It is a curious thing to find Ulysses, who, with respect to Telemachus, is a representative of the contemplative

life, in the same position as Hanno, who, with respect to the
Hesperides, is a representative of the active life. But the distinctive thing about Ulysses is that his whole life is conducted upon
the heroic plane. Unlike Tithonus and Tiresias he is not associated with the gods. When Tithonus says,

> Why should a man desire in any way
> To vary from the kindly race of men,
> Or pass beyond the goal of ordinance
> Where all should pause, as is most meet for all?

he seems to be the very opposite of Ulysses—and so in a sense he
is. But it is also clear that the cold marble palace of Aurora is for
him what the barren crags of Ithaca are for Ulysses, and that he is
as ill matched with his eternally youthful wife as Ulysses is with his
aged one. The only difference is that his "island" is divine,
whereas that of Ulysses is subhuman; the one is a world of pure
Being, the other of a kind of animal sloth that amounts to non-
Being. But both Tithonus and Ulysses want to be released into the
human world of Becoming, the world of change, movement,
activity, life—and death. Indeed, when the clouds part and give
Tithonus a glimpse of "that dark world where I was born," our
feeling is about the same as when the dark seas gloom upon the
mariners in *Ulysses*. Ulysses and Tithonus are both setting out
upon a voyage, though from opposite directions, and the goal
toward which they are moving is that of the eternally fluctuating
human condition.

It is the Lotos-Eaters, not Tithonus, who are the true moral
opposite of Ulysses, for they have rejected the open sea for the
island. They believe, of course, that the lotos will make them into
gods, but actually it has made them into vegetables, and thus their
terrestrial paradise, though superficially having little in common
with rockbound Ithaca, is morally the same. It is a place of decep-
tive luxuriance which diverts the hero from his normal activity of
the quest.

The island of the Hesperides, however, which superficially resembles that of the Lotos-Eaters, is truly a source of sacred wisdom, but of wisdom absolutely esoteric, not available to man even
to heal the ancient wound of the world. If Hercules, the type of
the active man, should attempt to steal it, he should be resisted,
for not only would the apples lose their virtue but he too would be
in jeopardy. At least that was the experience of Tithonus and

Tiresias when they attempted to wed themselves with the divine. It was by a divine carelessness that Aurora gave to her lover only half of what he needed to be happy, and it was by a divine anger and jealousy that Ares pursued the descendants of Cadmus and Athene blinded Tiresias. Clearly, in Tennyson the gods are not necessarily good, only sacred.[17] This is a central paradox in many of these poems, and Tennyson's main effort, as he moves into the middle thirties, is to bridge the gulf between the human and the divine. One may see him doing this in three distinct stages: first, in poems like *The Hesperides* and *The Poet's Mind*, where the poet-figure is a priest or goddess and the uninitiate are warned to stay away; secondly, in poems like *The Lady of Shalott* and *Œnone*, where the poet-figure is a "fairy" and longs to communicate with mortals but the mortals are inattentive or false; and thirdly, in poems like *Tiresias* or *Ulysses*, where a mortal who has had some experience of divinity is able to communicate that experience to another, who will translate it into reality. Clearly, the proper way to heal the ancient wound of the world was not for Hercules to steal the apples but for Hanno to listen to the music and then speak to Hercules about it. For Hercules is the equivalent of Telemachus in this poem, or, if that is too strange a thing to say, at least Telemachus undertakes his version of Herculean labors. And as for Ulysses, if he should not hear the music of the Hesperides on this voyage, we know that he has heard such music before. That, indeed, is why he is sailing on. But because he has always, both in his earlier voyages and now, conducted his quest solely on the heroic level, he is capable of bridging the gulf between the human and the divine. It is significant that by 1833 Tennyson had abandoned the isolated maiden singing in her tower and had given to a masculine figure, who is also a contemplative, the linear image which hitherto had been reserved for her absconding lover.

In the *Morte d'Arthur* the linear image is given to Arthur, who at the end of the poem is moving out in his barge toward the island-valley of Avilion. Arthur too is an old man—his fight, his struggle, his quest is over, and he is now seeking a place of rest where he can heal himself of his grievous wound. But Arthur differs in one respect from Ulysses, Tithonus, and Tiresias in that he is not a prophet-seer, a visionary who has delegated to others the task of realizing his vision in the world. He is a complete man, who has both conceived an order and brought it into being. "The vision of an ideal Arthur," said Tennyson, "as I have drawn him, had come upon me when, little more than a boy, I first lighted upon Malory."[18] But it is the first time that any such ideal figure has been represented in his poetry. Ulysses comes closest to it, to doing what Hallam and Tennyson said they must do—not lose sight of the real in pursuing the ideal[19]—but Arthur is a paradigm of the entire process. For far back in the recesses of the poem, at the very forefront of his history, stands the Lady of the Lake, who has created the most dazzling work of art in the entire Arthurian world. That Excalibur is a work of art is clear, for when Sir Bedivere looked upon its jeweled hilt he was so dazzled by its curious beauty that he wished to put it in a museum.

> "were this kept,
> Stored in some treasure-house of mighty kings,
> Some one might show it at a joust of arms,
> Saying, 'King Arthur's sword, Excalibur,
> Wrought by the lonely maiden of the lake,
> Nine years she wrought it, sitting in the deeps
> Upon the hidden bases of the hills.' "

What Sir Bedivere overlooks is that Excalibur, beautiful as it is, is a sword. True, the Lady of the Lake is a faery creature dwelling in a supernatural realm far removed from Arthur and his battles and closely associated with all that is most permanent in nature. She is to Arthur what the Lady of Shalott was to Lancelot, but whereas Lancelot ignored his Lady, out of the mysterious depths of this silent mere has come the source of Arthur's power. By Excalibur he has forged the Table Round, and if we may be permitted to see in its circularity, "which was an image of the mighty world," the fulfillment and perfection of what Telemachus was sloping toward, then Arthur is himself a Telemachean figure. He has subdued a savage race into a rugged people, but now he perishes by this people he has made. His wide world is narrowed to "a dark strait of barren land," and one may see this promontory, on one side of which lay the ocean and on the other a great water, as the equivalent of Ulysses' island. Indeed, it is even more harsh and sterile than Ithaca, for it is set in the depth of winter. There are sharp, jagged rocks, and a shrill wind whistles through the icy caves. On the barren strand are the tombs of the mighty dead and the broken symbols of religion. There is no living thing but the water flags, and when the Queens send up their lamentation to the stars, it is like "a wind, that shrills / All night in a wasteland, where no one comes, / Or hath come since the making of the world." And yet, when Arthur's barge moves out from this world of death it reminds us less of Ulysses' vessel than of the funeral barge of the Lady of Shalott, for just as her dying song was compared to that of the dying swan, so is the lamentation of the Queens. "Like some full-breasted swan / . . . fluting a wild carol ere her death," the barge moves from the brink, and unlike Ulysses' vessel, it moves not into the sunset but the sunrise. Though Arthur's faith is very muted ("for all my mind is clouded with a doubt"), yet he thinks he goes

> To the island-valley of Avilion;
> Where falls not hail, or rain, or any snow,
> Nor ever wind blows loudly; but it lies
> Deep-meadow'd, happy, fair with orchard-lawns
> And bowery hollows crown'd with summer sea,
> Where I will heal me of my grievous wound.

Ulysses, Tithonus, and Tiresias all envision for themselves some place of final rest, but theirs is not like this. For Tithonus it is simply human; for Tiresias and Ulysses it is heroic. Ulysses, if he touches on the Happy Isles, will "see the great Achilles, whom we knew"; and Tiresias yearns to be "gather'd to my rest, / And mingled with the famous kings of old." There he will no longer be oppressed by the petty "populace" of Thebes but will regain his sight and find

> The men I knew, and watch the chariot whirl
> About the goal again, and hunters race
> The shadowy lion, and the warrior-kings,
> In height and prowess more than human, strive
> Again for glory, while the golden lyre
> Is ever sounding in heroic ears
> Heroic hymns.

Avilion, however, is a feminine rather than a masculine place. It closely resembles the island of the Hesperides, and although the three Queens are not to be identified with the three sisters, Tennyson resisted their identification with any other figures. They are, and are not, Faith, Hope, and Charity, he said. "They are three of the noblest women. They are also those three Graces, but they are much more."[20] They are those who have in them the power to heal "the old wound of the world" whether they wish to do so or not. In a word, though our initial impression is that Arthur is to be associated with the linear image of Ulysses, actually his voyage is but one segment of a circle, not the small circle of the Table Round, the ordered and finished society, but the great circle of the cosmic process. Coming out of the great deep and returning to the great deep again, he illustrates the eternal recurrence and is a kind of symbol of the dying god. Tennyson has made this clear in many ways, primarily by the topography of the poem, in which the narrow strait of barren land, which is the symbol of life in this world, is flanked by the twin mysteries of Birth and Death, but also by the imagery of the revolving seasons. It was "one summer noon" that an arm "Rose up from out the bosom of the lake, / Clothed in white samite, mystic, wonderful," and presented Arthur with the sword. Now it is in the depth of winter and at midnight that he returns it whence it came.[21] Since Tennyson changed the time of the last battle from summer, as it is in Malory, to winter, it is likely that he intended it to be the winter solstice, when the old year is dying and the new year about to be reborn. Professor Paden believes that Tennyson's reading of Malory was suffused by suggestions of George Stanley Faber's Helio-Arkite mythology, a strange fabrication which Faber believed was developed by the descendants of Ham and spread over the western world and which involved the worship of the sun and the Ark.[22] Whether or not one accepts this view, it is clear that Arthur, whose lustrous curls made him in youth like a "rising sun" and who, though his face is now white like a "withered moon," is sailing into the sunrise again, is a kind of god whose death and rebirth signalize the death and rebirth of the year. So much is suggested not only by the imagery but also by the threefold structure of the poem—the three Queens, the three attempts of Sir Bedivere, the three wavings of the sword—which reproduces the threefold process of Birth, Death, and Rebirth that is the cyclic theme of the poem.

The theme, indeed, as Arthur makes clear in his far too explicit valedictory, is the passing of an old order—an old set of values— the recognition of this fact, and adjustment to it. But to say this is to state that Sir Bedivere, not Arthur, is the protagonist of the poem. True, Arthur is the one who passes, but it is Sir Bedivere who has the problem of surviving into the new world of "strange faces, other minds." It is he who has to relinquish Excalibur, which is the central action of the poem. Tennyson attempts to humanize the process by distinguishing, as Malory hardly does, between the first attempt and the second. In the first, Sir Bedivere's eyes are simply dazzled by the beauty and preciousness of the hilt, but in the second he is rather "clouded with his own conceit," as he attempts to rationalize his disobedience by appealing to pragmatic standards of value and a spurious antiquarianism. Ultimately, he has to close his eyes in order to relinquish the sword, and it is in his eyes that Arthur sees that it is done. For Tennyson uses the eyes in this part of the poem as a witness of the truth and a symbol of authority. Essentially, Bedivere has to learn to see spiritually, and when he does he is rewarded by an aurora borealis that is far more beautiful than the sword itself. Further, when he is called to bear Arthur himself down to the edge of the water, he achieves a heroic stature he had never achieved in life. Sir Bedivere

> swiftly strode from ridge to ridge,
> Clothed with his breath, and looking, as he walked,
> Larger than human on the frozen hills.
> He heard the deep behind him, and a cry
> Before. His own thought drove him, like a goad.
> Dry clash'd his harness in the icy caves
> And barren chasms, and all to left and right
> The bare black cliff clang'd round him, as he based
> His feet on juts of slippery crag that rang
> Sharp-smitten with the dint of armed heels—
> And on a sudden, lo! the level lake,
> And the long glories of the winter moon.

Tennyson well knew how to invoke the barrenness of the landscape in order to express the desolation of the heart. For Bedivere is desolate. As Arthur lies in the barge, "Then loudly cried the bold Sir Bedivere"—whose epithet "bold" has been an ironic note from the very beginning—

> "Ah! my Lord Arthur, whither shall I go? . . .
> For now I see the true old times are dead, . . .
> And I, the last, go forth companionless, . . .
> Among new men, strange faces, other minds."

Arthur's last speech explains, through the image of the fountain and the gold chain, how a new order may be created through prayer, but essentially he says, "Comfort thyself: what comfort is in me?" and moves off until he is a black dot against the dawn.

Biographically, there is nothing strange in the fact that Sir Bedivere is the protagonist of the poem. To Tennyson the "Morte d'Arthur" is the death of Arthur Hallam, and the poet is naturally cast in the role of the one who is left behind. But poetically it is strange, for we have not hitherto had figures like Sir Bedivere as the protagonist of Tennyson's poems. Of course, if this poem had been written in the form of a dramatic monologue, it would necessarily have been placed in his mouth. This is not entirely fantasy. Malory, in indicating his uncertainty whether Arthur had indeed died and whether he was buried at Glastonbury, says that he is merely reporting the story as Sir Bedivere told it. And when Tennyson joined the *Morte d'Arthur* to the rest of the *Idylls of the King* under the title *The Passing of Arthur*, he composed a brief introductory passage which began,

> That story which the bold Sir Bedivere,
> First made and latest left of all his knights,
> Told, when the man was no more than a voice
> In the white winter of his age, to those
> With whom he dwelt, new faces, other minds.

In other words, though he retained the third-person narrative, *The Passing of Arthur* (and also the *Morte d'Arthur*) is essentially a dramatic monologue in that it gives Sir Bedivere's experience of the events. But this is a striking departure from Tennyson's usual practice in that Sir Bedivere is distinctly a minor character. He plays a role comparable to that of Telemachus in that he is the successor, the one who is left behind, and he is not even as important as Telemachus since he is not a son or an enactor of vision but a mere retainer. But whereas in the earlier poem Tennyson identified with Ulysses, here he identifies with Sir Bedivere. One could, of course, imagine the story of Ulysses retold from the point of view of Telemachus. One would get an admiring account of the old king's past greatness, his painful dissatisfaction with his life on Ithaca, his decision to leave, the boy's cry, "What will become of me?" and Ulysses' reassuring speech, not about prayer but about government, and then the ship moving off till it is merely a black speck against the sunset. But it would not be a very "dramatic" monologue, and we have already seen that if Telemachus were to set up as a poet it would not be dramatic monologues that he would write but quatrains. *Hail Briton!* and *Love thou thy land* are, in fact, the poetry written by Telemachus, and Sir Bedivere's would presumably not be very different. (Its title is actually *In Memoriam*.) It would apply the gradualism that Telemachus applies to politics to the problem of human grief. And one has no doubt that that is what Sir Bedivere will do. He will fast and pray—as Malory tells us that he does—write quatrains about King Arthur, and gradually emerge from his grief into reconciliation.

6

The English Idyls

These little paintings in their costly frames.
Draft of *The Gardener's Daughter*

"Of this *Second* Vol:," says FitzGerald of the *Poems* of 1842, "the Morte d'Arthur, Day-dream, Lord of Burleigh, & Dora, were in MS in a little red Book, from which they were read to me & Spedding of a Night, 'when all the House was mute,' at Spedding's House, Mirehouse, by Basanthwaite Lake, in Cumberland. Spedding's Father & Mother were both alive: and his Father, who was of a practical turn, and had seen enough of Poets in Shelley and Coleridge (perhaps in Wordsworth also) . . . , rather resented our making so serious a Business of Verse-making, though he was so wise and charitable as to tolerate every thing & Everybody—except Poetry & Poets."[1] FitzGerald goes on to say that the frame to the *Morte d'Arthur,* which was published in 1842 under the title *The Epic,* did not exist at this time and therefore must have been added sometime between May 1835, the date of the reading, and 1842.[2] Since the ostensible purpose of the frame, which describes the reading of the poem to a group of college friends at Christmastime, is to provide an embarrassed apology for a poem so little relevant to modern life, and particularly for the anachronism of the style—"faint Homeric echoes, nothing worth"—one may think that it derives from this reading and that Parson Holmes is a distant allusion to Mr. Spedding, Sr. Actually, of course, the effect of the frame is firmly to assert the poem's worth, for although the parson, who has been "Now harping on the church-commissioners, / Now hawking at Geology and schism," fell asleep during the recital, this is a compliment rather than the reverse, and the other two listeners were deeply moved. Naturally, like the college youths they are, they will not betray their emotion. Francis Allen, "muttering, like a man ill-used, / . . . drove his heel into the smoulder'd log" and sent a blast of sparkles up the flue. The narrator was set by the tale to dream, but the real indication of his interest comes in the introductory part of the poem where, when mention is made that one book of Everard Hall's epic has survived, "I, tho' sleepy, like a horse / That hears the corn-bin open, prick'd my ears," for he remembered Everard's college fame and recognized the true source of his spiritual nourishment. What they had been discussing, these three youths and Parson Holmes, was how "the old honour had from Christmas gone, / Or gone, or dwindled down to some odd games / In some odd nooks like this"—forfeits and kissing the girls beneath the sacred bush—and the parson, "taking wide and wider sweeps" through the various issues of the day, had finally settled down "upon the general decay of faith / Right thro' the world . . . : 'there was no anchor, none, / To hold by.'" At this point Francis Allen, laughing, clapped his hand on Everard's shoulder and said, "I hold by him," and though Everard, ever playing the clown, says, "And I by the wassail-bowl," the clear implication of this is to anticipate Arnold's statement that in the modern world poetry will more and more take the place of religion. In the general decay of faith Francis Allen will hold by the poet, who will provide a new order, a new set of values, to replace the old.

This, as we have already seen, is what the poem does—not confidently, for Tennyson with characteristic agnosticism mutes the thought of Arthur's second coming. But there is enough said to enable the youths to see that Sir Bedivere's problem is their problem and that the proper solution is not, as Holmes would say, blindly to cling to the old but through prayer, labor, and imagination to prepare for the new. Indeed, the narrator is so impressed that when he goes to bed he dreams that Arthur does come again, "like a modern gentleman / Of stateliest port," and that all the people acclaim him. Now whether it be the stateliness of his port or the cheeriness of the church bells that ring him in, we feel that in this detail Tennyson has suffered a lapse of taste. His point, of course, is that, like Adam, the narrator awoke and found his dream was true. But the "dream" was the myth of Arthur embodied in Everard Hall's poem, and the youths found it true when, in their embarrassment, they kicked the log and acknowledged its bearing upon themselves. They did not need to dream it over again in the modern dress it had already assumed, and, in any case, if the modern gentleman is supposed to be Hallam, there is the objection that Hallam is dead and that it was his death and not his second coming that was the occasion of the poem. The last dozen or sixteen lines not only reduplicate the action unnecessarily, they also get ahead of the story.

Nonetheless, the frame is a real achievement. Without it Tennyson would have created a jewel, but with it he has placed this jewel in a setting which enhances its beauty by the play of reflected lights. It is not merely that the frame emphasizes the relevance of the Arthurian myth—though this has more point than usual because of the fact that the myth contains a cyclical view of history—but also that the *Morte d'Arthur* is transformed from the narrative of a king's death into a work of art, a poem. It is distinctly a piece of literature. It does not pretend to any other reality than this, that it is the eleventh book of an epic written by a young man and being read to an audience of which two are attentive and one is asleep. Thus, the poem as a whole is called *The Epic,* and its center is neither in the frame nor in the inset but somewhere between the two. It hovers back and forth between the reading of the poem, which is initiated by the first part of the frame, and its reception, which is detailed by the second— between these and the poem itself. Hence the poem's quality as art can actually be emphasized, and this is done by the heightened formalism and artificiality of the romance or epic style. Within the poem this courtly and ritualistic character—the archaic language, the epithets, the symmetry of the action, the repeated poetic formulas—is justified as the literary equivalent of the old order that is passing. But within the frame it constitutes a heightened and intensified beauty which is simply the beauty of art itself. For this reason the style of the frame is in sharp contrast with that of the inset—not archaic, formal, and ritualistic but the perfectly natural and cultivated language of Oxford and Cambridge undergraduates. At the same time there is nothing colloquial about it: it is limpid and graceful and it is written in blank verse. Thus, it too is art, though it is reality with respect to the artfulness of the inset, and so the whole question is raised, What is art and what is reality? What is the relation of the poet to society, of the myth to the moment? We are left with the impression that we do not know quite so clearly as we thought we did, and we are even aware that the problem does not stop here. For far within the center of the poem, dwelling "Upon the hidden bases of the hills", is another artist, the Lady of the Lake, who has fashioned in Excalibur a work of art that is far more dazzling even than the legend in which it is set. Yet this work of art is the means of the King's acting upon the world. So there is a work of art which impinges upon reality, which itself is a work of art which impinges upon reality, which, as we read it, impinges upon our reality again. By this device of a series of receding images—like the picture of an artist painting a picture of an artist painting a picture—Tennyson raises questions which he has been asking, but not so distinctly, from the very outset of his career.

He does this again in an even more complicated, though less substantial poem, *The Day-Dream*, which is precisely parallel to *The Epic* in that it too represents the poet as telling an old-world legend to a person who he at least hopes will be deeply affected by it. In this case the legend is that of the Sleeping Beauty and the person Lady Flora. The poem, which is a veritable *Tale of a Tub* for preliminary and concluding matter, consists of nine sections, which form an envelope structure in three stages successively recessed. It may be represented thus:

1. Prologue
        2. The Sleeping Palace
                    3.   The Sleeping Beauty
        4. The Arrival
        5. The Revival
        6. The Departure
7. Moral
8. L'Envoi
9. Epilogue

The fascinating thing about this structure is that Tennyson wrote the poem from the middle out. The first section written was *The Sleeping Beauty,* which was published in the *Poems, Chiefly Lyrical* of 1830 and which would have taken its place there among the "lady" poems as a pure aesthetic image. It was feminine, passive, absolutely immobile—"A perfect form in perfect rest." Then, sometime between 1830 and 1834, when Tennyson had become more interested in the social uses of beauty, he added the surrounding legend, sections 2 and 4–6. Section 2 presents a picture of the Sleeping Palace which concludes with the words, "When will the hundred summers die, / And thought and time be born again, / And newer knowledge, drawing nigh, / Bring truth that sways the souls of men?" The answer is given in the arrival of the fairy

Prince, who, led by a "Magic Music" that has beat within his heart since childhood, comes, "scarce knowing what he seeks," and kisses the Sleeping Beauty. She and all the palace awake (though some of the king's councillors rather reluctantly), and he carries her off to his father's court: "Through all the world she followed him." He is, in other words, precisely the kind of lover that the Lady of Shalott and Mariana longed for and never had, and as a result the roles can be reversed. For where the Lady of Shalott was the artist and did not even have a sympathetic listener, the Sleeping Princess is Beauty itself, who is brought out of her hidden bower by the artist imbued with love.

> All precious things, discovered late,
>   To those that seek them issue forth;
> For love in sequel works with fate,
>   And draws the veil from hidden worth.

This was the state of the poem when Tennyson read it to FitzGerald and Spedding in the famous session of May 1835. At least when FitzGerald says that "the Prologue & Epilogue" were added after that date,[3] we must probably understand him as referring to all the preliminary and concluding matter, for the Moral and Envoi, which refer to Lady Flora, would not have been intelligible without the Prologue, which introduces her. In this outermost frame Tennyson is again practicing imitative form. For just as the Prince took the Sleeping Beauty out into the world, so Tennyson now takes the legend of the Sleeping Beauty out into the world by telling it to Lady Flora. For Lady Flora, who in the Prologue is dozing by an open lattice, is herself a Sleeping Beauty, and as the poet watches her, he too has a dream which is the "day-dream" of his title. He dreamed "until at last / Across my fancy, brooding warm, / The reflex of a legend past, / And loosely settled into form." If she will but close her eyes he will tell it to her, but when he does, Lady Flora, whose "too earnest eyes" and "pensive mind" betoken a too serious approach to literature, demands the moral. The poet protests. "What moral is in being fair?" But if she will have one, let her consider how pleasant it would be to fall asleep for a hundred years, missing all the intervening wars and struggles, and then to wake upon a new state of science, poetry, and politics. So we should reap "The flower and quintessence of change." But really, anyone can make applications according to his humor, and to do so is to narrow art too much. Its use is in its beauty. In this case, where the poet would be the fairy Prince to his Lady Flora and wake her from the sleep of single life into the condition of wifehood, the poem is the kiss by which he would do it. Fashioned as a graceful compliment, it would itself accomplish the act of which it speaks. For it now appears that the Lady Flora is not merely dozing by the lattice, she is "all too dearly self-involved" and in that sense "sleeps a dreamless sleep to me"; and it is out of this solipsistic state that the poet, not entirely playfully, would wake her. Hence the rather frivolous poem. For just as the *Morte d'Arthur* provided for the young men the new order of imaginative experience which both they and Sir Bedivere required, so the legend of the Sleeping Beauty not only parallels Lady Flora's situation but is also the means of resolving it. And the resolution, as the poet is quick to point out, would combine her aesthetic with his, for if she would come out of her self-involvement into wifehood, that would be the "moral of [her] life" as it would be the "pleasure" of his.

Finally, Tennyson provided a brief frame for *Godiva*, written after passing through Coventry in June 1840. As so often, he throws the reader off the track by pretending that the poem is about something other than its true subject. Not only we, the modern generation, he says, who prate of rights and wrongs, have loved the people well, but she, Lady Godiva, actually suffered for them a thousand years ago and freed them from their tax. But when we come to the passage that is the emotional center of the poem, that in which Lady Godiva prepares to leave her inmost bower, and read the lovely description of her tender, shrinking modesty, her sense of shame, her reluctance to reveal her beauty to the world, then we realize that we are reading of the artist and that Tennyson was getting ready to publish once again. If one doubts this interpretation, one need only consult the Trinity College manuscript, where Tennyson turned Peeping Tom into the type of the critic.

> Nor do I trust the tale of peeping Tom:
> But if there were so gross a clown, be he
> Accursed! or if one of modern days
> Would turn this verse to scandal let him forge
> His own shame from it, Sathen helping him,
> Accursed! For she wrought a noble deed.[4]

Ultimately, Tennyson thought better about thus throwing down the gauntlet to the *Quarterly Review* and told the story of Tom in its traditional form. But he knew that by telling the story of Lady Godiva he was exposing himself to the same kind of ribald laughter that she had been exposed to in her ride. He thought, however, that he was doing it for the same good purpose—to serve the people—and hence the four lines of introduction:

> I waited for the train at Coventry;
> I hung with grooms and porters on the bridge,
> To watch the three tall spires; and there I shaped
> The city's ancient legend into this:—

The purpose of these lines is not, as Leigh Hunt says,[5] to inform us how casually Tennyson writes his poetry but to reinforce the theme of the poem by showing the poet mingling with grooms and porters, as Lady Godiva did, and the train counterpointed by the spires of the medieval cathedral.

Though the true subject of this poem is the artist's sensitivity, the mention of grooms and porters, trains and taxes, is not accidental. For beginning in the 1820s and continuing for perhaps thirty years there was a powerful demand on the part of many critics that the poet deal with the great realities of modern life instead of the outworn themes of Greece and Rome or the romance of the Middle Ages.[6] Trains and steam engines were as interesting as the monsters of antiquity, and the urban poor had their sorrows as well as the shepherds and shepherdesses of the Renaissance. Thus, when Elizabeth Barrett heard that Tennyson's new poem, *The Princess*, was "in blank verse & a fairy tale," she wrote, "Now isn't the world too old & fond of steam, for blank verse poems, in ever so many books, to be written on the fairies?"[7] And the *Westminster Review*, in noticing Tennyson's first volume, asked, "Is not the French Revolution as good as the siege of Troy? . . . The old epics will probably never be surpassed, any more than the old coats of mail; and for the same reason; nobody wants the article." The reviewer added that "a long story . . . is now always done, and best done, in prose."[8] Indeed, the real problem was not steam but the novel. The novel was usurping the dominant position previously occupied by poetry and was doing so precisely by its ability to deal, seriously and directly, with the issues of modern life. If the poet wished to compete with this rival, he would have to bestir himself. Hence some poets, such as Clough and Elizabeth Barrett, attempted the verse novel, whereas others, such as the Spasmodics, thought that a pretentious style and psychological violence would do the trick. Arnold, more thoughtfully, took the view in his Preface of 1853 that the important thing was not whether a subject was ancient or modern but that it involve actions which "powerfully appeal to the great primary human affections: to those elementary feelings which subsist permanently in the race, and which are independent of time."[9] He added that he was dropping his own *Empedocles on Etna* from his new volume not because it had an ancient subject but because it had a modern disease.

As usual, Tennyson took a mediatorial view. In his first two volumes there was little to provide comfort for the modernist, and there is no question that in his heart he was deeply drawn to the older legends and the traditionary forms. On the other hand, he was a proponent of change, and he certainly would have been startled by Elizabeth Barrett's remark, for in the "University of Women," as *The Princess* was originally called, he at least thought he was addressing the modern world. Aubrey de Vere, who heard him read from it in the spring of 1845, found him "denouncing exotics, and saying that a poem should reflect the time and place."[10] Of course, the way in which he did this was to write an old-world legend and place it in a modern setting, and we have already seen that in so doing he was not merely answering the call for relevance but was also devising complex poetic effects. He was, in fact, approximating a form which became one of the dominant forms of the Victorian period and that with which his own name is particularly associated—the idyl. For the idyl, as employed by Theocritus and Virgil, frequently involves two or three shepherds who come together and speak in artless and simple language about their everyday affairs. Then one asks the other to sing a song, or they engage in a song contest, perhaps of the "amœbœan" variety in which verse answers to verse, or they describe a beautifully carved bowl or other work of art, and then, after a brief interval, they part in subtly altered mood. It is difficult to say just what this Alexandrian and Neoteric form meant, for the scholars who have studied it most deeply are themselves not agreed. But one thing is certain: it was a highly sophisticated, not a simple form, and it had more to do with art than with shepherds. It was, indeed, a kind of coterie poetry, written by learned and highly cultivated men for their friends, and it was based on the premise that a delicate emotion expressed in a pure style came closer to the aesthetic experience than the most magniloquent emotion hammered home. It was, in other words, a poet's poem, highly conscious of itself as art, and if the idyls of Theocritus and the bucolics of Vergil have become world famous, it is probably because quietude and charm, tenderness and pure beauty, appeal as powerfully to the great primary human affections as does heroic action. In any case, it was this form, which in Tennyson's work grew out of his use of the frame, that served as his means of responding to the call for relevance.

The matter is paradoxical because, however "modern" or archaic the poems of Theocritus and Vergil may have been, certainly by the end of the eighteenth century the pastoral had acquired the name of the most sterile and artificial of poetic forms. It had been frozen in its own convention. Crabbe did the form a service by recalling it to truth and urging it to "own the Village Life a life of pain," and Wordsworth provided a new positive impulse to pastoralism by writing directly from nature. Indeed, when Wordsworth chose humble and rustic life as his subject because there the essential passions of the heart are more simply and accurately revealed, he was stating the true pastoral method. For pastoral is not a subject but a perspective. It is the perspective of one who has gone out of the city into the country and looks back upon his problems through the clear rural air. Hence, the tension of winter along with spring, of labor along with harvest, is essential, and these had always been included by Theocritus and Virgil. The latter especially found that he could treat vast social movements, such as the demobilization of armies, through the single instance of a shepherd threatened with dispossession of his farm. Through simple things, as Empson noted, complex things may be said.[11] Thus, when the impulse from a vernal wood which had been renewed by Romanticism met with the new industrialization and the urbanization of the early Victorian years, it was the perfect pastoral moment. On the one hand was the sense of a complex and sophisticated culture, of pressing national problems, and, on the other, of an older and greener world which was rapidly fading away but had not yet altogether been lost.

It is no wonder, then, that Theocritus came back into favor at this time, particularly at Cambridge. Asked whether Tennyson was a good classicist, the Master of Trinity is said to have replied, "He knew his Theocritus very well."[12] But so too did others. Among Tennyson's contemporaries at Trinity were a future translater of Theocritus and a future student of the Greek bucolic poets.[13] Possibly their attention was drawn to their subject by the publication in 1826–29 of a Cambridge reprint of the Kiessling edition of Theocritus, the most important English edition of the poet since Warton's in 1770. And of course all these men had known their Virgil since childhood. But the pastoral revival came from many sources, one of them being Germany. For in 1756 Salomon Gessner published his *Idyllen* which, though retaining Greek names, added touches from a north European scene and infused into the poems a modern sentimentality and morality. These *Idyllen* were translated into English as the *Rural Poems*, and when Robert Southey heard about them from William Taylor of Norwich, he determined to imitate them.[14] His *English Eclogues*, nine in number, are doubtless the formal precedent for Tennyson's English Idyls, that is, for the recreation of the classical form with modern English characters and manners, but spiritually their flat prosaicism hardly provides a model. For that, for the freshness and beauty, the sentiment and charm of the English countryside, Tennyson was indebted, apart from his own observation, to the newly emerging prose idyl. For in 1843, in *A New Spirit of the Age*, R. H. Horne noticed that "Within the last half century a somewhat new class of writing has been introduced into this country with great success, and most fortunately for the public taste, as its influence is most healthy and sweet, most refreshing and soothing, most joyous, yet most innocent. It is that of the unaffected prose pastoral."[15] Citing the delightful papers and essays of Leigh Hunt, and particularly one little work *The Months,* he acknowledged that Miss Mitford was the undoubted leader of this school, though William and Mary Howitt were strong supporters. The latter's *Rural Life of England* (1838) in two volumes, and Miss Mitford's *Our Village: Sketches of Rural Character and Scenery* (1824–32) in five, make us aware that the idyl, or "little picture," when naturalized into English, takes the form of the "sketch." It is this form, halfway between an essay and a narrative, which seems to have just the flexibility and inconclusiveness demanded by these materials. What Lamb's essays and the *Sketches by Boz* did for London, and *The Sketch Book of Geoffrey Crayon, Gent.* for other parts of England and America, the sketches of Miss Mitford and William Howitt, of Charlotte Smith and Thomas Miller did for the English countryside. The danger of these works, as Horne's encomium indicates, is that they may fall into mere prettiness on the one side or heaviness on the other. For as the origin of the term *sketch* indicates, there was, quite apart from Gessner, a considerable Dutch or German element in these idyls, a kind of domestic *Gemütlichkeit,* which made what had originally been an aristocratic into a middle-class form. The "little picture," in other words, may be a Cuyp instead of a Claude Lorraine, a Rembrandt instead of a Titian.

Tennyson did not altogether avoid these evils. *The May Queen,* which was universally beloved in the Victorian era, is to modern taste almost unreadable, and *The Lord of Burleigh,* though a fine "period piece," is also marred by condescension and superficiality. Even *Dora,* which many people admire, seems to me a mistake— not for Arnold's reason, that it sacrifices *simplicité* to *simplesse,* [16] but because its harsh Crabbean realism is at variance with the sentiment it ought to inspire. Tennyson's intention, in this tale adapted from Miss Mitford's *Our Village,* was to achieve the severity and simplicity of the Book of Ruth or the nobility of Wordsworth's *Michael.* But his harsh, bald style, in which (as in the third book of *Paradise Lost*) there is not a single metaphor or any descriptive passage, is the counterpart not of the loving mind of Dora but of the harsh vindictiveness of the old man. Since Dora's strategy is to soften the mind of her uncle by bringing the child to him in the midst of the harvest plenty, that strategy should also be practiced on the reader. Miss Mitford manages the matter better by having the tale told retrospectively by a feminine narrator in the midst of the harvest scene.

The best of Tennyson's English Idyls may be divided into two groups: on the one hand, *The Gardener's Daughter* and *The Miller's Daughter,* written about 1832–33, and on the other, *Walking to the Mail, Audley Court, Edwin Morris,* and *The Golden Year,* written about 1837–39. The former are dramatic monologues, focusing upon a feminine figure, and so closer to the poems of 1830–32; the latter involve a dialogue between two or more masculine figures and so are more Theocritean in structure.

The Gardener's Daughter is one of Tennyson's most luxuriant poems, but when we examine the manuscripts we find that it was once far more luxuriant, perhaps twice its present length and infinitely fuller not only of incident but also of description. [17] It was, indeed, not an idyl but a tale, precisely in the manner of *The Lover's Tale,* and so provides a link between that earlier Romantic mode and the Victorian idyl. Then as now, it told of the narrator's wooing of Rose, the gardener's daughter, but in the original there was much more about the paintings of Eustace, the narrator's friend, about the long-drawn-out difficulties of the courtship, and about the death of a younger brother. Fortunately, at a certain point Tennyson had the acumen to realize that the essence of his tale lay not in the narrative but in the picture which the narrator painted of Rose as she stood in her cottage door. And so it is on that picture that the poem focuses. We do not realize it at first, but by the end of the poem we are aware that the tale is not addressed to us as readers but to some unamed auditor to whom the portrait is being unveiled by the speaker years after his beloved's death. The poem thus belongs with Rossetti's *The Portrait* and Browning's *My Last Duchess* as a member of that Victorian subgenre, the portrait by the artist of a dead girl. But whereas Browning is horrified at the thought of a living woman being imprisoned in a dead work of art, and Rossetti is thrilled at the idea of a form which somehow imitates the object without constituting it, Tennyson believed that the soul could be captured in a portrait painted by Love.

For this portrait was so painted. The subtitle of *The Gardener's Daughter* is *The Pictures*. The other picture is Eustace's portrait of his betrothed, Juliet, of which the narrator said, "(half in earnest, half in jest,) / 'Tis not your work, but Love's.' " So the narrator is told that he will paint his masterpiece when he goes to see Rose, the gardener's daughter. For, less in jest than in earnest, Tennyson believes that one does paint beautifully only that which one truly loves. What does Tennyson love?

> Not wholly in the busy world, nor quite
> Beyond it, blooms the garden that I love.

Among all the rewritings and changes of the manuscripts these lines remain unchanged. For though the gardener's daughter appears in a garden that has some resemblance to the bower of the Sleeping Beauty or of the other sequestered maidens, it is not absolutely a *hortus conclusus,* cut off from the world. "News from the humming city comes to it / In sound of funeral or of marriage bells"; and although between the city and the garden lies a "league of grass, wash'd by a slow broad stream," this stream creeps slowly down, "Barge-laden, to three arches of a bridge / Crown'd with the minster-towers." Neither is Rose herself a Sleeping Beauty. True, "In that still place she, hoarded in herself, / Grew, seldom

seen." Still, her fame was widespread, and when the narrator
came to see her he found her, not warbling in her bower, but
engaged in a useful domestic task. A storm the previous night had
blown down one spray of a rose bush by the cottage door, and she,
as he entered, was reaching up to replace it. Society ladies in those
days assumed what they called "attitudes."[18] In a parlor or salon,
before a cluster of admirers and arrayed in cashmere shawls or
turbans, they threw themselves into a series of postures: they were
now Niobe, lamenting her children, now Ariadne, gazing out to
sea. "O Attic shape, fair attitude!" says Keats, but there is no fairer
one than that into which Tennyson froze the gardener's daughter.
For the real portrait is not that in pigments revealed by the
narrator at the end of the poem but that in words revealed by
Tennyson in the middle.

> For up the porch there grew an Eastern rose,
> That, flowering high, the last night's gale had caught,
> And blown across the walk. One arm aloft—
> Gown'd in pure white, that fitted to the shape—
> Holding the bush, to fix it back, she stood,
> A single stream of all her soft brown hair
> Pour'd on one side: the shadow of the flowers
> Stole all the golden gloss, and wavering
> Lovingly lower, trembled on her waist—
> Ah, happy shade—and still went wavering down,
> But, ere it touch'd a foot, that might have danced
> The greensward into greener circles, dipt,
> And mix'd with shadows of the common ground!
> But the full day dwelt on her brows, and sunn'd
> Her violet eyes, and all her Hebe bloom,
> And doubled his own warmth against her lips,
> And on the bounteous wave of such a breast
> As never pencil drew. Half light, half shade,
> She stood, a sight to make an old man young.

"It is the Center of the Poem," said Tennyson of the above
passage; "it must be full & rich. The Poem is so, to a fault, I know:
but, being so, this central Picture must hold it's [sic] place—"[19]
That is why he pruned the poem so drastically, eliminating
metaphors and descriptions, placing Eustace's self-portrait in an
Ante-Chamber, even, to FitzGerald's disgust, eliminating a lovely
bit of autumn landscape which had been taken from Titian's *Three*

Ages of Man.[20] For there are pictures within pictures within pictures in this poem. Like the Lady of the Lake and Godiva and the Sleeping Beauty, the Gardener's Daughter is framed within the narrative of her own wooing and by that successful wooing is brought out into the world. But then she is framed again by the husband's exhibiting her picture in later years and telling her story to the unnamed friend who listens.

The Miller's Daughter also focuses upon a picture, for as the squire, sitting over the walnuts and the wine, reminisces with his wife about their wooing, he recalls how, a listless and unhappy boy, he had thrown himself down one April morn by the mill pond. He had no thought of Alice but, like an absent fool, "angled in the upper pool." All seemed to be conspiring, however, to create their love. A love song he had somewhere heard beat time to nothing in his head, haunting him with the weary sameness of its rhymes. "Then leapt a trout." This was the precipitating moment, the tiny action, which, like the fluttering of the film of soot in Coleridge's flue, set the drama in motion. For as he watched the ripples clear, there in the level flood "a vision caught my eye; / The reflex of a beauteous form"—Alice, who was leaning out of her casement to tend some flowers on the ledge. He raised his eyes and they met hers, so full and bright that he has never forgotten the scene. The entire poem is, indeed, a re-creation of that moment and of the mood of love which it inspired, for as the poem closes, the two wander out across the wold to the old mill, where they watch the sunset "fire your narrow casement glass, / Touching the sullen pool below"—just as Alice had touched him long years before, just as the troubled waters, clearing to a mirror, had swept away the troubles of his youth.

And yet, this life has not been free from trouble. As the scene opens the old Miller has just died, and this event diffuses a tender sadness over the poem. They have also lost a child, though, as so often in Tennyson, this event is so obscurely expressed that one is hardly aware it happened. And the circumstance which had made the youth so troubled in boyhood was the early death of his father, which made him fear that he too would die young. Life gives much, but more is taken away, opines the squire, and this truth is illustrated by the two songs inserted into the narrative, one, an imitation of Anacreon, which he made for their bridal day, and "That other song I made, / Half-angered with my happy lot." The songs, so opposite in mood, re-create the pastoral structure, but this is perhaps even more effectively done by the second major picture of the poem, that of the old Miller himself. For though ostensibly irrelevant to the love that follows, it really establishes its mood. "I see the wealthy miller yet," begins the squire—

> In yonder chair I see him sit,
>   Three fingers round the old silver cup—
> I see his grey eyes twinkle yet
>   At his own jest—grey eyes lit up
> With summer lightnings of a soul
>   So full of summer warmth, so glad,
> So healthy, sound, and clear and whole,
>   His memory scarce can make me sad.

The poem is a little too sentimental, and one regrets the condescension of the mother, who, in learning of her son's choice, "wished me happy, but she thought / I might have looked a little higher." But these are minor faults compared with the warm twilight glow that is diffused through the picture, the golden haze through which even trouble is seen by the eyes of love.

The idyls are so closely connected with painting that it is perhaps desirable to say a little about Tennyson's knowledge of this art. The great public galleries did not, of course, exist in those days, but Tennyson nonetheless had managed to see a good many pictures and to acquire a taste for both the Dutch and the Italian school. His father had collected a number of quite tolerable old masters on his visits to Italy and had written a manuscript treatise on oil painting, with a list of some two hundred of the most famous painters of all countries.[21] At Cambridge the collection bequeathed to the university by Viscount Fitzwilliam was at that time housed in a building lent by Caius College, where Tennyson presumably would have seen it. Later he visited the Dulwich Picture Gallery, at that time the principal public gallery in England, which housed a collection of nearly four hundred paintings, chiefly of the Dutch school, but with some French, Italian, and Spanish masters. The National Gallery was not opened until 1838, but Mr. Angerstein's collection of thirty-eight paintings, the nucleus of the collection, presumably could have been seen in his ill-lighted rooms in Pall Mall. Tennyson, in fact, preferred private collections. In 1833 he and Tennant went to see Samuel Roger's gallery, in which there was a "superb Titian, very beautiful Raphael Madonna, and in fact all art gems." And in 1840, when he visited Warwick with FitzGerald, "nothing pleased me better on the whole than two paintings I saw in the castle: one, an Admiral van Tromp by Rembrandt, the other Machiavelli by Titian, both wonderful pictures, but the last grand beyond all words." Titian, indeed, was his favorite. "The first time he was in Paris," he told Miss Rundle, "he went every day for a fortnight to the Louvre, saw only one picture, 'La Maitresse de Titien,' the second time looked only at 'Narcissus lying by a stream, Echo in the distance and ferocious little Love.'" Hallam had somewhat broader tastes, and they used to argue about their favorites. "There is [at Cologne]," wrote Hallam to Emily Tennyson, "a gallery of pictures quite after my heart, rich, glorious old German pictures, which Alfred accuses me of preferring to Titian and Raffaelle." And in his last letter to Tennyson from Vienna, he wrote: "The gallery is grand and I longed for you: two rooms full of Venetian pictures only; such Giorgiones, Palmas, Bordones, Paul Veroneses! and oh Alfred such Titians! by Heaven, that man could paint! I wish you could see his Danaë. Do you just write as perfect a Danaë!" Tennyson's line, "Now lies the Earth all Danaë to the stars," is perhaps an answer to that request. It justifies Hallam's remark that "Titian's imagination and style are more analogous to your own than those of Rubens or of any other school."[22]

The later idyls are less dependent on painting than on poetry and song and so are more Theocritean in structure. E. C. Stedman, indeed, has shown how many of them reproduce the basic formulas of Theocritus. The opening of *Godiva,* for example, uses the same device for entering on the story of Godiva as the thirteenth idyl uses for introducing that of Hylas: "Not we . . . but she."[23] *Audley Court* is modeled on the *Thalysia* (VII), in which Eucritus, Amyntas, and Simichidas, going to a harvest festival, meet the goatherd Lycidas, vie in pastoral song, and then, continuing to the feast, spend an evening of perfect content amid the opulent summer harvest. *Walking to the Mail* is Tennyson's version of Idyl IV, a gossipy conversation between two rustics, Corydon and Battus, about their neighbor Ægon, who has gone to compete in the Olympic games and whose cattle are growing thin. The social themes of Tennyson's idyls, however, derive less from Theocritus than from Virgil, where the troubled political background in connection with the confiscation of estates provided an analogy to the troubles of the Reform Bill. Indeed, the significant thing about Tennyson's use of both Theocritus and Virgil is that he could use them so freely, simply reviving their forms in order to accomplish an analogous purpose in his own day.[24]

Even under this aegis the danger is that the idyls will be considered merely trivial. In *Audley Court*, for instance, two young men walk across the fields to picnic at Audley Court. They talk, argue a bit, sing a few songs, and then return through the dark to their boat. What is so wonderful about that? Nothing, unless, as in a story or drama by Chekhov, the quality of the experience is everything, the sense of a mood delicately achieved that is very fragile. For the poem begins in bustle and confusion.

> 'The Bull, the Fleece are cramm'd, and not a room
> For love or money. Let us picnic there
> At Audley Court.'

And so the friends move off through the fields and, settling down upon the grass, create a kind of Victorian *déjeuner sur l'herbe*. Tennyson does not muff the occasion but, in almost pre-Raphaelite manner, produces an intensely wrought genre painting of a Victorian picnic hamper.

> There, on a slope of orchard, Francis laid
> A damask napkin wrought with horse and hound,
> Brought out a dusky loaf that smelt of home,
> And, half-cut-down, a pasty costly-made,
> Where quail and pigeon, lark and leveret lay,
> Like fossils of the rock, with golden yolks
> Imbedded and injellied; last, with these,
> A flask of cider from his father's vats,
> Prime, which I knew; and so we sat and eat.

Under the genial influence of the cider they reminisce about old times, get onto the more dangerous present, argue heatedly about the Corn Laws, and come together again upon the king. For these youths, though friends from of old, are of diametrically opposed temperament and principles. The one, Francis Hale, is a farmer's son; the other, the narrator, "having wherewithal, / And in the fallow leisure of my life," was a "rolling stone of here and everywhere." Thus, when they sing their songs, they are of sharply contrasting temper. Francis Hale's is a cynical drinking song—"But let me live my life"—for in his view army, shop, public

service, and love are equally unrewarding. It is precisely the right
song to modulate from the quarrel into a happy mood again, but
the narrator's is precisely right to follow it. For it is a softly lyrical
nocturne, probably adapted from an Elizabethan song, of his love
for Ellen Aubrey. It modulates into the conclusion. For as they go
back across the fields and drop down the headland to the quay,
they find the town all hushed, the bay calm.

> the harbour-buoy,
> Sole star of phosphorescence in the calm,
> With one green sparkle ever and anon
> Dipt by itself, and we were glad at heart.

It was with these lines that the poem began. "This poem," says
Tennyson, "was partially suggested by Abbey Park at Torquay.
Torquay was in old days the loveliest sea village in England and
now is a town. In those old days I, coming down from the hill over
Torquay, saw a star of phosphorescence made by the buoy appearing and disappearing in the dark sea and wrote these lines."[25]
Such serenity, however, required a discord to precede it, something to suggest the commercialism that would later sweep over
the town. And so in the original version of the idyl Tennyson gave
a description of the snorting paddle boat on which Francis arrived, the crowded quay, the quacks and hawkers, the ranting
showmen, and the squealing bagpipes. There was even a third
character, "John the storyteller, John / The talker, steering
downward with a thumb / In either armhole."[26] But all this was
too much. The heavy picnic hamper was adequate balance to the
elfin phosphorescence of the sea, for these are among the antinomies that had to be reconciled in the poem. The two youths
are brought together, not simply by patriotism but by youth,
friendship, song, and the beauty of the evening. The scene is the
perfect equivalent of the serene harvest-festival at the farm of
Phrasidamus in Theocritus's seventh idyl.

Walking to the Mail, like Theocritus's Idyl IV, turns even more
on the subtly differing personalities of two friends. John, who is
apparently visiting the district after being long away, is established
as the pleasanter by his opening comment about the meadows.
James, we gradually gather, is a somewhat less attractive figure,
for he tends to pass harsh judgments on people and seems instinc-
tively to believe in punishment. He alludes to the younker caught
tickling trout—"caught *in flagrante*—what's the Latin word?—

/ *Delicto*"—and even in reference to his own youthful escapades
he seems to take satisfaction in the fact that he had to "pay."
"There was law for *us*; / We paid in person." Indeed, he
generalizes his remarks into one simple principle:

> but, sir, you know
> That these two parties still divide the world—
> Of those that want, and those that have: and still
> The same old sore breaks out from age to age
> With much the same result. Now I myself,
> A Tory to the quick, [etc.]

The immediate occasion for these remarks is Sir Edward Head,
whose house they are passing and for whom James feels a contempt because he allowed the Chartist violence so to infect his
dreams that he could not sleep and ultimately left the country.
John, though presumably a liberal, demurs at the harshness of
this judgment and, turning to the pleasanter subject of Sir Edward's wife, whom he once knew as a slight, modest girl, is rebuffed by the phrase, "A woman like a butt, and harsh as crabs." For
to James, who thinks in stereotyped phrases—"like breeds like,"
"Kind nature is the best"—such was bound to happen. She was a
cottager's daughter and, marrying into the gentry, was unable to
adjust: "Two parties still divide the world."

Indeed, the more we hear of James the less we like him. For one
thing, his language is laced with cruelty. If he mentions a willow, it
is "hump-back'd"; if a Chartist's pike, it is "venomous"; if Sir
Edward is ill, he is "vexed with a morbid devil." This habit culmi-
nates when he unconsciously condemns himself by telling of a
college prank. A farmer's sow was great with pig and several of
them hauled her up the stairs of the college tower and hid her on
the leads. When she littered, they killed the sucklings one by one
and ate them—"till she was left alone . . . , the Niobe of swine."
John makes no immediate comment on this but returns to Sir
Edward.

> Well—after all—
> What know we of the secret of a man?
> His nerves were wrong. What ails us, who are sound,
> That we should mimic this raw fool the world,
> Which charts us all in its coarse blacks or whites,

—and then the reproof to James—

> As ruthless as a baby with a worm,
> As cruel as a schoolboy ere he grows
> To Pity—more from ignorance than will.

But then the mail appears, "as quaint a four-in-hand / As you shall see—three pyebalds and a roan," which seems to support John's view that even in these days of Chartism and the Reform Bill, of Disraeli's Two Nations of the rich and poor, life is a mixed affair and people should strive to make it so, not by harsh, dogmatic judgments but by tolerance and reconciliation. Even the story of Jocky Dawes, which James tells, contributes to this interpretation. Jocky moved out of his house because it was haunted by a ghost, but when he found the ghost among the luggage, he decided to move back in and treat it like a familiar.

All the idyls share this spirit of reconciliation. *Edwin Morris,* written in 1839 against the background of the Llanberis lakes, contrasts two views of love, that of Edwin Morris, a kind of Admirable Crichton, too good to be true, who puts forth in languid aesthetic phrase a kind of Romantic Petrarchanism, and that of the fat curate Edward Bull, who declares that all this is nonsense: "God made the woman for the man, / And for the good and increase of the world." The narrator, an artist, declares immediately that the curate pitches the pipe too low, but, though he is impressed by Morris's fine phrases, he is also a little resentful, for he thinks that he too has the seeds of a genuine love within him but also "something of a wayward modern mind / Dissecting passion." This tinge of cynicism, mediating between the high-flown ideality of Morris and the gross materialism of Bull, will serve him well, for in his courtship of Letty Hill, ward of some cotton-spinning millionaires, he runs smack into the marriage of convenience. The episode is apparently the same as that which Tennyson treated more thunderingly in *Locksley Hall* and *Maud,* but here he treats it lightly. Despite the fact that the speaker has been hounded out of the country by the sheriff, he is not bitter. Indeed, as he begins to speak, he cries, "O me, my pleasant rambles by the lake, / My sweet, wild, fresh three quarters of a year," and he shows a friend the sketches he made during that period. There are two, which comprehend the antithetical elements of the tale. One is of

> curves of mountain, bridge,
> Boat, island, ruins of a castle, built

> When men knew how to build, upon a rock
> With turrets lichen-gilded like a rock.

The other is of

> new-comers in an ancient hold,
> New-comers from the Mersey, millionaires,
> Here lived the Hills—a Tudor-chimnied bulk
> Of mellow brickwork on an isle of bowers.

Nature and commerce, the old and the new, gross materialism and romantic ideality have all found their place in art, and so even the false little Letty is forgiven. Mixed with his memories of that youthful time,

> See seems a part of those fresh days to me;
> For in the dust and drouth of London life
> She moves among my visions of the lake.

The Golden Year is a product of Tennyson's same visit to Wales in the summer of 1839. The poem is modeled on the singing match between two shepherds, though in this case the "song" of one of them, as befits his character, is in prose. For the contest is, in a sense, between prose and poetry, and the fact that Old James, the down-to-earth realist, begins his answer to Leonard "in mimic cadence" sufficiently indicates their parity. To make the contest fair, of course, it cannot take place under a hawthorn or in a bower. The speaker of the idyl had wished for Leonard when he and James had climbed Snowdon, for it was from that visionary height that a poet might be expected to speak. But they did not find him until they descended to Llanberis, and then the three of them crossed between the lakes and "clambered half way up / The counter side." It was there, on the opposite side from Snowdon and only halfway up, that the debate took place. Leonard began in "measured words," by which one may gather that they were not only metrical but moderate. Indeed, Leonard was a poet who, like Tennyson himself, had been chided by his friends for not speaking out in these "feverous days," and his excuse had been that he was born too late, unsuited for modern times. Thus, when he comes to state the doctrine of progress, he does so in beautifully melodious but also muted phrase. As it is the law of all things to move, of the sun, the earth, the ocean, and the seasons, so it is man's law too; but it will be slowly, by ebb and flow, in a cyclical movement, that the Golden Year will come. Leonard looks particularly to the distribution of wealth, to education more widely disseminated, to less disparity between social classes, to free trade and universal peace. But Old James, who is a Carlylean curmudgeon with little faith in poets' dreams, "struck his staff against the rocks / And broke it." "What stuff this is!" The ancient poets placed their Golden Age in the past, the modern in the future. Both are dreamers, for the true Golden Year is that, here and now, which is well spent in work.

> He spoke; and high above, I heard them blast
> The steep slate-quarry, and the great echo flap
> And buffet round the hills, from bluff to bluff.

It would be a wise judge who would award the prize in this song contest. The blasting, echoing like Old James's staff buffeted against the rock, does reinforce the doctrine of work, and one can hardly doubt that the true Golden Year is the present moment well used. But is it better used in poetry or blasting? On the one hand, it is by these practical means that the world will be transformed. But, on the other, one has a feeling that Leonard's song will reverberate longer, for, as Tennyson says in *The Princess*, "Our echoes roll from soul to soul, / And grow for ever and for ever." In a passage not used by Tennyson, Old James leaves in the middle of the debate for some business in the town, and while he is gone Leonard privately expresses some doubts about his own doctrine. Would we be happier when the Golden Year comes? Even if we merged with the All would it be worth the loss of individuality? Tennyson was wise to omit this passage and simply allow the two "songs" to work themselves out within the dialectic of the poem.

Enough has been said to indicate that the English Idyls are not trivial poems but are works of a subtle and delicate art. In my opinion, they are among the finest of Tennyson's poems, certainly the most neglected in proportion to their merit of all of Tennyson's works. Their great value lies simply in the beauty and charm with which they invest their subject. There is a kind of golden haze, a lucent atmosphere, in which everything is enveloped. Though written at the same time as much of *In Memoriam*, they are by far the happiest of Tennyson's poems. The nostalgia and melancholy of the earlier lyrics is gone, the complacency of middle age has not yet descended. Preeminently they are poems of youth, of the heyday of one's existence, when love and art, nature and society are all clothed in a freshness which they will later lose. And yet they are not poems of escape. They solve the problem, better than Clough's *Bothie of Tober-na-vuolich* or Goethe's *Hermann und Dorothea*, of how to combine the persons and topics of everyday life with the heightened beauty which we look for in poetry. Granted that there are things they cannot do. Mystery and passion, ecstasy and magic they do not attempt, for they are poems of the middle range of life and of the middle class. But within these limits they are subtle and complex works, and they are not, as is sometimes said, of a cloying sweetness. Indeed, in their ironic juxtapositions and unresolved conflicts they have a dryness and classicality that is not achieved by any other of Tennyson's poems. They are less the product of the muse than of one who is "bemused," who does not quite know what to make of modern life but whose artless statement of its problems comes nearer to the truth than other people's conclusions. But for a full understanding of the form we need to turn to its larger embodiment in *The Princess*.

7

The Princess

The next that spoke was Arthur Arundel
The Poet: rough his hair but fine to feel,
And dark his skin but softer than a babe's,
And large his hand as of the plastic kind,
And early furrows in his face he had:
Small were his themes—low builds the nightingale—
But promised more: and mellow was his voice,
He pitched it like a pipe to all he would.
                    Fragment of Prologue to *The Princess*

Although Tennyson said he early came to believe that he would
have to make his mark by shortness, since almost all the big
subjects had been done and the men before him had been so
prolix, it is notable that in the 1840s and 1850s he began to
attempt longer versions of what he had already done on a smaller
scale. Thus, *In Memoriam* may be said to expand on *The Two Voices*,
Maud on *Locksley Hall*, the *Idylls of the King* on the *Morte d'Arthur*,
and *The Princess* on *A Dream of Fair Women* and *Edwin Morris*. In
the latter Edward Bull, the fat curate, expresses the same low view
of women that was expressed by the old King in *The Princess*, and
the former contains two stanzas that were widely quoted by
feminist writers in the 1830s:[1]

In every land I thought that, more or less,
    The stronger sterner nature overbore
The softer, uncontrolled by gentleness
    And selfish evermore:

And whether there were any means whereby,
    In some far aftertime, the gentler mind
Might reassume its just and full degree
    Of rule among mankind.

These stanzas were omitted when Tennyson republished the
poem in 1842, and one would like to know why. In its original
form *A Dream of Fair Women* had an elaborate introduction com-

paring the poet to a balloonist raised high above the earth by the "finer air" of his imagination. Like the apocalyptic poet of Tennyson's youth, he is "Selfpoised, nor fears to fall." What he sees from this height is

> Beauty and anguish walking hand in hand
>   The downward slope to death.

Nightmarish images swirl before him of all that women have suffered in the violence of history, till "I started once, or seemed to start in pain, / Resolved on noble things, and strove to speak." But just as his arm was raised to strike down a cavalier who offered injury to a lady,

> I know not how,

> All those sharp fancies, by down-lapsing thought
>   Streamed onward, lost their edges, and did creep
> Rolled on each other, rounded, smoothed, and brought
>   Into the gulfs of sleep.

What happened, one wonders, in this Lucretian picture of the mind, to smooth and round off the sharp images of violence so that, just as the poet was moved to strike a blow for woman's rights, he got diverted into an old wood and his poem became a female adjunct of *The Divine Comedy*? Of that and Ovid's *Heroides*. For although there are here women who suffered at the hands of men, notably Iphigenia and Jephtha's daughter, they alternate with women like Helen of Troy, Cleopatra, and Joan of Arc, who were reasonably well able to take care of themselves. Unlike Chaucer, Tennyson did not venture to assert that all his women were "good," merely "fair," and his poem is uncertain in its purpose and ultimately trails off without any proper conclusion. One feels that the suppression of the two feminist stanzas is related to the suppression, also in 1842, of the introduction in which Tennyson represented himself as a Shelleyan poet "selfpoised" and without fear of falling. For by that time he had fallen, in the sense that he recognized the subject was more complicated than he had imagined and that he needed a more complicated poetic structure to express his relation to it.

The subject was complicated because it was highly controversial in Tennyson's day and involved a variety of conflicting points of view. It had been introduced into the political arena by Mary

Wollstonecraft's *A Vindication of the Rights of Women* (1792), which brought with it not only the odium of Tom Paine's *Rights of Man* but an antifeminine prejudice as well. It had not been helped by association with the life and works of the godless Shelley, and at the moment when Tennyson was writing *A Dream of Fair Women* it was being most vociferously expressed by the socialist Saint-Simonians, whose missionaries in England made an unfavorable impression on almost everyone except the young Mill. After the collapse of the Saint-Simonians it would be carried on by the followers of Fourier and Robert Owen. Thus, it came associated with socialism, revolution, the French, atheism, free love, and other execrable ideas, as well as with more moderate and acceptable proposals for the education of women, equal employment, cheap divorce, the right to vote, and the right to have custody of one's property. The Apostles generally regarded the Saint-Simonians with aversion, and yet when the speaker of *Locksley Hall* dipped into the future and saw "the Vision of the world and all the wonder that would be, " that Vision included not only a warless, classless society created by the workers but also a world in which Amy would have been free from the tyranny of her father and her loutish husband. The "Golden Year" envisioned by the poet Leonard is also partly socialistic, and in *The Princess* that same phrase is used to denote the day when woman shall have achieved equality with man. On the other hand, much of the impulse toward this ideal came from quite a different source. Arthur Hallam, nourished on Plato, Dante's *Vita Nuova*, Petrarch, and the troubadour poets, evolved a highly spiritualized religion of love in which woman, worshiped almost in the way the Virgin Mary was worshiped in the Middle Ages, would serve almost that same purpose of elevating and refining the gross, unspiritual man. This idea, that woman was the Angel in the House, was adopted by a great many champions of woman of both sexes. On the other hand, many of the more realistic and politically sophisticated saw in this attitude precisely the kind of sentimental sop that was thrown to women in order to deprive them of their substantive rights, and in the 1830s and 1840s a number of militant feminists said so explicitly. Among them were Mrs. Anna Wheeler, Harriet Martineau, Mrs. Anna Jameson, Mrs. Mary Leman Grimstone, and Mrs. Caroline Norton. These were the rather formidable ladies who prepared the way for the suffragettes of later decades.

Caroline Norton, the beautiful and talented granddaughter of

Richard Brinsley Sheridan, was, like some of these other ladies, unhappily married, and in 1836 her husband carried his persecutions to the extent of bringing action against Lord Melbourne for the seduction of his wife. The jury found against Norton without even leaving the box, but in the ensuing separation the children were automatically in the custody of the husband. In the following years Mrs. Norton agitated in support of a bill put forward by Serjeant Talfourd which sought to give the courts power, in certain circumstances, to award the custody of infant children to their mother. In 1839, after initially being rejected by the Lords, the bill was passed by both Houses and became law.[2] As that was the year in which Tennyson first thought of writing *The Princess*[3]—in which the custody of the infant plays so important a role—one cannot but think that he was partly inspired by the case of Caroline Norton. Particularly does this seem likely when one learns that J. M. Kemble, with whom Tennyson was then occasionally dining, was fulminating against Mrs. Norton in the columns of the *British and Foreign Review*. To W. B. Donne he wrote denouncing "that most accursed heresy of Sexual Equality" and assuring his friend that "The Antichrist of the Women of our day is 'Intellectual Developement.' "[4]

To most people, however, the idea of the education of women was less controversial. It had been the main theme of Mary Wollstonecraft, and W. J. Fox, the Unitarian minister, in reviewing Tennyson's *Poems* of 1830, had said, "There is not a greater moral necessity in England than that of a reformation in female education."[5] He took the position that simply because of woman's influence on her husband and children she needed to be educated, but Mrs. Grimstone, an Owenite feminist, rose upon the winds of prophecy to a higher view. "I see not why civil offices should not be open [to women]," she declared in 1834, "especially chairs of science in colleges endowed for the education of their own sex. Why should moral philosophy come with less power from the lips of woman than of man? Why may she not fill a professorship of poetry as well as he?"[6] The answer was that there was no institution at this time where women could even be students, but in 1835 the Oberlin Collegiate Institute, in the wilds of Ohio, became the first institution of higher learning to open its doors to both women and blacks. As an alumnus of Oberlin, I would like to think that it had had some part in the education of *The Princess*, and since it canvassed widely in England for funds in

1839, it may be that it did. But the idea of such an institution was already abroad in England, and of course the accession of Queen Victoria to the throne in 1837 did much to favor the feminist cause. It was all too glaring an anomaly to have a woman in the highest office of the land when other women could not even vote for their parliamentary representative or be properly educated. Still, when the Queen's Maid of Honor, the Hon. Amelia Matilda Murray, began conversations with the Government in 1845 about establishing a college for women, it was initially to be limited to the training of governesses, and it was only after a larger group of people, including Kingsley and F. D. Maurice, were brought into the project that the Queen's College, in Harley Street, was founded in 1848.[7] As this was the year after *The Princess* was published, one would like to think that it was the practical outcome of Tennyson's speculations, but in reality the two were parallel but largely independent developments.

Given the complexity of the issues involved, it is obvious that Tennyson could not deal with the woman question in the visionary mode. In the first place, there was the necessity of deciding exactly what he himself believed, how much of the new he was willing to entertain, how much of the old he must keep; and then there was the rhetorical problem of leading people like Kemble as far along the road to an enlightened position as they would go. Hence he punctured his hot-air balloon, abandoned the real-unreal treatment of the medieval dream vision, and adopted the frame device which he had already perfected in *The Epic, The Day-Dream,* and *Godiva.* By choosing a romance that was as remote as possible from modern life and having it told by people of varying points of view he could actually incorporate into his poem the variety of feminist discussion. And yet the tale would work by its own logic to some kind of unified conclusion, and this, tentatively and varyingly received by the group, was probably as close to the truth as one could get.

The setting of the frame of the poem is the park of Sir Walter Vivian, which for one day he has opened up to his tenants, with their wives and children, and also to the members of the local Mechanics' Institute, which is having its annual outing. This was a strange affair in which "sport / Went hand in hand with Science," for the patient leaders of the Institute, who were instructing the multitudes in the various branches of useful knowledge, were doing so by means of practical demonstrations—a fountain on which danced a gilded ball, a toy cannon, telescopes, an electrical apparatus, a clockwork steamer that paddled about the lake, model steam engines, a tiny railway, a fire balloon, and an infant telegraph that "flash'd a saucy message to and fro." "Strange was the sight," says the poet, "and smacking of the time." Strange, indeed, for as we move about the scene its hybrid character will more and more appear. Along with the group from the Mechanics' Institute were six college youths, friends of young Walter, who were visiting him, and one of these, the poet of the group, Walter was showing about the house. It was Grecian in architecture but, like most Victorian houses, was filled with a strange gallimaufry of objects, "every clime and age / Jumbled together." Chief among these were relics of the Middle Age, particularly the arms of old Sir Ralph, who fought at Ascalon, and about whom the family kept a chronicle. Walter brought it, and the poet, who is also the narrator of the poem, was soon lost in tales "Half-legend, half-historic," not only of Sir Ralph but also of a lady warrior who, early in the family's history, rather than be married against her will, sallied forth and "beat her foes with slaughter from her walls." Called to join the rest of the party, the poet took the chronicle with him and found them seated in the midst of a Gothic ruin, formerly an abbey, which now made part of the park. There, propped against the wall, was the statue of Sir Ralph himself, whom Lilia, Walter's younger sister, "Half child half woman," had made her knight-errant by winding "a scarf of orange round the stony helm," so that "the old warrior from his ivied nook / Glow[ed] like a sunbeam." The poet read them a little about Sir Ralph and also about the family Britomart, and when Walter twitted Lilia with the question, "Lives there such a woman now?" Lilia, who, despite her name turns out to be "a rosebud set with little wilful thorns," replied, "There are thousands now / Such women, but convention beats them down."

> 'O I wish
> That I were some great princess, I would build
> Far off from men a college like a man's,
> And I would teach them all that men are taught;
> We are twice as quick!'

It is not difficult to see where Lilia has gotten her militant feminism. Her maiden Aunt Elizabeth had a little earlier taken the program of the Mechanics' Institute as text and "preach'd / An universal culture for the crowd," and doubtless she had also been preaching to Lilia in the manner of Harriet Martineau and Mrs. Jameson. The youths replied with knowing smiles that it would indeed be delightful to see "prudes for proctors, dowagers for deans," but, seeing that Lilia was too earnest to be put off with "Part banter, part affection," they told her, and the other young ladies from the neighborhood who had been gathered to make up the party, how desperately they missed them while at college. So much so that when they stayed up at Christmas to read for their examination they spent their whole time playing charades and riddles and "often told a tale from mouth to mouth / As here at Christmas." This pleasant game, in which one person began a tale which was then taken up in turn by the others, was likely, in the absence of an overall plan and with so many different tellers, to produce a monster, but this was just what all were beginning to feel was necessary. For in a situation which mingled old with new, the common people with the gentry, a Grecian house with a Gothic abbey, sport with science, the Cambridge colleges with the Mechanics' Institute, serious talk of women's rights with idle talk of college pranks, ladies with gentlemen, the lily with the rose, the scarf of orange about the stony helm, banter with affection, the child-woman with the woman-child, history with legend, the true heroic with the mock-sublime—in such a situation only a medley would do. And so a Medley (the subtitle of *The Princess*) is what they determined to produce. The seven youths would tell a tale on the theme of Lilia's college, and in between "the rougher voices" of the men, the ladies would sing ballads or songs. They would thus fashion a "summer's tale" to match the "winter's tale" they told last Christmas, and since they wish that they could "have him back / Who told the 'Winter's tale' " to do it for them, they doubtless take that mingling of pastoral and romance, of near tragedy and ultimate reconciliation, as their model.

The tale is of Tennyson's invention, though he has doubtless taken hints from various sources. Initially, it presents two diametrically opposed views of the position of women. At one extreme is the militant feminism of Princess Ida, who, betrothed in childhood to the Prince of a neighboring kingdom, has broken off her betrothal and, with the aid of Lady Blanche and Lady Psyche, established a women's college which it is death for men to enter. At the other extreme is the reactionary view of the old King, the Prince's father, who says bluntly,

'Man for the field and woman for the hearth:
Man for the sword and for the needle she:
Man with the head and woman with the heart:
Man to command and woman to obey;
All else confusion.'

In between these two are several varieties of intermediate opinion: Gama, Ida's father, who does not really approve her position but is too "swamp'd in lazy tolerance" to do anything about it; Arac, her hulking brother, all beef and no intellect but with enough loyalty to Ida to think she ought to be allowed to do what she wants; Cyril, the Prince's friend, a Mercutio-like figure whose lusty realism brushes aside all abstract theories of the relation between the sexes; and the Prince himself, whose refined idealism is ultimately found to be at one with the true views of Ida herself.

Initially, in books I–III, the college is satirized rather gently in the best manner of the war between the sexes. Old Gama puns outrageously, declaring that the ladies' view is that with "equal husbandry / The woman were an equal to the man." And the host of an inn near the college declares that for miles around all the fields are "till'd by women, all the swine were sows, / And all the dogs—," a sentence which he does not finish. But the principal method of satire is simply that of reproducing all the details of an Oxford or Cambridge college but with everything diverted to feminine uses. It is not merely that there are prudes for proctors and dowagers for deans but that the very desks are satinwood. When the Prince and his two friends, Cyril and Florian, enter the college disguised as young ladies from the northern kingdom, they are required to subscribe, not the Thirty-Nine Articles, but the statutes binding them "not for three years to speak with any man." They naturally then inquire which is the prettiest and most popular tutor and on being told, "Lady Psyche," enroll themselves with her. On entering her lecture room, they see

along the forms, like morning doves
That sun their milky bosoms on the thatch,
A patient range of pupils.

The only anomaly is that on the rostrum beside Lady Psyche is her infant, day nurseries not having yet been thought of. Her lecture deals as exclusively with the female accomplishments in human history as the normal lecture with male, and the statues adorning

the courts are all of famous women, not of men. Finally, when the
Prince and his companions are unmasked and have to scramble
over the college gates at night, they are pursued and ap-
prehended by two husky "daughters of the plough," who are quite
as efficient as any proctor's bulldog at Oxford or Cambridge. It
was Tennyson's original intention to have the second book, in
which most of this satire occurs, told by Walter Vivian, whose
affectionate but patronizing attitude toward his younger sister is
precisely the attitude taken toward Ida's college.

Gradually, however, the picture darkens. It is revealed, for
example, that anatomy is not included in the curriculum. Ida
herself wishes that children "grew / Like field-flowers everywhere!" and she apparently intends that this is what her pupils
should think. Whatever they think, they are not entirely happy
with their lot. The older of them lie about the lawns "and
murmur that their May / Was passing: what was learning unto
them? / They wish'd to marry; they could rule a house."
Moreover, it appears that not only was there discontent among
the undergraduates, there was also dissension among the tutors.
Lady Blanche, who had the care of Ida's youth after her mother's
death, claims that the original idea of the college was hers and that
she and Lady Psyche were to have been equal. But now Lady
Psyche has supplanted her in Ida's affections, has engrossed most
of the pupils for herself, and has plagiarized her plans. But if it is
true that the original idea of the college was Lady Blanche's, then
our attitude toward the entire institution changes. For Lady
Blanche had a bitterly unhappy marriage, and thus her plan for
female education may arise out of this bitterness and be simply
her revenge at having been "wedded to a fool." Tennyson does
not exactly employ the genetic argument that it is *because* the
militant feminist is so ugly and disagreeable that she cannot get a
husband and so has been led to her views, but he does employ
something like it. Certainly, Lady Blanche is disagreeable, and we
are intended to understand that whatever is perverted and wrong
about her plan is exclusively hers, and only what is right and true
about it is held by Lady Psyche and, ultimately, by Ida.

The fourth book, in Tennyson's original plan, would have been
told by "a wild November fool," an Irishman out of Clare, who
was "something like the Cyril in the tale." Therefore he it was who
was responsible for Cyril's wild outbreak which revealed to Ida
who the three were and led to their being seized and ejected from

the college. Meanwhile, the Prince's father, fearful for his son's safety, had crossed the border with an army and seized old Gama as hostage. Ida necessarily capitulated, and it was agreed that the question of the marriage should be decided by open combat, Arac and his two brothers against the Prince, Cyril, and Florian, each party being supported by fifty knights. It is likely that Tennyson was influenced in this encounter by one of the most fantastic episodes in the Victorian era, a full-fledged medieval tournament, complete with jesters, boar's heads, tilting grounds, and suits of armor, which the Earl of Eglinton held at his castle in August 1839. The Earl was careful enough to have the young gentlemen practice beforehand, and he fitted their lances with rockets, or flat pieces of wood, so that they would not get hurt.[8] Tennyson also inserted a line in the third edition (VI, 225) indicating that *he* did not intend anyone to get killed—but he did intend them to get hurt. This, indeed, was necessary so that the college could be transformed into a hospital and Ida could take up the more womanly occupation of nursing. She could then be softened by pity at the Prince's suffering into a condition where she would be willing to consider marrying him.

   The Prince is usually criticized as a weak and colorless hero, and it is generally thought that the "weird seizures" to which he was made subject in the fourth edition (1851) were a mistake. The seizures are explained on the naturalistic level as "catalepsy," but on the level of legend as an ancestral curse providing that "none of all our blood should know / The shadow from the substance." Tennyson says he added the seizures for two reasons, first, to account for the anachronisms and improbabilities of the tale (but these are adequately accounted for by the frame device), and secondly, to emphasize the Prince's "comparative want of power."[9] It is true that the Prince does require an element of effeminacy, corresponding to the excessive masculinity of Ida, which he will put off as he moves toward her, just as she will put off her false self as she moves toward him. But there is a third and more important reason, namely, that Tennyson was attempting in these seizures to create something analogous to the trancelike experience which he knew as a boy and which he always associated with poetic power. For the Prince is a poetic youth who is attempting to realize in his own life the vision of "All beauty compass'd in a female form." This ideal had its origin in his childhood betrothal, by proxy, to Ida, which fostered in his mind the thought that he was destined for some such union. It was then nourished by the picture, with a tress of dark hair, which he ever wore by his heart and contemplated in solitude. And it was further realized for him by his mother, who, like Tennyson's mother as portrayed in *Isabel*, was a saintlike figure who must have suffered much under her husband's roughness. As a result, his life had always been dominated by this ideal. As he will later explain to the Princess, in lines which recall Tennyson's youthful feeling about "The Passion of the Past,"

> when a boy, you stoop'd to me
> From all high places, lived in all fair lights,
> Came in long breezes rapt from inmost south
> And blown to inmost north; at eve and dawn
> With Ida, Ida, Ida, rang the wood.

Naturally, then, when the betrothal was broken off and his father proposed violence, he proposed a quest. It would be a quest for ideal beauty, and success in this quest would give him wholeness once again. For his seizures are, in a sense, simply this, that the vision of ideal beauty, which is the most intense reality he knows, is not embodied in the world about him, and, on the other hand, the world is comparatively unreal. And so when he went out into the woods and heard a wind which arose and said, "Follow, follow, thou shalt win!" he was but following the melody in his own heart. He was doing what Tennyson had done in several poems before him, leaving a cold northern kingdom for a kingdom in the warm south to seek the abode of clear poetic beauty.

It has been noticed that in his quest the Prince is not unlike the fairy Prince in *The Day-Dream*, who also comes, "scarce knowing what he seeks," led by "the Magic Music in his heart," to rouse the Sleeping Beauty with a kiss and take her out into the world. But the difference here is that it is Ida who rouses the Prince with a kiss. For after he was injured in the combat with Arac he fell into "some mystic middle state" which was but an intensification and prolongation of his seizures. In this state, in which all did look like "hollow shows"—even sweet Ida, who tended him—he cried,

> 'If you be, what I think you, some sweet dream,
> I would but ask you to fulfil yourself:
> But if you be that Ida whom I knew,
> I ask you nothing: only, if a dream,
> Sweet dream, be perfect. I shall die tonight.
> Stoop down and seem to kiss me ere I die.'

This is the culmination of the poem. If the figure that he sees or
thinks he sees above him is his visionary Ida, then he asks her to
fulfill herself. But if she is simply the false Ida he has known in the
world, he asks her nothing. Only, if a vision, let her, like a vision,
"*seem* to kiss me ere I die." But at this point vision and reality
merge.

> She turn'd; she paused;
> She stoop'd; and out of languor leapt a cry;
> Leapt fiery Passion from the brinks of death;
> And I believed that in the living world
> My spirit closed with Ida's at the lips.

In this moment the Prince is not only saved from death but is
cured of his weird seizures as well. Never again will the real be at
variance with the ideal in his world, and though his father was
doubtless right in saying that he must fight for Ida, must endure
the shock of battle for her, still it was not by forcing circumstance
that he won her. It was by envisioning her with sufficient intensity
so that she came into being. Like Adam, he awoke and found his
vision true.

But if the Prince was changed, so too was Ida.

> from mine arms she rose
> Glowing all over noble shame; and all
> Her falser self slipt from her like a robe,
> And left her woman.

White and red, the lily and the rose, have been used throughout
the poem to symbolize the antinomies of intellect and passion. But
now Ida divests herself of the influence of Lady Blanche and
becomes in her rebirth more like Lady Psyche. For it is not one or
the other extreme which is desirable in this poem but a balance of
the two. Indeed, as Ida looks back over her past course she sees
how partial she has been. Her situation has been not unlike that of
Paris on Mt. Ida in that, pretending to pursue knowledge, she had
actually sought power (VII, 221–23), when what she should have
sought was love. Or rather she should have sought all three, but
convinced that love is greater than knowledge and knowledge
greater than power. When she does learn this, then the birth of
the new self within her is described as like the birth of Aphrodite
out of the sea, but it is not the false Aphrodite that Paris chose,
rather the kindly goddess of true procreative power.

For what Ida has ignored above all is the child. Both Lady Blanche and Lady Psyche have children, the former a daughter of about college age, Melissa, the latter the infant Aglaïa. They perform a Solomon's judgment upon themselves, the one by abandoning Melissa without compunction, the other by pleading for her child when it is taken from her by Ida. But the care of the child, which Ida took up to provide one last disciple in her crumbling school, actually teaches her that she has that within her which is wilder than she knew, a mother's heart. And when she gives Aglaïa, whose name means "bright" or "shining," back to Lady Psyche, it goes without saying that she will have to have one of her own. Tennyson never ceased to point out that all the intercalary songs (except the sixth) turn on the child as the unifying element in the family,[10] and thus Lilia and the other ladies who sing the songs are either not all militant feminists or else are made to testify unconsciously against themselves.

By all these admissions of error Ida is almost too deeply humbled, but happily the Prince comes to her rescue by explaining that through his mother's influence he had already come to believe everything that she still retains of her plan. In her lecture Lady Psyche had at the close risen "upon a wind of prophecy, / Dilating on the future":

> 'everywhere
> Two heads in council, two beside the hearth,
> Two in the tangled business of the world,
> Two in the liberal offices of life,
> Two plummets dropt for one to sound the abyss
> Of science, and the secrets of the mind:
> Musician, painter, sculptor, critic, more:
> And everywhere the broad and bounteous Earth
> Should bear a double growth of those rare souls,
> Poets, whose thoughts enrich the blood of the world.'

All this the Prince would subscribe to. One would assume that it means, in practical terms, equal education, equal opportunity in employment, equality before the law, and the vote. What is more, the Prince recognizes that a major cause for woman's condition is not only the "barbarous laws" enacted by men but also the parasitic social forms whereby, thinking to exalt her, men have actually degraded her. All these must be swept away, and the responsibility for doing so is as much man's as woman's. For if woman remain

"small, slight-natured, miserable, / How shall men grow?" Women
are wives and mothers and therefore both by cultural and biological means—the latter enhanced, in Tennyson's view, by the inheri-
tance of acquired characteristics—they will transmit their qualities
to others. It is in man's interest as well as woman's that these
should be great, and therefore woman must be free to develop
her full potentialities in the highest degree. In this work the
Prince offers himself to Ida as a helper. The college, one has the
feeling, is going to be reopened with a partly male faculty and on a
coeducational basis.

The Prince has only one reservation. Women must be free

> to live and learn and be
> All that not harms distinctive womanhood.
> For woman is not undevelopt man,
> But diverse:

For this reason he would like to drop "this proud watchword . . .
of equal," partly no doubt because it smacks of the French *égalité*
and so suggests the abstract theories of the Saint-Simonians, but
also because it seems to suggest to those who use it the false
doctrine of Identity. "Separate but equal" has proved so unsatisfactory a formula in race relations that "equal but not identical"
will probably not recommend itself in feminist circles. But the
basis for rejecting the one is partly that blacks are a minority and
partly that it does involve separation, whereas in Tennyson's for-
mulation neither is the case. Woman *is* equal in all her relations
with other individuals in society, but in the marriage relation the
whole concept of equality, with its competitive connotations, is
irrelevant. "In true marriage lies / Nor equal nor unequal: each
fulfils / Defect in each." Indeed, if man and woman were equal in
the sense of being identical, then "Sweet Love were slain: his
dearest bond is this, / Not like to like, but like in difference."
Tennyson has probably been influenced by Plato's theory, as
propounded by Aristophanes in the *Symposium*, that every individual is but half a soul and that by love we seek to find our
counterpart. But he is more obviously influenced simply by the
bisexual character of human reproduction. In love

> each fulfils
> Defect in each, and always thought in thought,
> Purpose in purpose, will in will, they grow,

> The single pure and perfect animal,
> The two-cell'd heart beating, with one full stroke,
> Life.

Life for Tennyson involves the reconciliation of opposites, but it is reconciliation and not homogenization.

Nonetheless, though the Prince believes that man and woman are "distinct in individualities," he also believes that over the centuries both men and women should, without losing their distinctive virtues, remedy their defects by growing liker to one another. Whether he actually contemplates a physically androgynous type is uncertain,[11] but such an idea is not beyond the range of Tennyson's usual speculations, and, indeed, it is difficult to see how there could be significant modifications of the soul without some modification of the body. But it is spiritual qualities that he is primarily interested in. Various Victorian writers had developed the idea that there is such a thing as "woman-power" and "man-power," which both men and women have in different degrees. According to John Goodwyn Barmby, Joan of Arc is an example of a woman with great "man-power," William Cowper of a man with great "woman-power." Shelley and Mary Wollstonecraft both had "woman-man-power."[12] By the mid-1840s, when Tennyson was writing, the matter had become a delicate issue because of Tractarianism and its associated ideas of celibacy. Tennyson did not want to be connected with this movement and so wrote, and then deleted, the passage:

> And if aught be comprising in itself
> The man, the woman, let it sit [apart]
> Godlike, alone, or only rapt on heaven—
> What need for such to wed? or if there be
> Men-women, let them wed with women-men
> And make a proper marriage.[13]

Again, in the late poem *On One Who Affected an Effeminate Manner*, he wrote,

> While man and woman still are incomplete,
> I prize that soul where man and woman meet,
> Which types all Nature's male and female plan,
> But, friend, man-woman is not woman-man.

It may be difficult to see how the Prince, who put off a certain effeminacy in moving toward Ida, and Ida, who put off a certain mannishness in moving toward the Prince, are thereby furthering Nature's plan, but they had adopted the defects, not the virtues, of the opposite sex. The Prince had already indicated to his father that the defects of man are grossness and roughness, "slips in sensual mire," while the defects of woman are apparently a narrow mental outlook. Therefore man should become gentler and morally more pure without becoming effeminate, whereas woman should acquire a broader mental outlook without losing her femininity. Tennyson thought that his friend Hallam had achieved "manhood fused with female grace" in such sort that a child would trustingly put its hand in his; and he thought that Christ was the perfect type of humanity in that he represented "the union of tenderness and strength"—"what he called 'the man-woman.'"[14] Thus, at this point evolution and Christianity merge, and to imitate Christ is to further Nature's plan. Indeed, by typing Christ in their own lives the Prince and Ida will bring back the "statelier Eden" in which reign "the world's great bridals, chaste and calm," and from these will spring "the crowning race of humankind."

"To quite a solemn close," then, came the romance which had begun in banter, and presumably most of the youths were rather sobered by what they had produced. Not so Walter. From being a superficial antifeminist before the tale he had become a superficial militant now. "I wish she had not yielded!" he cries. But it was Lilia's reaction which especially pleased the poet:

> the sequel of the tale
> Had touch'd her; and she sat, she pluck'd the grass,
> She flung it from her, thinking: last, she fixt
> A showery glance upon her aunt, and said,
> "You—tell us what we are" who might have told
> For she was cramm'd with theories out of books
> But that there rose a shout—

for the Mechanics' Institute people were leaving. Lilia obviously perceives that she has been taken in by her own equivalent of Lady Blanche, and she is a little resentful. One feels that the romance which, in one of the manuscripts, Tennyson indicated was budding between Lilia and one of the youths, will now go forward a little more smoothly. Indeed, it begins to appear that the purpose of the whole exercise was, like that of *The Day-Dream*, to laugh Lilia out of her militant feminism and into marriage. This has the effect, perhaps, of tipping the balance of the poem a little in favor of the men, and one wishes that some of the youths had been shown to go away more soberly determined to work for the women's cause. Perhaps they could have taken the orange scarf which Lilia now unties from old Sir Ralph's statue and tied it to their own arm. But in the end the balance is restored. For as the group mounts up the slope to Vivian-place, they turn and look out over the landscape which, in its variegated beauty, seems to reinforce their view that life is a medley. The happy valleys, "half in light, and half / Far-shadowing from the west," show gray halls mingling with trim hamlets, a rustic tower "half-lost" in belts of hops, fields and streams, and on the sea "a red sail, or a white." Beyond, in their mind's eye, is France, and the Tory member's elder son congratulates Britain on the narrow sea which keeps her "whole within herself, / A nation yet, the rulers and the ruled," not like the French, who are forever going to the extremes of reaction or revolution, but combining reverence for the laws with some "patient force" to change them. And yet, despite the fact that this entire passage was written shortly after the revolution of February 1848,[15] Tennyson does not rest simply in self-congratulation. Rather, he has the narrator complicate his vision further by indicating what England owes to the leavening influence of France.

> "Have patience," I replied, "ourselves are full
> Of social wrong; and maybe wildest dreams
> Are but the needful preludes of the truth."

If Aunt Elizabeth heard this, she would have brightened a little, for it indicated that she too had played her needful role in the education of Lilia.

If the mixed character of English life validates the theme of the poem, it also validates the form. We are, of course, to understand that the tale was originally told in prose and that the narrator later "drest it up poetically" and gave it a more uniform style. But it had been written democratically. A series of short prologues to each book, which Tennyson ultimately rejected,[16] shows that the first book was to have been told by the poet himself, since that is the one that expresses the poetic character of the Prince's quest; the second, which contains the chaffing description of the college, by Walter, Lilia's brother; the third, in which the story doesn't go

much of anywhere, by the "steersman of our boat"; the fourth by
"the wild November fool" who was "something like" Cyril, since it
tells of Cyril's wild outburst; the fifth by "an easy genial fellow"
who agreed to be Lilia's knight and give her the battle that she
wished; the sixth by Arthur Arundel, the Poet, a Tennysonian
figure who evidently was thought appropriate to depict the soften-
ing of Ida; and the seventh by

> one we used to call
> The lady: ladylike he read the parts
> Of Viola, Beatrice, Hermione:
> We thought he fancied Lilia: who could tell?
> He colour'd at the name of any girl.

He, a Shelley-like figure who presumably had "woman-man-
power," voiced the Prince's view of true marriage and so brought
the poem to "quite a solemn close." It had, in truth, followed "a
strange diagonal" from mock-heroic to true-sublime, but though
doubtless it had not absolutely pleased any one of the group, it
had carried them all from a relatively superficial view of their
subject to a more profound one, and it had reconciled their
differences.

In her prophetic view of the future, Lady Psyche had said that
the Earth would everywhere produce "a double growth of those
rare souls, / Poets, whose thoughts enrich the blood of the world."
One might ask what kind of poetry they would write. If the matter
were left to Ida, it would clearly be not unlike that officially
approved by the Useful Knowledge Society, for Ida's suppression
of Love in her soul has led her also to suppress poetry. When she
and her party are out on their geological picnic and the sun sinks
in the west, flushing all the hills with rosy light, Ida says, "There
sinks the nebulous star we call the Sun, / If that hypothesis of
theirs be sound." She then calls for someone to sing, for the good
ultilitarian reason that "lightlier move / The minutes fledged with
music," and when a maid sings the most beautiful lyric in the
entire poem, "Tears, idle tears," she reproves her for lamenting
over the fruitless past when all things move toward the great
future of equal rights for women. The kind of poetry that this
prophetess of the female millennium wants is the poetry of
apocalypse, for when her champion triumphs over the Prince in
battle, she herself sings a song such as Tennyson might have

published at age twenty in *Poems by Two Brothers*. Standing high on
the roof of the palace, "like that great dame of Lapidoth," who
celebrated the avenging of Israel, she sang, "Our enemies have
fall'n, have fall'n," a work full of allusions to the Book of Judges,
Isaiah, and the Book of Revelation. But this is before she is
softened. After her iron will had been broken by the sight of the
Prince's suffering and her love for the little babe, she sits by the
Prince's bedside and reads to him the lovely *ghazal*, "Now sleeps
the crimson petal, now the white," which expresses the new unity
of being she has achieved. Finally, she turns the page and reads,
all in low tones, "a small sweet Idyl," which, as she knows very well,
is addressed to herself and contains the final message of *The
Princess*.

> Come down, O maid, from yonder mountain height:
> What pleasure lives in height (the shepherd sang)
> In height and cold, the splendour of the hills?
> But cease to move so hear the Heavens, and cease
> To glide a sunbeam by the blasted Pine,
> To sit a star upon the sparkling spire;
> And come, for Love is of the valley, come,
> For Love is of the valley, come thou down
> And find him.

Tennyson had written this lyric when he was traveling in Switzerland with Moxon in August 1846. To FitzGerald he wrote that the
sight he had of Mont Blanc at 4:00 A.M. "did not by any means
repay me for the toil of travelling to see him. Two other things I
did see in Switzerland, the stateliest bits of landskip I ever saw, one
was a look down on the valley of Lauterbrunnen while we were
descending from the Wengern Alp, the other a view of the Ber-
nese Alps: don't think that I am going to describe them. Let it
suffice that I was so satisfied with the size of the crags that (Moxon
being gone on before in vertigo and leaning on the arm of the
guide) I *laughed* by myself. I was satisfied with the size of crags, but
mountains, great mountains disappointed me."[17] It was just here,
of course, that Byron had been inspired to write *Manfred*, and
only two years after Tennyson's visit Arnold would be traveling
through this country and, while lamenting that it was spoiled by
the omnipresence of "that furiously flaring bethiefed rushlight,
the vulgar Byron,"[18] would be unable to resist his influence in
writing *Empedocles on Etna*. But Tennyson finds that great moun-

tains disppointed him. Mont Blanc, which had so inspired Shelley, was for him hardly worth the toil of traveling to see it, and he much preferred the delicious valley of Lauterbrunnen to the cold beauty of the Jungfrau. Therefore he addressed that maid and urged her to come down from yonder mountain height, for "Love is of the valley, come thou down / And find him."

Princess Ida, then, though a figure in a fable about the education of women, is also a symbol of the development of Tennyson's poetry. The Prince, listening to the music in his heart, had gone to the warm southern kingdom to seek her but found that she had returned to the borders of the north and taken up her stand on a frosty mountain. When he melted her heart and persuaded her to come down into the valley, marry, and have a child, he was essentially asking her to take up her abode in the English Idyl. For this form, based in love, centering upon marriage and the child, is that which he found most in harmony with his genius. Certainly it is that in which his poetic problems were ultimately resolved.

8

In Memoriam

> The character of a deceased friend or beloved kinsman is not seen,
> no—nor ought to be seen, otherwise than as a tree through a tender
> haze or a luminous mist, that spiritualises and beautifies it.
>
> Wordsworth, *Essay upon Epitaphs*

When Edward King died in 1637, Milton wrote a pastoral elegy. When Keats died in 1824, Shelley also adapted this form to his Platonic presuppositions. And when Arthur Hugh Clough died in 1861, Arnold, though habitually using the elegy as a means of repudiating an old self and giving birth to a new, still accomplished his purpose within the framework of the pastoral elegy. Tennyson was at least as traditional a poet as any of these, and he was probably more deeply versed than they in the poetry of Theocritus, Bion, and Moschus. The question arises, then, why he did not also employ the form for the tribute which he had determined from the very first to construct for his friend Hallam. The answer cannot lie in the view that Tennyson was questioning the very assumptions of pastoralism, for there is a great deal of pastoral imagery in *In Memoriam*, and Milton, Shelley, and Arnold were also deeply probing the idea of the benevolence of nature. It is true that Hallam was much closer to Tennyson than the other friends were to their elegists, but deep sorrow has never been absent from Arcadian fields. No, the true reason for Tennyson's avoidance of the pastoral elegy must lie in its most characteristic or distinctive feature, the elegiac reversal or peripeteia. At a certain point the poet must say,

> Weep no more, woful shepherds, weep no more,
> For *Lycidas* your sorrow is not dead.

Or, as in Shelley,

> Peace, peace! he is not dead, he doth not sleep—
> He hath awakened from the dream of life—

Even Arnold, for whom the momentary loss of the signal elm is symbolic of the loss of the way of life he and Clough had pursued, suddenly turns round and sees, "Bare on its lonely ridge, the Tree! the Tree!" For Milton the peripeteia was made possible by orthodox Christian values, for Shelley by a belief in Platonic or mythopoeic forms, and for Arnold by a humanism which was persuaded of the existence of absolute values even if one could never know them. Tennyson, however, did not enjoy this dogmatic temperament. Had he employed Arnold's image, the tree would have been swathed in mist and would alternately have appeared and disappeared through the swirling vapor. Not that Tennyson was a less orthodox poet than Arnold. On the contrary, in the matter of the immortality of the soul Tennyson assumed from the very first that Hallam was immortal and that he would see him again. In the very first section that he wrote, the "Fair ship" lyric (ix), he speaks of "Arthur, whom I shall not see / Till all my widow'd race be run"—which certainly implies that after it is run he will see him. But later on he is less certain—he "falters where he firmly trod"—and so the poem flows backward and forward, following the contours of human experience. Its movement is rather like the swimming vapor in *Œnone*, which "slopes athwart the glen, / Puts forth an arm, and creeps from pine to pine, / And loiters, slowly drawn." Like that vapor Tennyson in his mature poetry is grandualist rather than catastrophic in his assumptions. The pastoral elegy, on the other hand, is an apocalyptic or catastrophic form. Depending as it does on the sudden revelation or "discovery" that the beloved is not dead but in some sense lives on, it precipitates the speaker, not from joy to woe, as does tragedy, but from woe to joy. True, it does not appear to do this in real time—one has the feeling that the "discovery" was planned from the very beginning and that the whole exercise takes place artificially in space—but that is the more reason for distinguishing it from Tennyson's elegy. For *In Memoriam* does take place in time—the main function of the three Christmas poems is simply to mark the passage of time—and if we think that Tennyson requires a long time to move from grief to reconciliation, we should consider what Lyell required for the formation of mountains and seas in the exactly contemporaneous *Principles of Geology*. For *In Memoriam* is to *Lycidas* as Lyell's *Principles of Geology* is to the Mosaic cosmogony. It operates not by means of volcanic eruptions and deluges but by subsidence and erosion. True, there are little crises here and there, and there is a major one in section xcv. But at no place, as A. C. Bradley observes, is there a true reversal.[1] Tennyson is concerned with the slow healing of a wound that is reluctant to heal, with the gradual understanding of something that cannot be fully understood.

The significance of the form of *In Memoriam* may be seen the more clearly if we go back to two poems which are usually thought to lead up to it, the *Supposed Confessions of a Second-Rate Sensitive Mind Not in Unity with Itself* and *The Two Voices*. The most notable thing about the *Supposed Confessions* (apart from its title) is its rigidity and absolutism. It is the portrait of a mind vacillating between two extremes, the intellectual pride of the rationalist and the evangelical's conviction of sin. In the course of the poem the speaker makes no progress toward the solution of his difficulties but, by recalling his past life, simply reenacts his conflict. On the one hand, as a youth he held the bold creed that it is man's privilege to doubt. He should not live like the ox or lamb, oblivious of death, but should compare all human creeds until he found the true one, if true one there be. Then Truth would stand forth "an image with profulgent brows." On the other hand, he soon discovered that, whether this were the right solution for others or not, he himself did not have the strength to live without faith. For he is terrified by death, and thus he flies back and forth from one extreme to another with no rest and no hope of resolving his difficulties. Both in the positions themselves and in the imagery by which they are expressed we recognize the apocalyptic and revolutionary poets of Tennyson's youth, but it is clear that Tennyson had passed judgment upon them by calling the speaker a "second-rate sensitive mind." Presumably his suggestion is that if he were first rate he would find a way out of his difficulties. But, as Hallam observes, there is nothing second rate about his speculations,[2] and his difficulty is not that he lacks intellect but that he pursues both the principle of intellect and that of faith to their absolute extremes. What he needs to do is moderate the Understanding by Reason, the religious principle by some confidence in his own powers. Then he would be able to emerge from the "damnèd vacillating state" into one of reconciliation and balance.

He did this in *The Two Voices* but apparently not until the second version. It used to be thought that *The Two Voices* was inspired by the death of Hallam and that its happy ending represents Tennyson's working out of his own personal problem. One would not wish to doubt the sincerity of the poem in the larger sense, and indeed Tennyson says that while he was writing it he was "so utterly miserable, a burden to myself and to my family, that I said, 'Is life worth anything?' "[3] Still, we know that the poem was in existence at least three months before Hallam died and that it could not have been narrowly autobiographical since its original title was *Thoughts of a Suicide*. It was obviously in the same Romantic mode as the *Supposed Confessions*. J. M. Kemble, who read it at that time, described it to his fellow Apostle, W. B. Donne, as follows: "Next Sir are some superb meditations on Selfdestruction called *Thoughts of a Suicide* wherein he argues the point with his soul and is thoroughly floored. These are amazingly fine and deep, and show a mighty stride in intellect since the *Second-Rate Sensitive Mind*."[4] By the time Spedding read it in September 1834 it was very long, but it still was not finished, Tennyson "not having fully made up his mind," according to Edmund Lushington, "to what conclusion he should bring it. The termination as it now stands I first heard him read in my London chambers (i.e. 1837–38)."[5] It is obviously important that Tennyson decided not to kill off his protagonist, but one feels that the final version of the poem represents less Tennyson's evolving faith than it does his evolving conception of the kind of poem it was appropriate to write. Particularly, it reflects his decision to abandon the Romantic confessional mode in favor of the more formal debate with one's soul or with a Mephistophelean tempter. It was no doubt the growing popularity of *Faust*, whose hero also says, "Two souls, alas, are housed within this breast,"[6] which led him to this conclusion.

Paradoxically, by thus taking the two elements of the divided soul and objectifying them as "voices" Tennyson achieved a much more credible and human speaker than he had before. For the speaker in the *Supposed Confessions*, like Browning's similar creation in *Johannes Agricola*, is a mere abstraction, a kind of Elizabethan Vice who comes down front stage and simply spouts the extremes of Rationalism and Evangelicalism in a way no credible human being could do. But the speaker in the later poem is more realistic. He is genuinely miserable, and as he cautiously puts forth one tentative little hope after another, only to have each one knocked down by the "still small voice," our sympathies go out to him. We feel that he is imitating the subtle persistence of life itself. Like a blind, groping organism he puts forth feelers this way and that, beginning with short speeches which are cut off sharply by the "voice," but gradually gaining in confidence with longer and more complicated arguments. The one which finally turns the tide is that if all be dark, as the voice says, then our very doubt whether death ends all suggests that it does not. For sense deals in such absolute certainties, and the soul in such uncertainties, that if death ended all, the evidence of the senses would be clear. The question arises, therefore,

> Who forged that other influence,
> That heat of inward evidence,
> By which [man] doubts against the sense?

The voice cannot answer and so with his own weapon of doubt he is slain. It is not, as Bishop Butler said, that "probability is the guide of life," for there is no probability here. Rather it is the absence of negative certainty that is the license for life. Whereas the speaker in *Supposed Confessions* swung from ultrafidianism to ultrarationalism, the speaker in this poem moves slowly forward from one millimeter on the side of despair to one millimeter on the side of hope.

So buoyed, he is emboldened to answer the voice's last argument—that the soul did not exist before birth and so why should it after death—by appealing to those trancelike experiences he had known from boyhood.

> Moreover, something is or seems,
> That touches me with mystic gleams,
> Like glimpses of forgotten dreams—
>
> Of something felt, like something here;
> Of something done, I know not where;
> Such as no language may declare.

The ineffability of the experience is reinforced by the rudimentary quality of the language—"something" four times over is the best that he can do—but this is in harmony with the conclusion of the second voice, who at this point does not so much enter the discussion as indicate ("I may not speak of what I know") that there is "a hidden hope." Hidden, indeed, it is, for although we are now told that a power like a "rainbow" breaks from the speaker's heart, this power is actually imaged by a cloud. It is the feeling,

> altho' no tongue can prove,
> That every cloud, that spreads above
> And veileth love, itself is love.

Tennyson said later that the very obscurity which veils revelation is itself a revelation, and so here it is the very existence of doubt that is the evidence of the spiritual life.

Would that the poem had been allowed to remain in mists and uncertainties! Unfortunately, the final hope was sufficient to bring on the Sabbath morn and start the church bells ringing. Everyone deplores the Sabbath morn, everyone regrets the church bells. And as for the sight of the wholesome English family walking to church, if it warmed the heart of the speaker, it causes the blood of the modern reader to boil.

> One walk'd between his wife and child,
> With measured footfall firm and mild,
> And now and then he gravely smiled.
>
> The prudent partner of his blood
> Lean'd on him, faithful, gentle, good,
> Wearing the rose of womanhood.
>
> And in their double love secure,
> The little maiden walk'd demure,
> Pacing with downward eyelids pure.

Still, the picture does indicate that in this poem Tennyson has moved from the apocalyptic mode to that of the English idyls, with which its conclusion is exactly contemporaneous. Moreover, the little maiden demure, on whom the love of the father and mother is focused, is a symbol of the resolution achieved by the poem. Indeed, it is a curious fact, which has been noticed by several critics, that in this poem there are three voices, not two. Formally, the two voices are the "still small voice" which counsels despair and the "second voice" which urges the speaker to rejoice. But since the second voice does not enter the poem until line 427, when the debate is over, every reader approaching the poem for the first time is under the impression that the two voices are the "I" (the speaker) and the "still small voice." He is surprised and confused when he encounters the "second voice" at the end, and Tennyson cannot be absolved of some carelessness in allowing this to happen. Still, it does give to the poem a tripartite character corresponding to the resolution achieved.

In *In Memoriam* the two voices are multiplied to several score. "The sections," said Tennyson, "were written at many different places, and as the phases of our intercourse came to my memory and suggested them. . . . The different moods of sorrow as in a drama are dramatically given."[7] Many different voices, indeed, speak in this drama, not only the moods of sorrow but also the different points of view on science, faith, immortality, and social progress. It is widely recognized, indeed, that the structure of the poem is partly based on a series of correspondences between earlier and later poems, not only the formal "paired poems," like those on the old yew, the dark house, the Christmas poems, and the poems of "calm despair" and "wild unrest," but also those which take up again the same theme in sharply altered mood. There are also poems which are written only to be unwritten in the next section, and assertions which are made in the first half of a lyric to be denied in the second. Things and people, real and imaginary, become personalities in the poem, and so too do the various powers of Sleep, Grief, Death, Sorrow, Time, Hope, Love, and Use and Wont. If one were to make an index of the "voices" of *In Memoriam*, as of the characters in a novel by Dickens, it would be rather large, and yet it is also true that all these voices are aspects of a single mind.

For such a pluralistic and collective poem, which consists of a sequence of meditative lyrics, the critics have been concerned to find a model. Shakespeare's sonnet sequence has been suggested, and it is very likely that Tennyson did have it partly in mind. But because it is formally a love poem addressed to another person, whereas here the beloved is gone and the speaker is alone, it does not quite fulfill the condition. T. S. Eliot has compared it to a diary, and the comparison is a good one provided one adds, as Eliot does, that it is "the concentrated diary of a man confessing himself,"[8] for, compared to the ordinary diary, there is very little of quotidian matter in it. Alan Sinfield has said it is rather like a novel: the work opens with the central character musing about his loss; he walks down to the graveyard, where more of his meditations follow; he goes to bed, thinks about his art; early one morning he goes for a walk to the dead man's house, etc., etc. The only difference, says Sinfield, is that "the poem lacks all the linking passages we expect in a novel."[9] Perhaps we should say that it is like an epistolary novel, which, being written in letters, has both the inwardness and the disconnected character of *In Memoriam*. Tennyson would not be displeased by this comparison, for he

loved the great leisurely novels of Richardson and wished they
would go on forever. Still, most of *In Memoriam* does not consist of
actions but of thoughts, and in that respect it is more like a
commonplace book. One can hardly read it and not think of
Pascal and La Bruyère, of Joubert and the meditations of Ober-
mann. But perhaps the most apposite and historical comparison is
with three works published just before the inception of *In
Memoriam,* Coleridge's *Aids to Reflection* (1825), Keble's *The Christian Year* (1827), and Julius and Augustus Hare's *Guesses at Truth*
(1829).

"Tennyson's Poems," says J. A. Froude, the historian, "the
group of Poems which closed with *In Memoriam*, became to many
of us what *The Christian Year* was to orthodox Churchmen."[10] The
main difference between Tennyson and Keble (apart from the
quality of the poetry) is that Keble arranged his poems according
to the authorized formularies of the Church of England, so that
he has poems for the Second Sunday in Advent, the First Sunday
after Epiphany, and so on throughout the ecclesiastical year,
whereas Tennyson arranged his according to that inward calen-
dar of what he actually felt. Keble's poems are intended to prom-
ote not only "a sound rule of faith" but also "a sober standard of
feeling in matters of practical religion." He alludes to "that *soothing* tendency in the Prayer-book, which it is the chief purpose of
these pages to exhibit."[11] Froude, however, did not care to be
soothed. He and his contemporaries "determined to have done
with insincerity, to find ground under their feet, to let the uncertain remain uncertain, but to learn how much and what we could
honestly regard as true, and to believe that and live by it. Tennyson became the voice of this feeling in poetry, Carlyle in what was
called prose."[12] One would not call *In Memoriam* "The Agnostic's
Year" or even "The Honest Doubter's Year," but by being divorced from the institution of the Church it seemed to many of
Tennyson's contemporaries a much more authentic and human
document than Keble's.

Coleridge's *Aids to Reflection,* though it consists of prose
aphorisms rather than poetry, provides perhaps an even closer
parallel. For Tennyson is often called the poet of the Broad
Church Movement, and *Aids to Reflection* is the seminal document
of that school. Is it any accident that both works are fragmentary
or composite in form? Coleridge was a master of the fragment,
the isolated thought, the marginalium, and though it has been

argued that one must be a peculiarly systematic thinker in order to write a really fine fragment, still it is true that system in the obvious sense is the product of the Understanding and that Reason clothes itself most naturally in the aphorism, the lyrical paragraph, the *aperçu*. This is partly because it is only by moments that one can glimpse transcendental truth and partly because the need is not for the dead level of comprehensiveness but for the depth, the intensity, the *o altitudo* of a living faith. This too is the reason why *Sartor Resartus*, another work exactly contemporaneous with *In Memoriam*, takes the form not of an encyclopedic German treatise on Clothes but of rhapsodic paragraphs stuffed into paper bags to the despair of its English editor. All over England at this moment there was a sense that the intellectual and spiritual systems of the past, Locke's empiricism, Paley's utilitarianism, and orthodox Christianity, were moribund but that there was a new world of spiritual truth for those who could look into their own hearts and see it. Hence neither *The Friend* nor *Aids to Reflection* proposes to lay down a dogmatic system but rather to teach the reader to reflect upon his own mind so as to reproduce in himself those states of consciousness which are the ground of moral and religious truth. Initially, *Aids to Reflection* started out as a selection of the Beauties of Archbishop Leighton, the seventeenth-century Scottish divine, but ultimately Coleridge's meditations upon Leighton took over the major part of the work, and in the end it is the reader's meditations upon the meditations on Leighton that are principally held in view. The work is a method, an instrumentality, a Way—designed not to be read through but to be meditated upon and put into practice.

Julius Hare dedicated the second edition of *Guesses at Truth* to Wordsworth, but he indicated that, had the first edition not come out anonymously, he and his brother would have wished to couple with the name of Wordsworth that of Coleridge. "You and he came forward together in a shallow, hard, and worldly age,—an age alien and almost averse from the higher and more strenuous exercises of imagination and thought,—as the purifiers and re-generators of poetry and philosophy. It was a great aim; and greatly have you both wrought for its accomplishment."[13] It was Augustus who first began keeping a commonplace book, which Julius, on perusing, found so delightful that the two joined together in producing *Guesses at Truth*, two volumes of random reflections on religion, poetry, politics, language, scenery, prudential morality, the Poor Laws, Coleridge, Shakespeare, and indeed all aspects of human life. Once again the aim is to be suggestive, not definitive. "The best divine is he who well divines." This is one of the two mottoes on the title page; the other is from Lord Bacon. "As young men, when they knit and shape perfectly, do seldom grow to a further stature, so knowledge, while it is in aphorisms and observations, it is in growth; but when it once is comprehended in exact methods, it may perchance be further polished and illustrated, and accommodated for use and practice; but it increaseth no more in bulk and substance." So in the address "To the Reader" Julius warns: "If then I am addressing one of that numerous class, who read to be told what to think, let me advise you to meddle with the book no further. You wish to buy a house ready furnisht: do not come to look for it in a stonequarry. But if you are building up your opinions for yourself, and only want to be provided with materials, you may meet many things in these pages to suit you."[14] In later editions the work greatly increased in bulk, and Julius noted that he had often ceased to believe what he had written earlier. Nevertheless, he let it stand, for if the heart has often been compared to the needle for its constancy, should it not also be for its variations? The very contradictions in his work would prove its truth.

It is not certain that Tennyson ever read *Guesses at Truth*, but as Julius Hare was his tutor at Trinity College in the years immediately following its publication, it is very likely that he was acquainted with it.[15] The important thing is that in works like this and *Aids to Reflection* one finds the model for the form of religious speculation in the Broad Church school. The principal work of that school, Frederick Denison Maurice's *Kingdom of Christ* (1838), was first written in the form of letters to a friend and, even when recast in discursive form, was still characterized by its author as "only a collection of *Hints*."[16] *Hints, Aids, Guesses*—this is what the Broad Church theologian attempted to provide, not a definitive system of truth but a method which would place one in the way of finding that truth for himself. In the *Kingdom of Christ* Maurice distinguishes between *system* and *method*, two words which many people take to be synonymous but which seem to him "not only not synonymous, but the greatest contraries imaginable: the one indicating that which is most opposed to life, freedom, variety; and the other that without which they cannot exist."[17] "Method" is

Coleridge's term, in *The Friend, Aids to Reflection,* and the *Essay on Method*; "system" might be predicated of his opposite, Bentham. The terms are, indeed, useful for making distinctions throughout the century. Arnold was interested in "the method and secret of Jesus" and was criticized by Frederic Harrison for not having "a philosophy with coherent, interdependent, subordinate, and derivative principles."[18] Maurice himself might be distinguished from Herbert Spencer as a man of method rather than system. *In Memoriam* is certainly an unsystematic poem but it is not an unmethodical one. It places the reader in the way of coping with his own sorrow, though it by no means completes the process. For that reason Tennyson did not speak of it as an "elegy," but rather as "elegies" or "Fragments of an Elegy," or, with perhaps too much of order and direction, as "The Way of a Soul."[19] For its composite, graduated character is of its essence. It is a poem in process, not of product. As the Prologue indicates, it consists of "wild and wandering cries" that lead uncertainly, fitfully, gradually to a doubtful conclusion.

This being the case, it is no wonder that Tennyson adopted for his poem the verse form which he had already devised to express his political gradualism. The so-called *In Memoriam* stanza was first employed not in *In Memoriam* but in *Hail Briton!*, *You ask me, why*, and *Love thou thy land.* There Tennyson had developed the Telemachean philosophy of gradually, "through soft degrees," subduing a rugged people to "the useful and the good." It has already been noted that Sir Bedivere is the equivalent in the *Morte d'Arthur* of Telemachus in *Ulysses* and that in the same sense in which Telemachus could be said to be the "author" of *Hail Briton!* Sir Bedivere is the "author" of *In Memoriam.* At the end of the *Morte d'Arthur* it is his task to survive into the new world of "strange faces, other minds" and, by his meditations, to knit up the fabric of a new order. "But thou," says Arthur,

> If thou shouldst never see my face again,
> Pray for my soul. More things are wrought by prayer
> Than this world dreams of. Wherefore, let thy voice
> Rise like a fountain for me night and day.
> For what are men better than sheep or goats
> That nourish a blind life within the brain,
> If, knowing God, they lift not hands of prayer

Both for themselves and those who call them friend?
For so the whole round earth is every way
Bound by gold chains about the feet of God.

This is an accurate description of what Tennyson did from 1833 to 1837—he let his voice rise like a fountain for Hallam night and day, and by so doing he fashioned a gold chain or *catena aurea*[20]—or, to use the imagery of *In Memoriam* itself, a ladder or *scala*—leading up through the mist and darkness to the feet of God. The individual sections of *In Memoriam* are the links in that chain, the steps of that ladder.

The image occurs at the very opening of *In Memoriam*:

I held it truth, with him who sings
    To one clear harp in divers tones,
    That men may rise on stepping-stones
Of their dead selves to higher things.

"I believe I alluded to Goethe," wrote Tennyson in explanation of this stanza. "Among his last words were these: 'Von Aenderungen zu höheren Aenderungen,' 'from changes to higher changes.' "[21] The precise occasion to which Tennyson alludes is unknown, but in the second part of *Faust*, and indeed in many other places, Goethe presents his philosophy of a spiritual evolution through self-transcendence to higher and higher types. In common with Hutton, Lyell, and Saint-Hilaire and in opposition to Cuvier, Buckland, and Sedgwick, he held to the uniformitarian hypothesis, and he applied this process of biological metamorphosis to the human spirit when actuated by self-control and led forward by divine love.[22] That Tennyson did "hold this Goethean philosophy true" in the years before Hallam's death is indicated by a poem he addressed to a friend, probably R. J. Tennant, in 1829 or 1830. That friend had been suffering from religious doubt, and Tennyson reminds him of the advice he had given: "From the tomb / And charnel-place of purpose dead, / Thro' spiritual death we come / Into the light of spiritual life.' " So it had proved, and "When from change to change, / Led silently by power divine, / Thy thought did scale a purer range / Of prospect up to self-control," the poet's joy was as great as his friend's.[23] But now he cannot apply this wisdom to himself. Under the traumatic shock of Hallam's death he is plunged into a kind of catatonic rigidity, where "Love [would] clasp Grief lest both be drown'd" (i), and he emphasizes all the melodramatic attributes of Death—its "raven gloss," the drunken dance with death, and the old yew, whose stubborn absorption in the grave seems to present the poet with a model for his own behavior. Sorrow, seen now as a "Priestess in the vaults of Death" (iii), voices the same apocalyptic view of nature and the cosmos that Tennyson had held earlier, and although he suspects that her whispers come from a "lying lip," he is uncertain whether he should crush her as a vice in the blood or cherish her as his natural good. He is like a vase of tears which, chilled below the freezing point, is suddenly precipitated by a slight shock into ice, and it is in this frozen state that he would remain (iv). Even when he does rouse himself and feels he would not be the "fool of loss," he is in a half-numbed state (v), and his imagination, replying to some well-meant condolence, can only people the world with melodramatic instances of sons dying even as their parents pledge them, of lovers falling from their horse even as their betrothed awaits them at the gate (vi). Indeed, his imagination is gothic, not wholesome, and in the early dawn, when he is unable to sleep, he creeps "like a guilty thing" to the "dark house" of his beloved, thus reenacting *Hamlet* or some scene from a gothic novel, and there luxuriates in the emotions which he ought to be assuaging (vii).

It is clear from these opening sections that the general structure of *In Memoriam* is similar to that of *Locksley Hall,* where the speaker as a youth believed in the social progress of mankind but lost that faith under the double impact of Amy's falseness and the venality of the age, and only after long suffering recovered it. So here *In Memoriam* will end almost precisely where it began, in a Goethean faith in spiritual evolution to a higher and higher type, but the journey back is far more complicated than that in *Locksley Hall.* Indeed, the division of the poem into major phases by the three groups of Christmas poems or the two anniversaries of Hallam's death oversimplifies it. On the other hand, the truer method of pausing on every one of the 131 stepping-stones is no analysis at all. An intermediate method, historically sound and doing justice to the wavelike movement of the poem, is afforded by Tennyson's own division of the poem into nine "natural groups or divisions," as follows: i–viii, ix–xx, xxi–xxvii, xxviii–xlix, l–lviii, lix–lxxi, lxxii–xcviii, xcix–ciii, civ–cxxxi.[24] The first division is that already analyzed in which the poet is plunged into the rigidity of grief and only emerges in a slightly numbed condition.

In the second division (ix–xx), the "Fair ship" sections, the poet releases his imagination to follow the fair ship which is bringing the body of the beloved to England to be laid to rest in the churchyard. The sequence performs the function in the poem of the funeral ceremony in real life. As the outward ritual which releases and purifies the emotions, it beautifies and domesticates death so as to bring it into the round of human life. It is here presented as the result of imagination, for whereas all the previous sections may be presumed to record actual experiences—the poet walks down to the churchyard and addresses the old yew, he revisits the dark house in Wimpole Street—the sections in the "Fair ship" sequence are enacted in the imagination. The poet sends his spirit forth over the waters like a dove to hover above the vessel and guide it through all the "circles of the bounding sky" (xvii). Sometimes he sweeps so low that he is virtually on board the vessel.

> I hear the noise about thy keel;
>   I hear the bell struck in the night:
>   I see the cabin-window bright;
> I see the sailor at the wheel.   [x]

But it is only "in spirit" that he sees these things, for in point of fact they did not happen as he imagined. Hallam's body was not discharged in the Bristol channel, where the babbling Wye, hushed by the salt-sea tide of the Severn, made a perfect symbol for the poet's grief (xix), but at Dover, where Arnoldian images of the Sea of Faith might have prevailed. Neither was it buried in the churchyard, as Tennyson's sanative imagination envisioned, but in the church, and then not in the chancel but in the dark transept.[25] What is more, it was his "fancy" which averred, when a violent storm arose, that the vessel was passing over tranquil seas, and it was his concern for the vessel's safety which prevented him from poring and doting upon the cloud, as he would have done a little earlier when he was fixated in grief (xv).

This is a significant feature, because every phase in the evolution of Tennyson's grief is paralleled by a comparable phase in the evolution of the poetic imagination. In the first section, when he was absolute for death, he felt it "half a sin" to write poetry at all and was only reconciled to it because the "sad machanic exercise" of versification provided a kind of anodyne, numbing his pain. He was even led to disparage language as doing more to conceal than reveal the soul within, and to say that if he wrapped himself "in words, like weeds," it was for the utilitarian purpose just mentioned rather than for any symbolic one (v). But with the second division, when he releases his imagination to follow the fair ship, not only does concern for the "sacred bark" (xvii) spare him from becoming its antithesis, the "unhappy bark / That strikes by night a craggy shelf" (xvi), but it also gives him a symbol, with associations from the Egyptian funerary ships and the ships of classical antiquity for which fair weather was invoked, by which to control and order his imagination. As a result, this entire division with its highly stylized language, is one of the most serene and tranquil in the poem. It opens with a prayer (ix) and closes with a benediction (xvii), and by the time we reach the "ritual of the dead" in section xviii we feel that that ritual has already been accomplished, within the poem, by the "sacred bark" that brought the "precious relics" home.

It is likely that Tennyson was helped to this conception of his office by Wordsworth's *Essay upon Epitaphs,* which he would have read as a long note appended to book V of *The Excursion.*[26] The village churchyard, says Wordsworth, is the ideal place of burial because it is contiguous to the place of worship and yet combines the advantages of natural beauty. Tennyson too seems to derive comfort from the fact that Hallam's body will not rest at sea or in a foreign land but in English earth, amid the names and places of his youth, and "where the kneeling hamlet drains / The chalice of the grapes of God" (x, xviii). Moreover, he accepts Wordsworth's conception of what is required in a good epitaph. It should contain nothing that will be inconsistent with "the most serious and solemn affections of the human mind," and if it contains "some thought or feeling belonging to the mortal or immortal part of our nature touchingly expressed," it need not be original. Moreover, it should not be too specific.

> The writer of an epitaph is not an anatomist, who dissects the internal frame of the mind; he is not even a painter, who executes a portrait at leisure and in entire tranquillity; his delineation, we must remember, is performed by the side of the grave; and, what is more, the grave of one whom he loves and admires. What purity and brightness is that virtue

clothed in, the image of which must no longer bless our living eyes! The character of a deceased friend or beloved kinsman is not seen, no—nor ought to be seen, otherwise than as a tree through a tender haze or a luminous mist, that spiritualises and beautifies it.[27]

Should one say that this is not a true image of the dead? Wordsworth asserts that it is a true image but "truth hallowed by love—the joint offspring of the worth of the dead and the affections of the living!" The character of a good man contemplated by the side of the grave ought to appear "as something midway between what he was on earth walking about with his living frailties, and what he may be presumed to be as a spirit in heaven."[28]

This is as exact a description as one could desire of the tone and temper of *In Memoriam*. The muted quality of the stanzas, the subdued emotion, the mingling of general reflections with specific incidents—and those so clothed in decorum that one can tell little more about Hallam than that he was a person of high ideals and glowing eloquence—all this insures that the poem will be, as Tennyson said it was, an instrument through which the voice of the human race is speaking.[29] There is very little distance between the Wordsworth of *The Excursion* and the Tennyson of *In Memoriam*, and particularly is this true when we come to the subject of immortality.

But first there is a short group of poems (xxi–xxviii) that is unified by the image of the path—the Dantesque path of life which stretches back into the past and forward into the future. Primarily, the poet is looking back. His mind no longer occupied by the external ritual of the service, he recurs in memory to the beloved and thinks back to the "happy times" they spent together. It is, as the poet recognizes, a pastoral motif, and his muse in this section is primarily pastoral. "I take the grasses of the grave, / And make them pipes whereon to blow" (xxi). But though gracious, it is a slender muse, capable only of the lesser griefs which are associated with the babbling Wye (xix), and with the servants of the house rather than the children (xx), and he is defensive about it as he imagines the criticisms of him that may be made. "I do but sing because I must, / And pipe but as the linnets sing" (xxi). The path back, however, implies the path forward, and he realizes that the Wordsworthian "haze of grief" (xxiv) may have the same effect as the mist on the Brocken or in the Westmoreland hills, of magnifying the object. The pastoral method idealizes the past, which, viewed clearly, had the same burdens as the present (xxv). The only difference is that Love was there to help him bear those burdens, and so what he must do is see that Love continues, even though its object is gone. He longs now to meet this challenge, "to prove / No lapse of moons can canker Love" (xxvi), and so, as he turns from the past to the future, he recalls and rejects his position in section i. There, fearful lest Love should weaken, he had convulsively clasped Grief "lest both be drowned." Only so could he avoid the scorn of the victor Hours, who would cry, "Behold the man that loved and lost, / But all he was is overworn." But now it is his own proper scorn and the eye of God that he fears, and so he sees that the image of the path rather than the cage is what he wants. If he is the linnet, he is the linnet deprived of its young, not the caged linnet. The captive void of noble rage, the beast imprisoned in its own bestiality, anything that "stagnates in the weeds of sloth," he repudiates: "Tis better to have loved and lost / Than never to have loved at all" (xxvii). What is more, he "holds this true" (using the same phrase he had used of Goethe's philosophy) "in any moods" and "whate'er befall." He recognizes that many of his verses represent a momentary feeling, but this is something staked out and established in the poem once and for all. The compulsive fixation in grief of section i is rejected, and he commits himself now and forever to change, growth, life, and time, wherever they may lead.

We have arrived at this point at the end of the third of Tennyson's divisions, approximately one-fourth of the way through the poem, after three months in the poetic year. The effect of the first of the Christmas poems is to confirm that life must go on, for when the Christmas bells begin to ring, "Four voices of four hamlets round," the message of their balanced lines is one of peace and order. If only for the sake of old times, the festivities must be continued, and so, sitting in a circle, the family sang three songs, first, a merry one that Hallam liked, then one of gentler feeling, and finally, "our voices took a higher range" (xxx), and with this, the theme of immortality, which will form the main subject of the long group of poems from xxviii–xlix, is introduced.

Immortality is not a subject with which most people are concerned today, and for the average reader this portion of the poem seems dated. One feels that Tennyson is puzzling his head about questions that are trifling or nonexistent or that involve a pecul-

iarly literal-minded conception of religion. Do the dead remember us on earth, he asks, and will we know them again in
heaven? Alas, in Hallam's case he will be ascending through
higher and higher spheres, and so, even when I rejoin him in
death, I will always be a life behind. Foolish thought! It was only
"place" that united us here, and so it will be there, he instructing
me still. But perhaps the souls of the dead do not advance but
sleep till a general awakening. Or perhaps they have only a dim
consciousness of their earthly life, like our recollection of earliest
infancy. Such are the questions that Tennyson raises in this portion of the poem, and one cannot read it without thinking of
Arnold's strictures on the narrowness and parochialism of the
English religious imagination.

Still, one must recognize that the subject of the immortality of
the soul was of tremendous importance to Tennyson and to his
age. At the end of the Gifford Lectures on *The Varieties of Religious
Experience* (1902) William James explains why he has said not one
word about immortality. He regards it as a secondary matter. But
he recognizes that for most people the main practical difference
made by the existence of God is personal immortality. "Religion,
in fact, for the great majority of our own race *means* immortality,
and nothing else. God is the producer of immortality; and whoever has doubts of immortality is written down as an atheist
without farther trial."[30] A hundred and sixty years earlier Bishop
Butler in his *Analogy of Religion Natural and Revealed* (1736) began
his dissertation on Personal Identity by saying, "Whether we are
to live in a future state, as it is the most important question which
can possibly be asked, so it is the most intelligible one which can be
expressed in language." It is "the foundation of all our hopes and
of all our fears; all our hopes and fears, which are of any consid-
eration."[31] Tennyson, living midway between these two
philosophers, agreed with Butler about its importance, but not
about its intelligibility. Talking to Edward FitzGerald in the spring
of 1842, he said: "I would rather know I was to be damned
eternally than not to know that I was to live eternally." Walking in
St. Paul's Cathedral, he said, "This is a Symbol that Man is immortal," and, going along the fields to Dulwich, in answer to some
remark of FitzGerald's, "Depend upon it, Milton shot up into
some grim Archangel, Fitz." "No Great Man," he added, "could
doubt of the Soul's Immortality."[32] But though agreeing with
Butler about the importance of the doctrine, he would more

nearly have agreed with James that religious experience was the ground on which to base it.

For up to the latter part of the eighteenth century the main argument for the immortality of the soul was the metaphysical one of its simplicity or "indiscerptibility." This was the position taken by Samuel Clarke in his pamphlet warfare with Henry Dodwell, Sr., and Anthony Collins in the first decade of the century, and it was elaborated by Moses Mendelssohn in Germany. But the argument was attacked by Kant in the *Critique of Pure Reason* as a serious logical paralogism, and in the *Critique of Practical Reason* (1788) he made immortality a postulate of the practical reason. Holiness, "the perfect accordance of the will with the moral law," demands an endless progression, and this "endless progress is only possible on the supposition of an *endless* duration of the *existence* and *personality* of the same rational being (which is called the immortality of the soul)." Not demonstrable as a theoretical proposition, the immortality of the soul "is an inseparable result of an unconditional *a priori practical* law."[33] This teleological argument, that immortality is necessary for man to realize the full potentiality of his spiritual nature, was adopted by Goethe in *Faust* and became the standard argument in the nineteenth century. It obviously harmonized with the age's faith in progress and with the newly emerging belief in biological evolution. It was deemed by both Emerson and Renan to be essential to the preservation of morality because, if one did not posit immortality, then one either fell into laxity in the pursuit of the moral law or into an excessive righteousness. The one middle way between antinomianism and sensualism was this capability of the soul for continuous striving.

This is the view of immortality that Tennyson accepted: it was not Eternity that he desired but an eternity of continual progress. In *Wages,* written in December 1867, he declares that if the wages of Sin is death, the wages of Virtue, whose glory is "to fight, to struggle, to right the wrong," is "going on." "She desires no isles of the blest, no quiet seats of the just . . . / Give her the wages of going on, and not to die." "I can hardly understand," said Tennyson, "how any great, imaginative man, who has deeply lived, suffered, thought and wrought, can doubt of the Soul's continuous progress in the after-life."[34] How Ulysses, who was such a man, could have said, "Death closes all," when he had "toil'd, and wrought, and thought" with his companions is not clear. Perhaps it was because he was a pagan, and perhaps we are intended to think that that note of melancholy would have been absent in his Christian counterpart. Certainly, that was the defect in Tithonus's immortality, that it consisted in stagnation not in striving, that he withered in Aurora's arms rather than growing in her love. For the main way in which Tennyson developed Kant's argument was in emphasizing not the moral law but love. "Love had not been, / Or been in narrowest working shut," if death had been seen from the very beginning as the end of all. This idea Tennyson could have found more fully elaborated in Wordsworth's *Essay upon Epitaphs,* where the sense of immortality is made a "twin birth with Reason" and where it is asserted that "from these conjoined, and under their countenance, the human affections are gradually formed and opened out."[35] It is inconceivable to Wordsworth that the sympathies of love could survive a repeated experience of death if they had not been supported by the prior feeling of immortality.

It would have been well had Tennyson left the subject in the purely philosophic and poetic form in which Kant and Wordsworth stated it, but he lived on the verge of an age of science when there was a desire to bring such concepts into relation with what was known of the physical world. Or to put it another way, just as positing the existence of God inevitably gives rise to questions about his nature and so leads to a system of theology, so positing the immortality of the soul gives rise to questions about the state of the soul after death and so leads to a science of immortality. It was with this tender and inchoate science that Tennyson attempted to deal in sections xxxi to xlix. That is why he begins with Lazarus. Lazarus was an important figure for mid-nineteenth-century poets, for Tennyson, Browning, and Arnold all make some use of his story. Arnold alludes to it in the "miracle" wrought by Empedocles in supposedly bringing Pantheia back to life after she had been dead for several days. In Arnold the miracle obviously did not happen and merely illustrates the superstitious fear with which the ordinary sensual man grasps at straws instead of confronting the fact of death with dignity and courage. In the *Epistle of Karshish* Browning uses the story to comment on the revolutionary implications of the doctrine of the Incarnation as indicating that the All-Powerful is the All-Loving too; but he also recognizes that if we had certain knowledge of another life it would have the effect of incapacitating us for this life. Tennyson takes a simpler view. When the miracle happened, no one asked Lazarus what it was like on the other side of the grave, or, if they did, they did not bother to record his reply. Curious oversight on the one occasion in history when this momentous problem might have been solved! But actually, his family was just glad to have him back, and they rejoiced in the Love which made this possible. How much better this simple faith than the "subtle thought," the "curious fears," that might have been exercised on the problem. Tennyson accepts this self-rebuke, and doubtless had Hallam risen from the grave he too would simply have rejoiced in the recovery of his friend. At least for the first two or three days he would, but it is hard to imagine that, after that, both he and his friend would not have exercised all the subtle thought of which they were capable on this grand scientific experiment with which they had been miraculously provided.[36] For that is precisely what Tennyson attempts to do in the sections that follow.

In this he had plenty of help, for there were many other Victorians who were also exercising their ingenuity on the problem of immortality, and it is difficult to believe that Tennyson had not read some of their works. The big question, of course, was whether the departed were conscious of their friends on earth, could communicate with them, and whether we would know one another in afterlife. Samuel Drew, in "An Essay, to induce the Belief that we shall know each other in a Future State," published in the *Amulet* in 1826, gave a comfortable reply to these questions. So too did the anonymous author of *An Essay on the State of the Soul after Death,* published in Edinburgh in 1825. He notices the assertion that "the souls of the departed sleep, in utter unconsciousness, from death to judgment," but declares that "for this cold and cheerless doctrine there is no authority in Scripture whatever." He is therefore inclined to believe that "there is an intermediate state of reward and punishment between death and judgment, and that the souls of the departed are, in this intermediate state, capable of recollecting the friends whom they left on earth, and deeply interested in their fate."[37]

Richard Whately, Newman's mentor at Oriel, was more skeptical. In a series of twelve lectures to unlettered parishioners published as *A View of the Scripture Revelations concerning a Future State* (1829), Whately noted that the whole subject is very confused. People commonly speak of the departed as "in heaven," but actually "we are not expressly told any where in Scripture what becomes of a man immediately after death." We know that there is a long interval between that time and the final resurrection at the great Day of Judgment, when we shall resume our bodies, but we are not told where we are or what we are doing during that interval. There are two alternatives. "It must either be a state of enjoyment and of suffering, respectively, to the faithful and the disobedient . . . or else a state of perfect insensibility—a profound sleep." The awkwardness about the former supposition is that it involves anticipating the final judgment. "It seems strange that a man should first undergo his sentence, and afterwards be brought to trial;—should *first* enter upon his reward or punishment, and *then* (perhaps many centuries after) be tried,—and then judged, and acquitted or condemned." On the other hand, the objection to the other supposition is "that it seems as if there were a tedious and dreary interval of non-existence to be passed"— though Whately informs us that this is more an objection to the imagination than the reason, for "a long and a short space of time are exactly the same to a person who is insensible."[38] For this reason—and also because, if we think of the departed as conscious, we are very likely to pray to them and so be led into Roman Catholicism—Whately inclines toward the second of the two alternatives, that we sleep till the great day of our resurrection. Tennyson contemplates this possibility in section xliii, where he notes that if the spirit in its "intervital gloom" (the period intermediate between this life and the next) should "slumber on; / Unconscious of the sliding hour," when it awoke along with "the total world since life began," at least there would have been nothing lost to man. Having been placed in a kind of spiritual deep freeze, neither he nor Hallam would have expended love in vain. But he does not find the idea very attractive.

He is more at one with Whately when the latter turns to the state of the blest after the resurrection. "It has been asserted by some . . . ," says Whately, "that in heavenly society, there will be no mutual knowledge between those who had been friends on earth; nor even any such thing as *friendship* towards one person more than another." He finds this idea "not very alluring." Tennyson too finds the idea of remerging in the general Soul "faith as vague as all unsweet" and is confident that "I shall know him when we meet" (xlvii). It is also thought, says Whately, "that the heavenly life will be one of *inactivity,* and perfectly *stationary,*—that there will be nothing to be *done,*—nothing to be *learnt,*—no ad-

vances to be made;—nothing to be *hoped* for,—nothing to *look forward* to, except a continuance in the very state in which the blest will be placed at once. Now this also, is far from being an alluring view, to minds constituted as ours are. It is impossible for us to contemplate such a state . . . without an idea of tediousness and wearisomeness forcing itself upon them. The ideas of *change,— hope,—progress,—improvement,—acquirement,—action*—are so intimately connected with all our conceptions of happiness . . . that it is next to impossible for us to separate them."[39] Tennyson and Kant would certainly agree.

The work which presents the closest analogy to *In Memoriam* in its arguments concerning the immortality of the soul is an anonymous work entitled *Immortality or Annihilation? The Question of a Future State Discussed and Decided by the Arguments of Reason* (1827). Its method, that of a personal meditation by one seeking guidance in grief, its strict adherence to Reason (more so than Tennyson), its arguing pro and con, giving now one side and now the other of the question, its arguments from psychology, physiology, and the other sciences, its homely examples, its idealistic tone and pure language, and its general Kantian position are all such as would have been attractive to Tennyson, and, if he did not read it, he at least produced a poem rather similar to it.

The author, for example, confronts the same problem that Tennyson does of the waste and prodigality of nature. "So careful of the type she seems," says Tennyson, "So careless of the single life" (lv). Similarly the anonymous author cries, "Survey the earth; every thing upon it is certainly contrived for the immortality of the different species, but not for the immortality of individual beings."[40] Like Tennyson, who finds that "of fifty seeds / [Nature] often brings but one to bear," he too declares, "How many fruit-buds drop from the trees? How frequently does it happen that not one in ten of the blossoms on a cherry-tree sets for fruit? . . . In the vegetable kingdom, too, what immense numbers of seeds of all kinds never find their way to the earth!"[41] Like Tennyson, he believes that without the assurance of immortality there is no reason for not being a mere sensualist, and like him he ultimately takes refuge in the Kantian argument that man needs immortality in order to achieve his destiny.

Must not this evident vocation of man to truth on the one hand, and this impossibility of completely attaining truth on the other, involve a tacit promise that in a future higher state he shall certainly arrive at it? . . . Must not in like manner the evident vocation of Man to virtue on the one hand, and the impossibility of completely possessing, enjoying, and applying virtue on the other, involve a tacit promise that in a future higher state he shall certainly arrive at it?[42]

"My own dim life should teach me this," says Tennyson, "That life shall live for evermore" (xxxiv), and the speaker in *Immortality or Annihilation?* observes,

It is precisely [man's] moral nature which furnishes the strongest argument for his existence after death. . . . Which position deserves the preference—that a being which is capable of advancing to eternity in wisdom and virtue . . . shall . . . be suddenly and cruelly stopped . . . ; or, that it shall here, agreeably to its faculties and wishes, acquire only the first rudiments of wisdom . . . . , and then, as a reward for having done so, be removed to a higher state, where it shall allay its thirst of wisdom, gratify its desire of being perfectly virtuous, find a sphere opened for it in which it shall exert the utmost activity . . . [and] feel inexpressibly happy? . . . By my reason, I swear, the latter![43]

This final meditation clinches the argument for the speaker of *Immortality or Annihilation?* and at the end of the book he ascends a lofty eminence whence he looks out over the beauty of the earth. It is, he declares, "only the first world for Man; the first mean by which he is to arrive at wisdom and virtue . . . and when he at last quits the earth . . . , he soars to some other orb, where higher arrangements are destined to conduct him to higher wisdom and virtue."[44] This too is the vision that Tennyson has for the soul of Hallam.

> Rapt from the fickle and the frail
>   With gather'd power, yet the same,
>   Pierces the keen seraphic flame
> From orb to orb, from veil to veil. [xxx]

Like a maiden who leaves her father's home to enter upon "other realms of love," Hallam will be given "A life that bears immortal fruit / In those great offices that suit / The full-grown energies of heaven" (xl). He is imagined as communing with all the wise of past ages, including Shakespeare (lxi), and as being led by the "great Intelligences fair" (lxxxv) through all the stages of future knowledge until, "Upon the last and sharpest height" (xlvii), he fades away into the Universal Spirit.

It is apparent that Tennyson wishes us to take this conception of the ascent of Hallam's soul through the various grades of spiritual being as in a certain sense literally and even physically true. Though he tells us we should not mock the "early Heaven" (xxxiii) of the naively religious, it is clear that he wishes to bring his conception of heaven into accord with the scientific ideas of his time. He realizes that the dead live in "unconjectured bliss"—that nothing certain can be known about their state—and he also re- alizes that poetic decorum requires him to be general. Still, latent in his language and in his images are certain scientific speculations current in his day, particularly those concerning the plurality of worlds.[45] That the moon, the planets, possibly the sun and the fixed stars are inhabited by rational creatures not unlike man was a speculation entertained by the earliest Greeks, and it survived throughout antiquity until it was finally put down in the Middle Ages by the combined authority of Aristotle and the Church. Giordano Bruno raised the question again in the sixteenth cen- tury, and it was given wide currency by Fontenelle in his lively *Entretiens sur la pluralité des mondes* (1686). Throughout the eighteenth and the first half of the nineteenth century it was the accepted view, being favored by scientists and most theologians and used by imaginative writers simply as a matter of course. Tennyson would have encountered it in Milton, Pope, Thomson, Edward Young, and Byron, and, with more of scientific detail, in Thomas Chalmers's *Astronomical Discourses* (1817).

> Why then suppose that this little spot, little at least in the immensity which surrounds it, should be the exclusive abode of life and intelligence? What reason to think that those mightier globes which roll in other parts of creation, and which we have discovered to be worlds in magnitude, are not also worlds in use and in dignity? Why should we think that the great Architect of nature, supreme in wisdom as he is in power, would call these stately mansions into existence, and leave them unoccupied?[46]

On the other hand, the strict Christian noticed that the inhabit- ants of these other worlds were not mentioned in the Bible, and it did seem odd, if the earth was so insignificant, that it should have been selected by God as the theater of the Christian drama. It was

on these theological grounds that the hypothesis was attacked by
Alexander Maxwell, a Scot, in 1820. The first serious attack,
however, based on an analysis of the conditions necessary to
support life, was made by Tennyson's former tutor, William
Whewell, in an *Essay of the Plurality of Worlds,* published in 1854.
Tennyson "carefully studied" Whewell's book and pronounced it
"anything but satisfactory." "It is inconceivable," he declared,
"that the whole Universe was merely created for us who live in this
third-rate planet of a third-rate sun."[47] Clough too believed that
"there are more things in heaven and earth than are dreamt of in
the inductive philosophy."[48]

   Tennyson was probably more pleased with Sir David Brewster's
reply to Whewell, *More Worlds Than One* (1854), for Brewster
applies the conception of the plurality of worlds to the problem of
immortality. Before the rise of modern astronomy, he says, the
Christian supposed his future life would be "in heaven." Now he
supposes it will be on other planets. Indeed, says Brewster, writing
in the post-Malthusian world, some such conclusion is almost
necessary, for we know that man in the future state is to rejoin his
body, and if so, where is he to live? The population of the world
now exceeds 1,000,000,000. Add to this all past and future generations, and it is clear that they must dwell on other planets of the
solar system. In a final chapter on "The Future of the Universe"
he speaks of the "warm and affectionate interest" with which the
Christian contemplates the sidereal bodies. "He looks to them as
the hallowed spots in which his immortal existence is to run."
Scripture has not told us specifically where we are to live, but
"Reason has combined with the scattered utterances of Inspiration, and with a voice, almost oracular, has declared that He who
made the worlds, will in the worlds which He has made, place the
beings of His choice." When Christ said, "In my Father's house are
many mansions," it was doubtless to the planets that he referred.[49]

   When one combines the idea of the departed as dwelling on the
various planets or other sidereal bodies with the idea that they are
continually moving upward through the grades of spiritual being,
one creates a problem. Bulwer-Lytton expressed this problem in
his novel *Zanoni* (1842). "For her and thee will there be even a
joint hereafter? Through what grades and heavens of
spiritualised being will her soul have passed, when thou, the
solitary loiterer, comest from the vapours of the earth to the gates
of light?"[50] Tennyson too felt a spectral doubt "that I will be thy

mate no more." For though he might follow "with an upward mind" Hallam's spiritual course "thro' all the secular to-be," still he would, like the hero of *Zanoni*, always be "a life behind." For that reason he sometimes wished to "leap the grades of life and light, / And flash at once, my friend, to thee" (xli). But that was impossible, and, in any case, his doubt was probably mere fancy. Hallam was as far ahead of him on earth as he will be in heaven, and just as it was only place that united them here, so it may be that Place will unite them there. But generally throughout the poem Tennyson imagines the spirit of Hallam, in whatever "after form" it may assume, mounting up by a vast spiral course from orb to orb until it attains the "landing-place" where individuals fade into the Universal Soul. The language is vague, and when Tennyson calls for Hallam to come from "the abyss of ten-fold complicated change," one feels that it harmonizes neatly with the Dantesque or Ptolemaic heaven.

Tennyson's departed, however, cannot simply lean over the gold bar of heaven, as the Blessed Damozel does, and know what the beloved on earth is thinking. Tennyson's great quarrel with Death is not that Hallam has been translated to another sphere, for he knows that the body, like the chrysalis of the butterfly, is but one state the spirit assumes and that Eternal Process must move on. His quarrel is rather that Death has "put our lives so far apart / We cannot hear each other speak" (lxxxii), and hence much of the poem is concerned with how, consistent with intellectual integrity and the dictates of reason, he can believe that they do communicate. The state after death is so different from this life that the only analogy to it is the soul's preexistence, but at this point Tennyson is not ready to draw on the Intimations of Immortality from recollections of early childhood. Rather, more modestly, he will draw on the psychological observation that our memories of our earliest childhood are lost after the sutures of the skull grow closed. Yet at times there come to us dim intimations of this forgotten life. Oh, if Hallam, ranging with his peers in heaven, should feel such intimations, might he turn round and allow the poet's guardian angel to speak to him and tell him all!

Such is Tennyson's effort, based upon the psychology, the physiology, the pneumatology, the philosophy, and above all the astronomy of his day, to construct a science of immortality. It is not very successful and he felt that it was not.

> If these brief lays, of Sorrow born,
>> Were taken to be such as closed
>> Grave doubts and answers here proposed,
> Then these were such as men might scorn. [xlviii]

But there is no attempt to "part and prove" or write a systematic treatise on the subject. He is merely drawing from art, from nature, and from the schools such random influences as may illuminate the subject. Previously, Urania, the muse of heavenly poetry, had reproved him for speaking of things beyond his ken, and Melpomene, the tragic muse, had excused him on the ground that Hallam loved to speculate on these matters. But Tennyson is not attempting a complete theodicy such as Hallam wrote in the *Theodicæa Novissima* or Pope in the *Essay on Man*. Rather he offers "short swallow-flights of song," mere guesses at truth, which dimple the surface of his pool of tears but do not penetrate to the depths.

This section on immortality, then, should be construed as a first faltering attempt to accomplish by means of the rational intellect what will be accomplished more perfectly, in lyric xcv, by the visionary imagination. The section has its place in the poem, for even Tennyson's misguided efforts are a part of his experience. But the central problem of his grief is not touched by his fabricating a physiology of souls or a geography of the afterlife, and that is why, after he has done so, the poem immediately collapses into its darkest and most poignant moan:

> Be near me when my light is low,
>> When the blood creeps, and the nerves prick
>> And tingle. [1]

For the next division of the poem, sections l–lviii, calls into question everything that had been tentatively settled up to that point.

It does this by returning to the theme with which the poem opened, the "trust that somehow good / Will be the final goal of ill." This trust, however, is immediately undercut by the poet's proclaiming it a "dream" and himself "An infant crying in the night / . . . And with no language but a cry" (liv). Thus, where previously the poet "firmly trod," now he "falters,"

> And falling with my weight of cares
>> Upon the great world's altar-stairs
> That slope thro' darkness up to God,

> I stretch lame hands of faith, and grope,
> And gather dust and chaff, and call
> To what I feel is Lord of all,
> And faintly trust the larger hope. [lv]

The reason for this sudden shift is that Tennyson has turned his attention from the moral nature of man, which provides the chief argument for the immortality of the soul, to the waste and prodigality in nature, which provides the chief argument against it. Tennyson, on looking into a microscope at the Zoological Gardens, had said, "Strange that these wonders should draw some men to God and repel others. No more reason in one than in the other."[51] This, indeed, was the trouble with the argument from design: it could very easily become the argument from undesign—as Paley learned to his cost when his phenomena were reinterpreted by Darwin. Tennyson was writing before Darwin, even before the publication of Robert Chambers's *Vestiges of the Natural History of Creation* (1844), but the subject had been adequately treated by Bishop Butler, Malthus, Lyell, and the anonymous author of *Immortality or Annihilation?*[52] Eleanor Mattes supposes that Tennyson had first read in Butler about the destruction of individuals and then gone on to Lyell on the destruction of entire species. It is not necessary to suppose that historically this is what occurred, but it is true that the structure of that single poem which constitutes the two sections lv-lvi does give the impression of deepening and darkening experience. For whereas after lv the poet falters and but "faintly trusts" the larger hope, after lvi he cries, "O life as futile, then, as frail!" It is not merely that individuals perish and that man himself may go the way of the dinosaur, but also that man is in a sense more a monster than they. For whereas they knew that ravine was the law of nature, man believes that love is nature's final law. Man has implanted in his breast a belief in immortality, and if this belief is not true, then God is a liar, man is a monstrous discord, and there is no meaning at all in the universe. Or if there is, it is "Behind the veil, behind the veil."

These two sections mark the lowest point in the poem, and it is here, if anywhere, that there is a peripeteia. For the next section begins, "Peace; come away: . . . we do him wrong / To sing so wildly": but the words of farewell which the poet utters are the same he later recalled in his elegy to his brother—the "Ave atque

Vale" of Catullus, which he regarded as unequaled in pathos because of the Roman's lack of belief in immortality.[53] With these words echoing like water dripping in a catacomb the poet is inclined to conclude his poem, but the high Muse urges him to "abide a little longer here" so that he may take a "nobler leave."

The new, more cheerful note is struck in the next group of poems, sections lix–lxxi, which are conducted in terms of the English Idyls. Just as those poems often turned on the condescension with which the hero stooped to marry one beneath him, so here Hallam is compared to one of nobler rank and Tennyson to the lowly village maid, or Hallam has moved out of his native village to become one of the great ones in the land and the question is whether he ever pauses to remember his early plowboy friend. It is appropriate that the group should be introduced by a section, addressed to Sorrow, which is deliberately made parallel to section iii, but in which Sorrow, if she is to be the poet's constant companion, must not be a tempestuous mistress but a "wife." For it is the homely domestic character which qualifies at least the first half of this group. The second half consists of dreams. Since one does not normally dream five memorable dreams in a row, with no daytime experience intervening, one feels that Tennyson has here departed from his usual custom of ordering the sections by experience and has simply grouped them mechanically by subject matter. A few of them, particularly lxvii, are memorable and most are psychologically interesting, but some are purely literary or allegorical dreams. It is as if Tennyson were preparing the way for the more adequate visionary experience of xcv. There is more of quotidian matter in this part of the poem than elsewhere, and its function seems to be to separate the dark stanzas of lv–lvi from the visionary section xcv. If the former is Tennyson's Everlasting No and the latter his Everlasting Yea, the group comprising sections lix–lxxi is his Center of Indifference.

The seventh group (lxxii–xcviii) opens with the first anniversary of Hallam's death and closes just before the second, the first poem being the conventional rhetorical accusation of the day, the second the far more moderate memorial which testifies to the distance traveled during this poetic year. For after some miscellaneous sections the poet enunciates his main quarrel with Death that "He put our lives so far apart / We cannot hear each other speak" (lxxxii). This complaint is to be resolved in section xcv, but the sequence of sections leading up to xcv is almost as important as the resolution itself. For it is essential that this victory should not be achieved too easily. When the author of *Immortality or Annihilation?* has finally convinced himself of the immortality of the soul, he repaired to his father's grave and there invoked his spirit. "Dost thou, O father, really continue to live—to live in loftier regions of light and perfection? If so, O appear to me in the still twilight of this serene evening—here, at this to me so sacred spot!" But then, alarmed at his own presumption, he cries:

> What do I ask of thee? Thou canst not appear to me even if thou dost continue to exist. In this case thou art no longer on the same planet with me. The falling-off of thy earthly garment enabled thee to take thy flight from off the earth; in order to sink to it again thou must be enabled to re-assume a gross body like that which thou hast quitted. And shouldst thou ever show thyself to me, and should I at the moment believe that I had obtained the strongest evidence in favour of a future state, would this appear to me to-morrow upon cooler reflection as any evidence at all? Should I not, nay, must I not consider thy appearance as a mere illusion of my imagination?[54]

So it turns out, for on the following day he declares, "Yes, now I clearly perceive what I yesterday suspected, that I should to-day be obliged to consider any apparition of my father that might have manifested itself to me at the grave as nothing more or less than a mere phantom of my imagination."[55]

Tennyson is equally concerned that there should be no hint of the supernatural in his communion with Hallam, but, on the other hand, he is not content with the purely rationalistic approach of the author of *Immortality or Annihilation?* He thus prepares the way for his own visionary experience by a series of poems in which he does two things. First, by addressing various aspects of nature— the reluctant spring, the ambrosial airs that sweep away the storms, the wild nightingale that mingles joy with its sorrow—he reestablishes a relationship with nature that had been broken in lv–lvi and infuses into himself its healing power. Secondly, through the purely natural powers of love and memory he recovers his life with Hallam. He thinks of the domestic bliss that would have been his had Hallam married his sister. He revisits Cambridge, lingers outside the door of Hallam's room, and remembers their youthful debates on art, science, and the state. In a poem which virtually anticipates section xcv he recalls Hallam's visits to Somersby and their happy days together, picnicking in the woods and reading the Tuscan poets on the lawn. By this means he is ready, like the author of *Immortality or Annihilation?*, to invoke the soul of Hallam to appear. This he does in a beautiful section in which the mode of his friend's appearance is to be regulated by the seasons. In spring, he is to come in the form in which the poet knew him in time among his peers. But in summer, which is presumably the season in which he is writing, he is to come

> not in watches of the night,
> But where the sunbeam broodeth warm,
> Come, beauteous in thine after form
> And like a finer light in light. [xci]

And yet he would not have this vision misunderstood. For in the very next section he declares,

> If any vision should reveal
> Thy likeness, I might count it vain
> As but the canker of the brain. [xcii]

Even if it appealed to things known only to the two of them, he might count it but a phenomenon of memory, and if it spoke of future events which actually came to pass, it need not be considered supernatural but merely his own "presentiments, / And such refraction of events / As often rises ere they rise." In other words, there will be a psychological explanation. Tennyson, as his early unfinished essay on *Ghosts* makes plain, did not believe in ghosts. "Within a week after his father's death," we are told, "he slept in the dead man's bed, earnestly desiring to see his ghost, but no ghost came. 'You see,' he said, 'ghosts do not come to imaginative people.' "[56] Ghosts are the refuge of the weak without imagination, just as the disbelief in the ghostly is the delusion of the strong without imagination.

Tennyson is neither one nor the other, and so, though he begins the next section with the flat statement, "I shall not see thee," he is concerned to differentiate his position from that of the rationalist author of *Immortality or Annihilation?* For that speaker, though persuaded that his father lives on, believes that it is impossible for them to communicate with one another. Not so Tennyson. Though he is clear that "No *visual* shade of someone lost" will appear, still,

> he the Spirit himself, may come
> Where all the nerve of sense is numb
> Spirit to Spirit, Ghost to Ghost. [xciii]

Because the visual sense is so closely associated with superstition, and perhaps also because the sense of touch is more intimate and the verb *to feel* is connected with the emotions, Tennyson exchanges the one sense for the other.

> O, therefore from thy sightless range
> With gods in unconjectured bliss . . .
>
> Descend, and *touch*, and enter . . .
> That in this blindness of the frame
> My Ghost may *feel* that thine is near. [xciii]

This is Tennyson's revised invocation to the spirit of Hallam, and he makes clear what he means by it in section xciv. The Gospel tells us that only the pure in heart shall see God. Tennyson amends this to the "pure in heart and sound in head." Only those who combine religion with science, imagination with the absence of superstition, shall hold communion with the dead. For it now appears that although the spirits of the departed may inhabit the moon and the planets they also have their dwelling on earth.

> They haunt the silence of the breast,
> Imaginations calm and fair,
> The memory like a cloudless air,
> The conscience as a sea at rest.

The true precondition for communing with the spirit of Hallam is to have one's own spirit at peace. Glendower had blustered, "I can call spirits from the vasty deep!" To which Hotspur replied, "Why, so can I, or so can any man; / But will they come when you do call for them?" So Tennyson declares,

> In vain shalt thou, or any call
> The spirits from their golden day
> Except, like them, thou too canst say,
> My spirit is at peace with all.

It is not that Tennyson's spirit will be set at peace by union with Hallam, rather that he will achieve that union because his spirit is at peace. Moreover, that state of inward quietude was achieved, not suddenly but by a long process of ordering and cleansing and restoring the imagination.

There is reason, then, for considering the scene on the lawn at Somersby, as described in the opening stanzas of section xcv, as an interior landscape. It reflects the perfect calm of the speaker's mood, and yet there is just that little quivering movement which gives a sense of ghostly presences. The flame flickers under the urn, the "filmy shapes" of bats and moths wheel in the dusk, and the white kine glimmer in the field. Spiritual echoes have already been started by the old songs which peal from knoll to knoll, and the trees, in a soft protective gesture, "laid their dark arms about the field." Gradually, the others withdrew and left the poet to the solitude he required. His heart hungered for the one absent figure, and, taking out the letters of the dead friend, he began to read them. Tennyson does not say that he read them aloud, and yet, "strangely on the silence broke / The silent-speaking words." He does not say that he repeated any particular phrase over and over, and yet the threefold repetition of the word *strange*— "strangely on the silence broke / . . . and strange / Was love's dumb cry . . . and strangely spoke"—gives us a sense of repetition. We feel the weird potency of language to realize itself in magical form, for once again it was by a kind of verbal spell that this trance was induced.

> So word by word, and line by line,
>   The dead man touch'd me from the past,
>   And all at once it seem'd at last
> His living soul was flash'd on mine,
>
> And mine in his was wound, and whirl'd
>   About empyreal heights of thought,
>   And came on that which is, and caught
> The deep pulsations of the world,
>
> Æonian music measuring out
>   The steps of Time—the shocks of Chance—
>   The blows of Death.

It is unfortunate that in this passage Tennyson's language does not rise to the incantatory height to do for the reader what Hallam's language apparently did for him. Of course, he admits as much. "Vague words! but ah, how hard to frame / In matter-moulded forms of speech" the transcendental experience he has had. As an example of the difficulty, he had first written, "*His* living soul was flash'd on mine, / And mine in *his* was wound," but later this reading "troubled me, as perhaps giving a wrong impression." Perhaps it was not Hallam's soul but "the Deity," or "The greater soul may include the lesser."[57] And so he changed it to read, "*The* living soul was flash'd on mine" and "mine in *this* was wound." The first change is certainly an improvement since it easily accommodates both interpretations and is more mysterious and vast, but the second is perhaps a mistake since no demonstrative is required and it does not meet the real need for ambiguity. The problem is not "vague words" but words that are too limited for the vagueness of Tennyson's religious imagination. In *Armageddon* Tennyson rendered his vision adequately, but in this gradualist poem language and style are not well adapted for its one apocalyptic moment.

For what is attempted is nothing less than mystical union, through the intercession of Hallam, with Absolute Reality—"that which is"—but it should be noted that for Tennyson Absolute Reality is not Eternal Being but Eternal Becoming—"The deep pulsations of the world"—and moreover that the music of the spheres is here the "Æonian music" of eternal change. The last time Tennyson used the word "Æonian" (xxxv) it was of geologic erosion, but now he has gained the insight into reality which enables him to see change as creative, not destructive. He has thus simultaneously solved all his problems, reorienting himself toward time, achieving the communion with Hallam essential to his personal life, and doing all this through an imaginative insight which is restorative to his powers as a poet. If the loss of Hallam was for Tennyson the loss of Joy, then through this experience he does not so much recover Joy—for Joy is never recovered—as recover that wholeness of spirit which will enable him to go on. And so when, after a moment, the trance is canceled, "stricken through with doubt," and he redescends into the phenomenal world, he finds the white kine glimmering and the trees with their dark arms still laid about the field. But in place of the absolute calm and tentative vibrations of the opening scene there has arisen a "correspondent breeze," which is nature's response to his effort, Hallam's way of saying he has been heard. The dawn then mingles with the lingering light of the west in a way that is physically possible in these far northern latitudes. The naturalistic explanation, however, is not the true one. It is, in the language of

The Ancient Sage, "as if the late and early were but one," for in this passage the implications of "Far—far—away" have been realized.

After the visionary experience of section xcv the main movement of the poem is centrifugal: the poet turns outward upon the world and concerns himself with the two themes of social change and natural evolution. The short group of poems, xcix–ciii, which chronicles the family's move in 1837 from Somersby to High Beech, Epping Forest, is initially a kind of reexperiencing of death, in that it involves a rupture with all that is associated with the past. But in the end it takes the poet out into the great world and provides just that sense of a new and larger sphere of activity that is needed. This seems to be confirmed by the dream which the poet says he had on the last night before the move—"says," because again it is one of those frigid allegorical dreams which one doubts ever arose from the unconscious. It shows the poet sailing down the river of life to the sea of death, where the Muses, who have accompanied him, are invited on board a gleaming ship by a supernatural Hallam. The meaning seems to be that the poet's powers are thus sanctified and approved, that he may take them with him into the next world, but, coming as the dream does in the context of the move, it also seems to suggest that his powers are not tied to place, as some poems had suggested, but can be taken with him into the larger world. Indeed, the theme that the Muses sing, as they drift down the winding stream, is that of "the great hopes of humanity and science"[58]—and this is the double theme of the remainder of the poem.

Hence it is that in the last major group (civ–cxxxi) Christmas, which previously had been celebrated for old times' sake, is now not celebrated because of the rupture with the past, and is rather displaced by New Year's, which rings out the old and rings in the new. The old includes not merely the poet's "mournful rhymes" but also all social ills, and the new not merely the "fuller minstrel" he intends to be but also the events leading to the Golden Year. The anniversary of Hallam's birth now for the first time replaces the anniversary of his death, and this leads into a series of poems in which we are given a portrait of the man (cix–cxiii). Our first thought is that we should have had this portrait much earlier. We are now getting for the first time an account of the qualities of the man whom we have, for a hundred sections, been lamenting. But is only now that the poet can talk about him objectively—about his social and intellectual qualities, particularly about the wisdom he represented. Hallam thus provides a model for what people should do and be in the world, and under the impact of this model the poet cries, "I will not shut me from my kind" (cviii). Rather than engage in the religious and metaphysical speculations which he now sees as barren and solipsistic, he will "take what fruit may be / Of sorrow under human skies," for it is our humanity and its future development that is the important thing. In the two sections that surround the portrait of Hallam, sections cviii and cxiii, Tennyson contrasts the wisdom that we have gained in sorrow with the wisdom that we have lost in Hallam, for though Tennyson knew that Hallam was no poet, he did believe that he would have been one of the great political figures of the age.

Wisdom is the key point, and thus the next section, cxiv, concerns itself with establishing this faculty as the one appropriate for solving human and philosophical problems. Knowledge, the instrument of science, is esteemed by everyone, and it will lead to the "power" over the external environment that was promised by Herè to Paris. But we must remember that it is "earthly of the mind." It is based upon sense impressions and so informs us only of the material world. Wisdom, however, is "heavenly of the soul." With the eye of Pure Reason it looks directly upon the world of spirit and so leads not to power but to reverence and charity. Cut off from reverence and charity (or faith and love), Knowledge is not a Pallas born from the brain of Jove but some wild phantom of herself, born from the brain of Demons. She is second in the hierarchy of the powers, not the first, and if she is not guided by her elder sister, she will lead us astray. Tennyson's analysis derives ultimately from Coleridge's distinction between Reason and the Understanding as interpreted by the Broad Church school of Sterling, Maurice, Carlyle, and Hallam. His coming to it at this point in the poem is certainly the result of section xcv, which was an exercise of the Pure Reason. But the distinction between Knowledge and Reason was first developed by Tennyson in the political poems, *Hail Briton!* and *Love thou thy land*, in *Œnone, The Palace of Art*, and *Locksley Hall*, where "Knowledge comes, but wisdom lingers." In *In Memoriam* "wisdom" is brought into the poem most prominently in the sections cviii–cxiii, which make up the portrait of Hallam, and there the word is not capitalized. It is, in other words, a gradualist conception, involving depth of spiritual experience as well as insight, and even when it is capitalized in section cxiv, it still is not a pure intuitive flash but is the empiricism of the inner life. It is grounded in sorrow and has as its precondition love. It is superior to Knowledge, but it is not to be thought that it should be exercised in the absence of Knowledge. In the Prologue to *In Memoriam,* where Tennyson gives his final statement of the matter, he says,

> We have but faith: we cannot know,
>   For knowledge is of things we see.

Still, Knowledge is presumably from God, and therefore,

> Let knowledge grow from more to more,
>   But more of reverence in us dwell;
>   That mind and soul, according well,
> May make one music as before,
> But vaster.

It is now Tennyson's task to apply this newly recovered harmony to the matters which Knowledge, acting upon alone, had distorted for him in sections lv–lvi.

He does this in section cxviii, where Wisdom, "contemplating" all this work of Time, arrives at a conception of evolution which does not contradict that presented by Knowledge in lv–lvi but supplements it with a spiritual dimension. Essentially, it distinguishes among three different types of evolution. There is, first, the evolution of the spirits of the departed through higher and higher phases of being which Tennyson had established as at least a reasonable hypothesis in sections xxviii–xlix.

> But trust that those we call the dead
>   Are breathers of an ampler day
>   For ever nobler ends.

Secondly, there is the physical evolution of the universe and the various forms of life upon it as described by the scientists. For Tennyson tentatively accepts what "they say," namely, that the nebular hypothesis of the origin of the solar system is probably true, that our planet has gone through a number of apparently random cataclysms, with successive forms of life replacing one another "till at the last arose the man." But at this point there commences a third type of evolution, which is moral and social. For man is certainly not the final product of evolution but is merely "the herald of a higher race." The history of this "great race, which is to be" is something which Tennyson's Muses had already sung in the dream of ciii, and it is prophesied again in the Epilogue. The question is whether man is himself to evolve into this higher race or whether he, like so many other species, is to be cast aside and replaced by another. Tennyson, in conversation with Sterling, declared, "I should consider that a liberty had been taken with me if I were made simply a means of ushering in something higher than myself."[59] In less flippant moods, however, he knew, as did Shaw in *Man and Superman,* that such a liberty was perfectly possible. Man was "the herald of a higher race," but he would be "of himself in higher place" only "If so he type this work of time / Within himself." Man's ability to prefigure this future development by his own moral evolution depends on two processes: striving and suffering—being refined in the central volcanic fires of sorrow. The fact that Tennyson included this latter process in his vision not only pays tribute to what he had been through but also indicates that he did not eliminate personal and social catastrophe from his concept of future evolution. Indeed, in two dark sections, cxxvii and cxxviii, he seems to transfer the violence of a "Nature, red in tooth and claw," to society by imagining that "the red fool-fury of the Seine" might thrice again be unleashed in tumult. If so, it will be the greatest cataclysm of all time. His vision includes crags trembling, spires of ice melting down into a flood, fortresses crashing, the brute earth lightening to the sky, while "the great Æon sinks in blood." In the midst of this, however, Hallam and Tennyson are seen smiling through the storm because they know that "vast eddies in the flood / Of onward time" must be, and that ultimately "all is well." Cataclysm is thus subsumed within the gradualism of Tennyson's spiraling evlotuion. But finally, all depends on man.

> Arise and fly
> The reeling Faun, the sensual feast;
> Move upward, working out the beast,
> And let the ape and tiger die. [cxviii]

It is the present moral evolution of man that is crucial to his future development.

Having thus acknowledged that God is not to be found in the world of nature—that Natural Theology, as Newman too believed, is a most jejeune and shallow discipline—and that he is not to be found in abstract metaphysical or theological speculations, Tennyson is ready, under the aegis of Wisdom, to regain that faith in himself which he had lost. "Fool," cried Carlyle, "Unbelief in thy God is unbelief in thyself!" And so, whenever the poet heard a voice crying, "Believe no more,"

> A warmth within the breast would melt
>   The freezing reason's colder part,
>   And like a man in wrath, the heart
> Stood up and answer'd, "I have felt." [cxxiv]

But then the poet corrected himself. No, not like a man in wrath but "like a child in doubt and fear." Tennyson was remembering his earlier image of the infant crying in the night and stretching its lame hands of faith up through the darkness to God (liv–lv). But this time "out of darkness came the hands / That reach thro' nature, moulding men."

This being so, the validity of the child's dream is reaffirmed. In section liv this "dream," that "somehow good / Will be the final goal of ill," was stigmatized as illusion, the mere wish of "an infant crying in the night . . . / And with no language but a cry." But now that infant has cried to such effect, its language has proved so adequate to the occasion, that even in the midst of reasserting the doctrine of Æonian change—

> The hills are shadows, and they flow
>   From form to form, and nothing stands—

the poet reaffirms his dream:

> But in my spirit I will dwell,
>   And dream my dream, and hold it true;
>   For tho' my lips may breathe adieu,
> I cannot think the thing farewell. [cxxiii]

The "nobler leave" that the high Muse had promised has now been achieved.

How does one conclude a poem written in sections? In a way, it cannot be concluded, and Tennyson once contemplated writing a sequel that would give the other side of the question. Still every experience must be brought to an end, and the Epilogue is a device for doing that. Part of the tragedy of Hallam's loss was that it frustrated Tennyson's hope for his friend's marriage with his sister Emily. Now, almost exactly nine years later, another friend, Edmund Lushington, is to be married to another sister, Caecilia, and Tennyson takes this as a natural and proper means of bringing to an end the period of mourning. He has now found "a gain to match" the loss of section i, has caught "the far-off interest of tears" that he could not catch at that time. Thus, the Epilogue, as it is often called, takes the form of an epithalamium, and if it were a better poem it would have fulfilled its function. For the need, both here and in the Prologue, is to widen out the vision from the poet's personal sorrow to some larger, even cosmic dimension. It is very likely that Tennyson was thinking of some conclusion like that of *Faust,* where the soul of Faust is borne up through the heavenly spheres by a band of angels.[60] It was Goethe's philosophy of spiritual metamorphosis through eternal striving which Tennyson had accepted before the trauma of Hallam's death, and it is to that philosophy that he now returns. Hallam had seemed to him a precursor of that higher race into which we or our successors are to evolve, and his soul has been seen winging its way through the realms of light to God, who is his home. Meanwhile, detaching itself from the vast is another soul, which Tennyson sees as entering into the earthly chrysalis conceived for it that very night. As an embryo it will go through all the phases of lower life that result in man, be born and "think / And act and love" and by that threefold activity become "a closer link / Betwixt us and the crowning race" of those who know truth directly. Thus, by these three types of evolution, natural before birth, spiritual after death, and moral within one's lifetime, man is drawn forward by Love, which *is* creation's final law, toward that "one far-off divine event, / To which the whole creation moves."

9

"Maud or the Madness"

> What is called mania and melancholia, are for the most part effects of the same power being overactive, but overactive in different directions. If the distressing passions are overactive, we have melancholia,—if the animal propensities, we have furious mania,—and if the exhilarating passions, we have an exuberance of joyous activity.
>
> This excitement of the depressing and exhilarating passions alternatively, is the most striking characteristic of the insane.
>
> Dr. Matthew Allen,
> *Essay on the Classification of the Insane* (1837)

Aubrey de Vere, in his superficial way, observed to Tennyson that in *In Memoriam* he had written the first two-thirds of a *Divine Comedy* and "suggested that perhaps he might at some later time give to the whole work its third part, or Paradise." To which the poet replied gruffly, "I have written what I have felt and known; and I will never write anything else."[1] Part of the reason for Tennyson's gruffness may have been that he himself felt that he had already written a kind of *Paradiso* in the Epilogue to *In Memoriam* and that what was lacking was the *Inferno*. "It's too hopeful, this poem," he said to James Knowles, "more than I am myself. I think of adding another to it, a speculative one . . . , showing that all the arguments are about as good on one side as the other, and thus throw man back more on the primitive impulses and feelings."[2] *Maud* is, in a certain sense, that poem.[3] Not that it is speculative, but it does throw man back on the primitive impulses and feelings and show that the arguments are about as good on one side as the other. Moreover, it is curiously parallel to *In Memoriam* in form. Both are composite poems, consisting of a series of meditation or lyrics arranged in a certain order. *Maud*, according to Tennyson, is a "monodrama," whose peculiarity is that "different phases of passion in one person take the place of different characters."[4] But *In Memoriam* is also a sort of monodrama. "The sections were written at many different places," says Tennyson, "and as the phases of our intercourse came to my memory and suggested them. . . . The different moods of sorrow as in a drama are dramatically given." *In Memoriam* is, of course, written in the first person, but Tennyson was eager to establish that " 'I' is not always the author speaking of himself, but the voice of the human race speaking thro' him."[5] It is, he said to Knowles, "a very impersonal poem as well as personal."[6] *Maud,* on the other hand, though written in dramatic form, is a very personal poem as well as impersonal, and readers are not easily persuaded that "I" is not often the voice of the author speaking through the hero. *Maud* deals almost exclusively with the social relations of man, whereas *In Memoriam* is concerned with the solitary individual in relation to nature and God.

To continue the contrast, *Maud* is a catastrophist poem, whereas *In Memoriam* is uniformitarian. *Maud* opens with the reported suicide of the hero's father, who has apparently killed himself when a "vast speculation had failed," and although the hero gradually recovers from this trauma through the ministrations of Maud, he is again plunged into madness through the violence of the duel with her brother and is only redeemed therefrom by the collective violence of war. Toward the end of *In Memoriam* Tennyson had qualified his faith in progress by asserting that there would be "vast eddies in the flood / Of onward time" and that these would be social in character. *Maud* deals with one of those eddies. It deals, in other words, with the cataclysm which in *In Memoriam* is subsumed under the law of progress. *Maud* and the related poems *Locksley Hall* and *Locksley Hall Sixty Years After* also ultimately assert a faith in progress, but their immediate focus is on the cataclysm, the epicycle, the social violence which interrupts it. In a certain sense they are the obverse of the English Idyls. Like the idyls they are modern in subject matter—*Maud* may be called a verse novel as the idyls are verse tales—and they generally treat situations in which young people are frustrated in their love by the barriers of social class. But whereas the English Idyls breathe a spirit of reconciliation in an effort to bring the two classes together, *Maud* and *Locksley Hall* treat these matters more angrily. Tennyson seems to be saying that just beneath the surface of English life lurks an element of violence, madness, and bestiality which hitherto has not entered very largely into his poetry. Why should it enter now?

Some have said that *Maud* is Tennyson's "spasmodic" poem and so have attributed it to literary fashion. The Spasmodics were a group of poets, never so much as a school, who flourished from about 1839 to 1854 and who represent the last galvanic twitchings of Romanticism. They derive from Byron's *Manfred* and Goethe's *Faust* and are the endeavor, without the talent necessary for the operation, to elevate the poet to the status of a prophet-hero. Their own self-appointed prophet, the critic George Gilfillan, urged them to wrestle with the great problems of the age, to be modern and relevant, to probe the deep recesses of the soul, and to give voice to the scientific-pietistic mishmash that was their philosophy. They succeeded in producing a number of very long poems that were for the most part pretentious and dull, in sub-stituting psychological violence and dubious morality for insight and truth, and in losing all sense of what Arnold called "architec-tonics." They were ultimately laughed out of court by William Edmondstoune Aytoun's parody of them in *Firmilian* in 1854, and it seems odd that Tennyson would have imitated a style that was just on the point of being discredited. On the other hand, he had already begun *Maud* before *Firmilian* appeared,[7] and he did ad-mire the Spasmodic poets. He praised John Philip Bailey's *Festus* when he first read it in 1846, and he thought Alexander Smith, the author of *A Life Drama* (1852), "a poet of considerable prom-ise." He pointed out the "real merits" of Sydney Dobell's *Balder* when it appeared the following year, and he was nettled by the refusal of George Gilfillan to consider him a great poet.[8] Moreover, *Maud* does have Spasmodic characteristics—the gloomy egoistic hero, the psychological violence, the dubious morality, and the ranting tone—and the critics had no hesitation in including it among the productions of the school. They were only sorry that the laureate had succumbed to temptation.

Apart from the question of literary fashion, there is the ques-tion of the autobiographical element in *Maud*. In recent years Sir Charles Tennyson and Professor Ralph Rader have made us aware how much of morbidity and violence is to be found in Tennyson's background and how specifically *Maud* and the re-lated poems reflect it.[9] There are three major elements. Tenny-son's father, though the eldest son, had been virtually disinherited by his father, the "old man of the wolds," in favor of a younger son, Charles, who was set up in splendor in Bayons Manor, took a coat of arms and a French name (Tennyson d'Eyncourt), and generally occupied the station in life that his more talented but less stable brother ought to have occupied. This act of injustice was bitterly resented at Somersby and, as it rankled in the mind of Dr. Tennyson, contributed, along with the pressure of poverty and an uncongenial vocation, to the alcoholism which resulted in his mental breakdown and early death. There was mental instability in several of the Tennyson children, one of whom went actually insane, and so Tennyson's youth was overshadowed by precisely the morbid resentment and fears of madness represented by the hero of *Maud*. Secondly, Tennyson as a youth had several love affairs with young ladies of the neighborhood which could not possibly have culminated in marriage, had such a thing been thought of, because of the disparity in social and economic status. The most serious of these was with Rosa Baring, the daughter and stepdaughter of a wealthy couple who in 1825 settled two miles from Somersby in Harrington Hall. In 1838, about the time *Locksley Hall* was written, she married Robert Duncombe Shafto, scion of a wealthy Durham family, and so may have been the original of Amy in that poem. Tennyson has several poems addressed to her, and roses throughout his poetry glow with the physical beauty of her presence. A second, less serious affair was with Sophy Rawnsley, daughter of the rector of Halton Holgate, a good friend of Tennyson's father, whose lighter, more intellectual nature provided Tennyson with a contrasting image. She was the original of "airy, fairy Lilian," perhaps also of Lilia in *The Princess*, and in general lilies in Tennyson's poetry often carry suggestions of Sophy.

Finally, in 1838 Tennyson became acquainted with a Dr. Matthew Allen, who ran a private lunatic establishment near High Beech, in Epping Forest, and a few years later was persuaded by Allen to invest his entire patrimony of £3,000 in a wood-carving scheme which was to make them both rich. By 1843 all was lost and Tennyson was precipitated into an intense depression. *Sea Dreams*, which reflects this episode, shows that Tennyson objected to Dr. Allen's oily religiosity as much as to his unscrupulous business methods and that he saw his own credulousness in this "get-rich-quick" scheme as the worldly equivalent of evangelical Christianity.

All these elements in Tennyson's life contributed to *Maud*, and in that sense one may say that the poem is autobiographical. Every poem is autobiographical in the sense that the poet could not have written it if he had not in some degree known and experienced the emotions with which it deals. But that does not mean, as one critic has claimed, that the writing of *Maud* was "an act of cathartic recapitulation by which [Tennyson] defined and judged his early life and attempted to put it behind him."[10] There is no evidence that the bitterness still rankled in 1854 or that at that date the difficulties of his youth were still of moment to him. What was of moment was the purely literary question of how to express the passionate morbidity which he felt infected the land. Both on the national and the international scene there was a festering evil, the product of a peace that was no peace and a prosperity ill divided, that he felt was corrupting the national life. Thus, when in January 1854, a month before beginning the composition of *Maud*, he invited Frederick Denison Maurice to Farringford, he indicated that what they would talk about was "the Northern sin / Which made a selfish war begin" and also "How best to help the slender store, / How mend the dwellings of the poor." The Spasmodics had been right in attempting to express these "spasms" in the national life, but they had not found the proper form. The form that Tennyson found was dramatic, but because the drama with which he was concerned was an inward one, a psychomachy within the national soul, it was a monodrama, a poem in which "successive phases of passion in one person take the place of successive persons."[11]

This form was invented by Rousseau in 1762. Rousseau at this time was deeply concerned about the problem of French opera and particularly about the inadequacy of its artificial style to express the passions. The actor was inhibited by the demands of the music from delivering his lines in a natural and expressive manner, and the singer was unable fully to exploit the power of music because of the constraints of language. Rousseau determined to separate the media one from another and use them alternately. Thus he wrote a short dramatic piece entitled *Pygmalion* in which Pygmalion, alone on the stage, speaks a few lines, which are then followed by a passage of instrumental music which underlines and interprets his mood. He speaks again, and again there is a short passage of music. This "mood music" is obviously related to melodrama, and melodrama (literally, "musical drama") did in fact grow out of this form. Rousseau's situation, however, was not melodramatic. He was interested in the exploration of the passions, and so in the twenty-six short intervals of spoken language and instrumental music which make up his piece he had Pygmalion run through the entire gamut of the passions. Beginning in lassitude and ennui, he rises through the stages of a growing love for his own statue of Galatea, horror at the thought of so unnatural a love, anger, self-reproach, ecstasy, wonder as the statue begins to move, fear that he is going mad, quietude, and death. These feelings succeed upon one another with dazzling rapidity, and Rousseau's drama perfectly fits Tennyson's definition of monodrama as a poem in which "successive phases of passion in one person take the place of successive persons."

Out of Rousseau's *Pygmalion* arose an art form which flourished for over half a century in the theaters of France, Germany, Italy, and Spain. Goethe was interested in the form and we are told that Mozart was tempted. The most famous of the European monodramas were Johann Christian Brandes's *Ariadne auf Naxos,* with music by Georg Benda, and Benda's later *Medea.* As these examples indicate, there was a tendency to take one's subjects from classical legend or history, particularly from Ovid's *Heroides,* where the laments of the abandoned heroines provided a fine display of passion. Œnone would have made a good subject for a monodrama, and indeed Tennyson's poem, though often called an epyllion, may be so considered. The form was introduced into England by William Taylor of Norwich and his friend Dr. Frank Sayers in 1792 and was quickly imitated by Southey and "Monk" Lewis. Because it did not often achieve stage representation, however, it soon lost the connection with music, and by the 1840s the term *monodrama* was commonly used of any dramatic performance intended for a single actor or, indeed, any dramatic poem placed in the mouth of a single speaker. It was used where we would use the term *dramatic monologue.* R. H. Horne, for instance, speaks of Tennyson's "powerful monodrama of 'St. Simeon Stylites,'" and a writer in the *Eclectic Review* (1849) says, "The entire sum of [Browning's] poetry may be said to be dramatic, though much of it, like so much of Tennyson's, simply *mono*-drama."[12]

There is, nonetheless, a difference between monodrama and the dramatic monologue which it would be well to revive and retain. The latter form, which did not really become established as a genre until the late nineteenth century and then on the basis of Browning's work more than Tennyson's, emphasizes the ironic distance between the speaker's actual words and the reader's understanding of those words. The Bishop in ordering his tomb gives to us and his "nephews" a very different understanding of his character than he himself possesses. The dramatic "conflict" of

such a poem, one would say, is the conflict between the conscious
intention of the speaker and his unconscious self-revelation. In
monodrama, however, there is no such ironic distance. We do not
need either to sympathize with or to judge the speaker but only to
wonder at the range, variety, and power of the passions and at the
remarkable linguistic (and musical) resource with which they are
displayed. The tradition here is a rhetorical tradition, deriving not
only from Ovid but also from Richardson, from the great virtuoso
soliloquies on the English stage, and from choral odes like *Alexander's Feast* and Collins's *Ode on the Passions*.

This is the tradition that Tennyson follows in *Maud* and *Locksley
Hall*, and it would be well to illustrate its use in the shorter poem
before we return to the major work. In *Locksley Hall* the immediate model which Tennyson had before him is not the European monodrama but Sir William Jones's translation of the Moâl-
lakát, the seven Arabian poems hung up in the temple of Mecca.[13]
Remote as these poems may appear to be from so English and
Victorian a work as Tennyson's, most of them do indeed follow
almost exactly the pattern of *Locksley Hall*: the poet, coming upon
the place where the tent of his beloved had formerly been raised
but which is now desolate, dismisses his companions and alternately cries out upon her faithlessness and upon his own weakness
in still being affected by her. In a wild Oriental manner he darts
from subject to subject and mood to mood with an extravagance
hardly equaled by Rousseau. In one instance the scene is even
terminated by a thunderstorm, as it is in *Locksley Hall*. The poems
are certainly the original of that poem but they are also Arabian
versions of monodrama, and one notes that Jones's translation
was published in 1799, just as the interest in monodrama was at its
height.

It has even been suggested that Tennyson's choice of his long,
loping couplets was determined by the long, rhythmical cadence
of Jones's prose translation, though Tennyson himself says that he
wrote the poem in this meter because "Mr. Hallam said to me that
the English people liked verse in trochaics."[14] If so, they do not
like it any more, but this is probably because we do not know how
to read trochaics any more. If the poem is read slowly, understres-
sing rather than overstressing and with great attention to the
pauses, then the true character of this meter comes out, which is
that it can accommodate itself to any mood. It can be stately or
passionate, furious or tender, angry or elegiac, and this is what it

is called upon to be. For *Locksley Hall* is a true monodrama in that, like *Pygmalion*, it is an exploration of the passionate heart of man. The modern reader, approaching it as a dramatic monologue and looking for some evidence of ironic intention, finds none and so leaps to the conclusion that the poet is to be identified with the hero and is to be condemned for that character's extravagance. But the true element of complexity in the poem is not the ironic detachment of reader from speaker but the internal conflict among the speaker's various voices. "Well—'tis well that I should bluster!" "But I *know* my words are wild." There are seven or eight places where the speaker rounds sharply on himself, repudiating what he has just said and introducing a new line of meditation. The orchestration of these moods, leading from the idyllic recollections of childhood with Amy through a series of bitter outbursts which gradually are mingled with efforts toward calm, until at last the speaker's faith in progress is restored—this is the structure of *Locksley Hall*. It is a musical structure which can easily be understood in musical terms. Needless to say, there is also a narrative element, in that, by moving through these phases of feeling, the speaker recapitulates the phases of his past life. Born with a faith in the future, he has been deeply embittered by the social injustice of the age, and he now vacillates between locking himself into this bitterness and freeing himself from it so he can join in the march of mind again. The essential problem is the recovery of the visionary imagination. As a boy, "nourishing a youth sublime / With the fairy tales of science and the long result of Time," he had

> dipt into the future far as human eye could see;
> Saw the Vision of the world, and all the wonder that would be.—

When that couplet is repeated a hundred lines later, but deepened and expanded by the vision of "the Parliament of man, the Federation of the world," the speaker can cry,

> O, I see the crescent promise of my spirit hath not set,
> Ancient founts of inspiration well through all my fancy yet.

With this perception he can put Locksley Hall behind him, knowing that his destiny lies not in brooding over the past but in working out this vision of the future.

Unfortunately, the vision did not materialize. Sixty imaginative years later (actually it was fifty) Tennyson published *Locksley Hall*

Sixty Years After, in which we see all these same events from the point of view of an octogenarian living not in 1837 but in 1887. Amy's husband has now died, and we learn that she herself had died in childbirth many years before. Indeed, in all likelihood she was already dead while the youth was fulminating outside her Hall. He himself has married Edith, whom he had first seen in early childhood when she looked out of a casement window and he, fool that he was, did not have the wit to realize that she was far superior to the shallow Amy. The one son she gave him, Leonard, has died at sea, heroically trying to save the lives of others, and his grandson has now come down by rail to meet him at the funeral. He is late because some mischievous boy had put an object on the track—so it appears that "the ringing grooves of change" are subject to minor derailments. He is to be the heir of Locksley Hall, but out of delicacy they will not stay there tonight—rather in the one decent hostel the town still affords. Then tomorrow they will attend the service and after that the grandson would do well to imitate the virtues of Amy's husband, for it now appears that he was not a clown but a very worthy squire. If anyone was a clown, it was the speaker himself who in his arrogance once refused to take his rival's proffered hand.

The grandson, who has just been jilted by his lady love, as the speaker had been sixty years before by Amy, is informed that the cases are not parallel. His passion was not the equal of the speaker's, and whereas Amy was weak, Judith is a worlding. In fact, the world in general has deteriorated, and as the speaker moves out into larger considerations, he finds more comfort in the immortality of the soul than in the cry of "Forward." That cry should be muted now, for the marvels of his day have grown stale through repetition and, in any case, there is no moral progress to keep pace with that of knowledge. Chaos alternates with Cosmos, and although the old man still retains his faith in progress, he remembers "how the course of Time will swerve, / Crook and turn upon itself in many a backward streaming curve." The present age, with its absurd doctrine of equality and the debased literary ideals of France, is certainly one of those backward curves.

T. S. Eliot has said that the creation of any new work of art alters the meaning of all previous works, and that is particularly true in the case of a sequel like *Locksley Hall Sixty Years After*. We learn from this poem that the speaker of the previous poem was simply wrong in many of his facts and judgments. Does this mean

that Tennyson has written a palinode or that he has produced a
bitterly sardonic account of how the youthful liberal turns into an
archreactionary in old age? Probably neither one nor the other,
but it is certainly true that with the accession of the second poem
we cannot read the first as readers did in 1842. Each poem enters
into relation with the other, so that the two together form a
diptych, enclosed within a common frame. Like *L'Allegro* and *Il
Penseroso*, they are a kind of Youth and Age, and this means that
each ceases to some degree to be a monodrama and becomes, with
respect to the other, a dramatic monologue. The irony that was
lacking to the first poem is provided by the second, and although
the second claims to supersede the first, it cannot supersede it in
our mind or in the mind of the young grandson looking on. Thus,
the two poems taken together are relativistic and historical. Tennyson dedicated the second poem to his wife because he thought
that "the two 'Locksley Halls' were likely to be in the future two of
the most historically interesting of his poems, as descriptive of the
tone of the age at two distant periods of his life."[15] Lord Lytton
agreed. "The old lover, . . ." he says, "is exactly what the young
man must have become . . . if he had grown with the growth of
his age.—For that reason alone, the poem in its entirety [he is
apparently regarding the two poems as one] has a peculiar historical importance as the impersonation of the emotional life of a
whole generation."[16]

Locksley Hall, however, is not a diptych but a triptych, for its
large central panel, positioned in 1855, almost exactly halfway
between the first poem and the second, is *Maud*. And it too was
asserted by Tennyson to be historical. "I took," he wrote to Archer
Gurney in December 1855, "a man constitutionally diseased and
dipt him into the circumstances of the time and took him out on
fire."[17] By this he did not mean to deny that there were autobiographical elements in *Maud*. "In a certain way, no doubt, poets
and novelists, however dramatic they are, give themselves in
their work. The mistake that people make is that they think the
poet's poems are a kind of 'catalogue raisonné' of his very own
self, and of all the facts of his life, not seeing that they often only
express a poetic instinct, or judgment on character real or imagined, and on the facts of lives real or imagined."[18] *Maud* contains much that is real but a great deal more that is imagined.
    Yet this is what the British public was unwilling to grant.

Though not all reviews were unintelligent or unfavorable, many
were, and Tennyson perceived that they had not understood the
form. "As it is a new form of Poem altogether," he wrote to Mr.
Ticknor in October 1855, "the critic not being able to make it out,
went at it: why not? he is anonymous." To Charles Weld on
November 24 he wrote: "It is a poem written in an *entirely new
form,* as far as I know." And a few weeks later to Archer Gurney:
"The whole was intended to be a new form of dramatic composition."[19] The name of this new form Tennyson did not publicly
apply to the poem until 1875, when he added the subtitle *A
Monodrama* to the edition of that year, apparently in reaction to an
uncomprehending review in a Liverpool newspaper. "Thanks for
your Liverpool paper," he wrote to R. C. Hall on January 17,
1873. "*Maud* is a drama—a monodrama—& what is said in it is
dramatical."[20] It has usually been assumed that Tennyson got the
term from a pamphlet, *Tennyson's 'Maud' Vindicated: An Explanatory Essay,* published by Robert James Mann, a physician, in 1856.
For in that pamphlet Mann gives a full explanation of the form of
Maud and calls it a "mono-drama." We have seen, however, that
the term was current in England in the 1850s and that Tennyson
would not have had to learn it from a medical man. Indeed, it is all
but certain that not only the name "monodrama" but also the
entire substance of Mann's pamphlet derived from Tennyson. For
Tennyson was a near neighbor of Mann's on the Isle of Wight,
and in the spring and summer of 1855 used to walk over to his
house and look at the stars through his telescope. One night they
looked at Orion and Dr. Mann drew a diagram of the constella-
tion which Tennyson sent to his wife. "Look out at Orion," he
wrote, "at a faintish star under the lowest star of his belt. That is
really 8 stars, all moving in connection with one another, a system
by themselves, a most lovely object thro' the glass." "Orion low in
his grave," in the third and final sections of *Maud* may owe
something to this evening. So friendly did Tennyson become with
this "clever, interesting doctor" that before he purchased Farringford he thought of living in one of the houses on the Bon-
church Terrace, near Ventnor, occupied by Dr. Mann, for then,
he explained to his wife, she would have "a 'most careful' physician always at hand & ready to serve you. I think him a most
excellent & pure-minded man—from whose society everyone
must reap advantage."[21]

Certainly Tennyson reaped advantage, for in October 1855, as the bad reviews came in and he became more and more exasperated at being confounded with his hero, he received a letter from Dr. Mann accompanying the loan of his valuable telescope. "Many thanks," wrote Tennyson, "but it is a loan that I shall accept with fear and trembling." And then he added, "I am curious to hear your 'plan' touching Maud."[22] One can hardly doubt that Dr. Mann's plan was that he should put forth under his own name an explanation and vindication of *Maud* the substance of which he had undoubtedly received from Tennyson. (One may suppose that Tennyson had read the poem aloud to him, as he later did to James Knowles, with full explanation and commentary.) Mrs. Tennyson, it should be noted, was "utterly against that Defense Vindication as it was called, however kindly meant," declaring that *Maud* "must stand or fall of itself."[23] However, Dr. Mann went ahead, and when he finished, he sent the proofsheets to Tennyson to look over and emend. "It is very difficult to recriticize a critique on oneself," wrote Tennyson. "I don't quite like your 'word-sculpture' but if you choose let it stand. I don't quite think that the lines *jar*; they rather rush with the impetuosity of passion, jarring perhaps once or twice. However, 'recalls clearly' is wrong—the memory [presumably of the hero's betrothal in part I, section vii] is a phantasmal one, which he cannot trace to its origin." Type and style he thought did very well, but he declared, "If I were with you, we could settle it together viva voce much better than by letter."[24]

Settle it they did, for when the pamphlet appeared, Tennyson gave it his official blessing: "No one with this Essay before him can in future pretend to misunderstand my dramatic poem, *Maud*."[25] It is, indeed, one of the best critiques of the poem that has ever been written, and the central passage about the monodramatic form is as follows:

Maud is a drama;—that is, an action. . . . The *dramatis persona* of the action,—for there is but one individual who is ever brought forward in it *in person*,—exhibits his story through the mental influences its several incidents work in himself, and this exhibition is made, not directly and connectedly, but, as it were, inferentially and interruptedly, through a series of distinct scenes, which are as varied as the circumstances involved. It is in this peculiarity of the poem,—the one person revealing to the reader his own sad and momentous history,

by fits and starts, which are themselves but so many impulsive
utterances naturally called forth from a mind strung to the
pitch of keen poetic sensibility,—that its absolute originality
and the surpassing skill of the Laureate are displayed. Nothing can be more exquisitely consonant to the proceedings
of nature than that such utterances should be made in fitful
and broken strains, rather than that they should march stead-
ily on to the measure of equal lines, and regularly recurring
rhymes. . . . Every utterance, whether it be of sentiment,
passion, or reflection, is an impulsive outburst; but it is an
outburst that involuntarily clothes itself in language of the
most appropriate character and vivid power. Such, both in
the matter of sense and of music, is the language of *Maud*.
The syllables and lines of the several stanzas actually trip and
halt with abrupt fervour, tremble with passion, swell with
emotion, and dance with joy, as each separate phase of mental experience comes on the scene. The power of language to
symbolize in sound mental states and perceptions, has never
before been so magically proved. In the successful employment of this kind of word-music, the author of *Maud* stands
entirely unrivalled, as, in its general form of severe dramatic
uni-personality, the poem itself is absolutely unique.[26]

Clearly, Dr. Mann is right in declaring that the central feature of
Maud is the dazzling variety of mood as expressed in the varied
forms of the individual lyrics. When Maud smiles upon the
speaker, he is ready to fall at her feet, but when his dark imagination broods upon the significance of her smile, he is plunged into
gloom. When he sees her in church, he is exalted; but when he
sees her riding upon the moor with his rival, he is like a spark
extinguished in the night. Even within the lyrics the mood shifts
abruptly from one state of feeling to another. In part I, section ii,
when the hero first sees Maud, he exlaims, "Long have I sigh'd for
a calm," but then observes bitterly, "It will never be broken by
Maud," whose cold and clear-cut face is "dead perfection, no
more." "Nothing more," that is, "if it had not been / For . . ."—
and he then enumerates all the interesting little beauties with
which he is already half in love, until, drawing himself up short,
he declares, "From which I escaped heart-free"—adding the ad-
mission, "with the least little touch of spleen." Every lyric and part
of lyric can be analyzed in this way, as if spoken by the Two Voices

of Tennyson's earlier poem, or by the several voices of love, resentment, jealousy, pique, moodiness, melancholy, tender longing, self-depreciation, anger, whimsy, playfulness, lyric exultation, and mad pride. The basic conflict in part I is between the hate with which the poem opens and the love in which it closes, between morbidity and health, madness and sanity, violence and calm—ultimately, between life and death—and this is its dramatic action. Though ultimately the conflict is objectified in the characters, particularly the speaker and Maud's brother, primarily the "different phases of passion in one person take the place of different characters."

Moreover, the sequence of the passions in *Maud* follows a common monodramatic formula. Beginning in morbidity and bitterness, it rises through the alternating moods of dark suspicion and growing love to the exaltation of the garden scene. It then plunges down through the remembered violence of the duel into the madness of part II and reemerges with the hero calm but shattered in part III. The final scene, where the hero resolves his problems by embarking for the Crimean War, has been criticized as unsatisfactory, and from a moral point of view it is. But French and German monodramas often resolved themselves in spectacle at the close, and something of that sort seems to be happening here. If the work were performed on stage, there is no doubt but that the hero's dream, in which Maud is seen to separate herself from the band of the blest and pronounce a benediction upon the war, would actually have been performed in the upper regions of the theater; and the lines in which the hero "stood on a giant deck and mix'd my breath / With a loyal people shouting a battle cry" would have been accompanied by a panorama of ships-of-the-line passing across the rear of the stage much as Tennyson saw them move down the Solent as he was writing this scene. The whole would have been accompanied by martial music, the booming of guns in the distance, fireworks, and other displays of theatrical machinery. It is, indeed, a pity that we cannot see *Maud* performed. Skeptics who heard Tennyson read the poem were normally convinced, and Hallam Tennyson's account of his father's reading emphasizes the variety of intonation. "The passion in the first Canto was given by my father in a sort of rushing recitative," but with the section "I have led her home, my love," "my father's voice would break down," and in the garden scene his eyes, "which were through the other love-passages veiled by his drooping lids, would suddenly flash as he looked up and spoke these words, the passion in his voice deepening in the last words of the stanza."[27] From the little disc issued by the Tennyson Society, which reproduces a recording made by Tennyson on wax cylinders in 1890, one may confirm Hallam Tennyson's impression.

On the other hand, one cannot claim that *Maud* is pure monodrama, for Tennyson has created an "objective correlative" for the emotions of his hero which is far more extensive than was ordinarily the case. Ordinarily, monodrama dealt with classical figures whose character and situation were sufficiently well known that they did not need to be developed. Had Tennyson written a Hercules Furens or Orlando Furioso, he would have had a proper monodrama. But instead, he has taken a slice of modern bourgeois life and treated it realistically as in a novel, and in so doing he has created a plot which asks to be judged in accordance with the normal canons of dramatic action. The puzzling thing about this plot is that it moves through two cycles. The hero is moved from the disorder occasioned by his father's death to order through "the holy power of Love."[28] But then he is plunged back into a deeper disorder by the duel and is redeemed from that through what we can only call the holy power of war. Why this second movement? Tennyson said that *Maud* was akin to *Hamlet*,[29] and there is an analogy with Hamlet's morbidity, occasioned by his father's death, with the possibility of redemption through Ophelia's love, and the tragic conclusion of the duel with Laertes. But Shakespeare ended the drama at that point. He did not have Hamlet recover and go to war with Fortinbras. One feels that Tennyson could also have so managed it that, although the "dreadful hollow" once again reechoed with the violence of hate, the values of the garden would have been reestablished in the poem. Tennyson also compared the work to the *Oresteia*, and although that does provide a parallel for the curse between the two houses which goes on in cycle after cycle, Aeschylus had a means of terminating the cycle in the emergence of a new conception of justice. As it stands, what Tennyson's drama seems to mean is that the evils of the age are so great that they cannot be assuaged gradually by the holy power of love but only catastrophically by the holy power of war.

This may well be what Tennyson meant, and one could argue that he was merely unlucky in his choice of war. If he had set his poem in the Middle Ages and had his hero go off on the Crusades, no one would have objected, for it has always been considered legitimate for a hero to solve his personal problems by giving himself to some larger cause. But Nolan's blunder at Bala-klava, the state of the hospitals at Scutari, plus modern pacifism have effectively ruined Tennyson's symbol, and it is idle to say that anyone can now read the final scene of *Maud* and like it. Moreover, Tennyson *was* quite bellicose at this time. Every since the coup d'état of Louis Napoleon in 1852, when Tennyson felt that the government had allowed the national defenses to deteriorate to the point where England was dangerously exposed to invasion, he had been writing violent anonymous poems for the newspapers—poems so violent that, as he humorously observed to his wife, some of them might in themselves be a cause for war.[30] If *Maud* is a national and historical poem, as on one level it certainly is, it urges that post-Romantic English youth, who have very properly been brooding on their social wrongs, particularly upon that central evil the marriage of convenience, should not confirm themselves in morbidity but come out of their shells and give their lives for England. In *The Charge of the Light Brigade* and the slightly later poems *Havelock* and *The Defence of Lucknow*, which describe the gallant stand of a little band of Englishmen against a horde of Indian rebels, Tennyson gave models of how he expected his hero to act. It is undoubtedly true that he did not expect him to return alive.

But the great model he had already given, just a year and a half before, in the *Ode on the Death of the Duke of Wellington*. The theme of that stately utterance is that "the last great Englishman is low." Not once does Tennyson address his subject by name. With befitting generality he is the Great Duke, our chief state-oracle, the statesman-warrior, the man of amplest influence, the foremost captain of his time, the great World-victor's victor. Neither is Nelson, whose rest in the crypt of St. Paul's is broken in upon by the procession, called by name.

> Mighty Seaman, this is he
> Was great by land as thou by sea.

The poet then reviews his hero's career from the early charge at Assaye to the late defense of Lisbon, culminating in "that world-earthquake, Waterloo!" For such a man the "Civic muse," the muse of Tennyson's early political poems, preserves a broad approach of song, for, thanks to be God! "we are a people yet." The word "people" had for Tennyson a special meaning. It connoted

that law consonant with liberty which was imposed upon a nation
by itself. Unlike foreign nations, where "brainless mobs" and
"lawless Powers" contend, the English cherish

> That sober freedom out of which there springs
> Our loyal passion for our temperate kings.

The only danger is lest the English be not vigilant to preserve
freedom, for only so can mankind be preserved. To do this they
must look to their seaward walls. The poem falters a little toward
the close, but in its stateliness, its lofty dignity and sense of national purpose, and in the solemn rhythms and sonorous rhymes
by which this is conveyed, it is one of Tennyson's great public
utterances. Had he been able to strike the same note at the end of
Maud, instead of the slightly jingoistic note he has struck, he
would have ended his drama more worthily.

Still, the final scene makes it apparent that the hero rises at this
point from a purely personal conflict to one in the national interest. This is betokened by the fact that the wraith, which has
dogged him ever since the duel, now leaves him and is replaced by
the Spirit of Maud in Heaven. In the drama itself the distinction
between the wraith and the Spirit is not made entirely clear, but in
the original version of "O that 'twere possible," the lyric out of
which *Maud* grew, it is clear that the wraith is a purely sensuous
and psychological phenomenon. It is precisely of the same character as the ghost that Tennyson says in *In Memoriam* he will *not* see
because it would not be truly spiritual but a mere product of his
own brain. So this shadow that flits before him is "not thou, but
like to thee." As contrasted with the "happy Spirit" of the beloved
in Heaven, this "dull mechanic ghost" is a mere "juggle of the
brain," an obsessive, compulsive memory of the beloved, a product of the "blood" rather than the "will." It is clearly a manifestation of disease, and one gets the impression that the cause of this
disease is wasting sexual desire.

Once the protagonist frees himself from his disease, then the
Spirit of Maud appears in his dream and pronounces a benediction on the coming war. This scene would correspond to section
xcv in *In Memoriam*, where the poet is united with the spirit of
Hallam, and although in *Maud* it is merely a dream, not a true
mystic trance, still the hero had to achieve wholeness for it to
happen. When it does happen, the phantom flies off into the
North, the devil's quarter.

The question arises, then, what is the nature of the madness of the hero in *Maud*? for it is clear that madness is central. Tennyson says that the original title of the poem was "Maud or the Madness," and there is evidence that even after publication he thought of reverting to that title.[31] It is an odd one for several reasons. It is odd, in the first place, to call the poem after the lady rather than the protagonist and particularly odd (and inconvenient) to leave him nameless. But then it is odd to add a subtitle which stands as if in apposition to Maud but obviously is in opposition to her, and finally it is odd to use an abstract noun and definite article, as if the phrase alluded not to a person but a condition—the condition of England. It is like Camus's *The Plague* or the madness that infuses Pope's *Dunciad*. For it is not merely the protagonist who is mad but Maud's brother, the young lord, the two feuding fathers, the shopkeepers and mine operators, the baker who adulterates his bread, the lying politicians, the Quaker who does not know peace from war, the treacherous and tyrannical czar— all are mad, and there is a sense in which the protagonist, who alone seems to perceive this fact, is the only sane person among them. Certainly, when he enters the asylum, he finds it an image of the mighty world, with the lord, the statesman, and the physician performing in their usual way, only with a certain exaggerated clearness. Tennyson was very proud of his delineation of madness and quoted again and again the letter of the asylum doctor who told him it was "the most faithful representation of madness since Shakespeare."[32] The doctor was an excellent literary critic, for Tennyson's representation of madness is not only the best since Shakespeare—it is right out of Shakespeare. It cannot really have owed very much to his visits to Dr. Allen's establishment, where his reaction, as reported to Spedding, was that he was "delighted with the mad people, whom he reports the most agreeable and the most reasonable persons he has met with."[33] This is in line with his method—employed also by Shakespeare—of having his madman speak home truths but in a slightly crazed and translucent way. To Archer Gurney he wrote,

> I do not mean to say that my madman does not speak truths too: witness this extract from an enlightened German, quoted in one of our papers about the state of all England, and then think if he is all wrong when he calls our peace a war, and worse in some respects than an open civil war—"Every day a murder or two or three—every day a wife beaten to death by

her husband—every day a father or mother starving their children, or pinching, knocking, and kicking them into a state of torture and living putrefaction." Then he asks, "Has this always been so? or is it so only of late?"

"Is not the true war that of evil and good?"[34]

The madness in *Maud* manifests itself on three levels: first, that "nature is one with rapine," secondly, that man has modeled himself upon this natural world, adding thereto his own refinements of civilized cruelty, and thirdly, that the hero, by brooding upon these evils, has created within himself a world of lust and anger, violence and hate. All this is due to the absence of God, for if *In Memoriam* is a poem where God is perpetually sought, *Maud* is a poem where he is perpetually neglected. "The drift of the Maker is dark," says the hero, "an Isis hid by the veil," but the only ones who attempt to ascertain his drift are the three sainted women, who mediate between the hero and his maker. Hence at the very end of the poem he "embrace[s] the purpose of God and the doom assigned," but previously he had employed God's name primarily as an imprecation.

The process by which the hero is gradually restored involves both a growth in self-knowledge and a more accurate knowledge of the external world. As his dark suspicions of Maud are dissipated and he comes to know her better, he discovers that a hazy, phantasmal recollection he has of two men betrothing their children over the wine was true: he and Maud had been destined for one another from the very beginning. Further, in the intervening years, when Maud's family was abroad, the mother had ever mourned the rift between the two houses and on her deathbed had expressed a wish that it might be healed. So there arose in the heart of the child, as a kind of sacred duty, the desire to fulfill this wish of her mother, and the hero was amazed to learn that, while he was raging and cursing, these silent forces for good were at work in the land. He even learned, though with some skepticism, that her brother was "rough but kind," and under this new perception of reality he began to perceive himself differently. He realized that he had a kind of self-tormenting imagination that could easily destroy him if he did not control it—that there were two men within him and the one had better die if the other was to live.

Indeed, all is deeply ambiguous in this divided soul. When he first saw Maud, her cold and clear-cut face appeared in his dreams passionless, pale, deathlike, and yet it so troubled his spirit that he arose and flung himself out into the night, finding solace in the deep, ship-wrecking roar of the tide and the scream of the mad-dened beach. Because of her connection with her family Maud was associated in his mind with Death, but by virtue of her own person she was the incarnation of Love. This paradox was inten-sified for him when he heard her singing a battle song "in the happy morning of life and of May." That Maud "in the light of her youth and her grace" should be "singing of Death, and of Honour that cannot die" was so strange that he was fain to distin-guish in his mind between her and her voice, being both drawn and repelled by both one and the other. This theme of Love and Death is further emphasized in the lovers' moment of supreme felicity when they seem to sense that this felicity will be short.

> O, why should Love, like men in drinking-songs,
> Spice his fair banquet with the dust of death?

To which Maud replies,

> The dusky strand of Death inwoven here
> With dear Love's tie, makes Love himself more dear.

Death is symbolized throughout the poem by the pallor of the lily, as Love is by the ardor of the rose. But both symbols are ambigu-ous, for the lily also symbolizes the purity and spirituality of Maud, as the rose symbolizes the blood and passion that unsealed their love. Maud in her wholeness and balance is "Queen lily and rose in one," and the hero, after oscillating wildly between ex-tremes, is finally brought to rest in a similar, if precarious, bal-ance. The culmination of this movement is the beautiful lyric, "I have led her home, my love, my only friend."

In form this lyric is an epithalamion, breathing memories of Spenser's Epithalamion and the Song of Songs, and it seems likely that Tennyson intended us to understand by his use of this form that at this point their love is consummated. The brother has been away for a week, they have just enjoyed "twelve sweet hours that past in bridal white," and whether the bridal rites were actually celebrated or not, certainly the poem breathes the peace and serenity of sexual fulfillment. Vows have been exchanged, the hero has promised "to bury / All this dead body of hate," and they are in effect man and wife. By contrast the rose-garden scene, which Lewis Carroll so easily parodied in *Alice in Wonderland*, throbs with the frenzy of sexual passion. It is early dawn, after the ball to which the hero has not been invited, and he is frustrated and impatient. These are the lines which Tennyson read, according to his son, his voice dark with passion.

> She is coming, my own, my sweet;
>   Were it ever so airy a tread,
> My heart would hear her and beat,
>   Were it earth in an earthy bed;
> My dust would hear her and beat,
>   Had I lain for a century dead;
> Would start and tremble under her feet,
>   And blossom in purple and red.

The lines are strangely prophetic in that they foreshadow the hero's own insanity when he fancies he is buried under the city street and hears the trample of feet above him, and in that they foreshadow the "blood-red blossom of war" about to burst forth in miniature in the dreadful hollow.

The brother cried, "The fault was mine!" and doubtless it was, but the hero is not willing to exonerate his own "guilty hand." Dueling was widely condemned in Victorian society, and the hero joins in that condemnation of "the Christless code, / That must have a life for a blow." He recognizes that the duel was occasioned by "wine and anger and lust," wine on the part of the brother, anger on the part of both, lust on his own part. He has exchanged vows with Maud which he has essentially broken. If she by her singing had attempted to enlist him as her knight in some great chivalrous cause, he has acted like Lancelot by not listening, not attending, by turning away. And so, instead of her song, what he now hears is a passionate cry that arises out of the darkening land, for it is not simply the cry that Maud will utter when she learns of her brother's death, and the cry that his own mother has uttered when she learned of her husband's death, but the cry that all tender, loving things utter when they suffer from violence and crime. And the ghastly Wraith that glides out of the "joyous wood"—a wood that has been made joyous by their love—is not the true Spirit of Maud (which will go to heaven) but the ghastly creature of "sunk eye" and "dreary brow"[35] that he has created by killing their love. This creature will not leave him. It is the madness that infects him and all of his countrymen, and as he moves from the hilltop to which he had fled immediately after the duel, to Brittany, and then back to England again, it follows him. It will not leave him until he learns that "lawful and lawless war / Are scarcely even akin." One may observe that they are akin by virtue of being violent, and when Tennyson excuses himself by saying that surely the true war is the war between good and evil in the human heart, one may agree but still feel that gradualism has been put aside in this poem in favor of the old apocalyptic stance.

"And most of all," cried the hero of *Maud*, "would I flee from the cruel madness of love." "If I cannot be gay," he continued, "let a passionless peace be my lot . . . like a stoic, or like / A wiser epicurean." The story of this "wiser epicurean" is told in one of Tennyson's most successful dramatic monologues, *Lucretius*, written ten years after *Maud*, from October 1865 to January 1868. It is based on a legend told by Jerome in the Eusebian Chronicle that Lucretius "was rendered insane by a love potion and, after writing, in the intervals of insanity, some books, which Cicero afterwards emended, he killed himself by his own hand."[36] One may fancy, after reading the description of the frenzy of love in the *De rerum natura*, that the potion was brewed in his own veins, and indeed Tennyson's statement that the wicked broth tickled "the brute brain within the man's" indicates that it merely released something that was already there. This is Lucretius's tragedy. His tragedy is the deeply ironic one of a man who has lived all his life by a philosophy which now fails him, who finds himself racked by a passion that is the very opposite of his ideal, who discovers to his horror that there is a wild, irrational element in his own nature, a driving sexual frenzy, which destroys him, with some suggestion that a more adequate, less superficial philosophy might have saved him. Lucretius's ideal has been that of the "Passionless bride, divine Tranquillity." "O ye Gods, . . ." he cries,

> I thought I lived securely as yourselves—
> No lewdness, narrowing envy, monkey-spite,
> No madness of ambition, avarice, none:
> No larger feast than under plane or pine
> With neighbours laid along the grass . . .
> Nothing to mar the sober majesties
> Of settled, sweet, Epicurean life.

Such had been his ideal.

> But now it seems some unseen monster lays
> His vast and filthy hands upon my will,
> Wrenching it backward into his; and spoils
> My bliss in being.

The process by which he has discovered this is the Freudian one of dreams. A vast storm in the night, corresponding to the turbulence in his own nature and the civil war within the state, has given him three dreams, of which only the first he recognizes. That was of atoms "ruining along the illimitable inane"—a fearsome sight, but his own conception of the universe. That dream "was mine, . . . I knew it— / Of and belonging to me . . . : but the next!" All the blood that Sulla shed came raining down on earth to produce, not the warriors he expected, but "girls, Hetairai, curious in their art, / Hired animalisms"; and then, last dream of all, from out the gloom appeared the breasts of Helen, and, hovering near, a sword pointed to pierce, which "sank down shamed / At all that beauty." Lucretius needs no analyst to explain the significance of these dreams—he is only horrified to discover them his. For though with one half of his mind he repudiates them—"twisted shapes of lust, unspeakable, / Abominable, strangers at my hearth / Not welcome"—with another he knows the mind could not clasp these idols to itself unless it loved them. And so, when the disease invades his waking life and he suddenly sees a naked Oread pursued by a satyr, he cries, "A satyr, a satyr, see . . . ; but him I proved impossible; / Two-natured is no nature"—though his own double nature is all too apparent. Indeed, as the creatures are about to fling themselves upon him, he does not know what he wants—"do I wish— / What?—that the bush were leafless? or to whelm / All of them in one massacre?" For this mixture of sex and sadism, of love and violence, is thoroughly his own.

His effort had been to free men from fear by proving that the universe operates according to fixed laws, by showing that there is no life after death of which one need be afraid, that the gods, though they do exist, do not intervene in human affairs, and that the only thing to be concerned about is human passion, which presumably can be controlled by reason and moderation. But now he has been proved tragically wrong. He has vastly underestimated the wild, irrational element in human life, and it is clear that if he had allowed it a freer play and not tried to repress it, and if, on the other hand, he had acknowledged the immateriality of the soul and the existence of an afterlife, along with the concern of the gods for man, he might have established the spiritual values by which to control passion. As it is, when his wife, who has administered the potion, suggests that she has failed in duty to him, he can only say, "Thy duty? What is duty? Fare thee well!"

Tennyson's friend, W. Y. Sellar, noted in his *Roman Poets of the Republic* (1863) that Lucretius was a distinctly modern figure.[37] His atomism anticipated the scientific thought of the nineteenth century, and his epicureanism was the ancient equivalent of Utilitarianism. He represented the modern rationalistic, positivistic approach to life, and if there is no single nineteenth-century figure whom he can be said to represent, it is because Tennyson has caught him in a moment of crisis. Too much Mill, Tennyson seems to be saying, has given us Swinburne. Too much reason has produced licentiousness. Too much of the spirit of 1832 has produced the spirit of 1867, for it was just at the time of the political anarchy preceding the passage of the Second Reform Bill that Tennyson was writing. Lucretius was perfectly aware that the unruly passions welling up within himself had a political dimension. They are like

> crowds that in an hour
> Of civic tumult jam the doors, and bear
> The keepers down, and throng, their rags and they
> The basest, far into that council-hall
> Where sit the best and stateliest of the land.

Precisely such throngs Arnold had described in *Culture and Anarchy,* and his solution was to educate the lower classes before they became our masters. Carlyle's solution in *Shooting Niagara, and After?* was to drill the raw recruits of the world in platoons. Tennyson undoubtedly thought that a more spiritual philosophy that would give man a firmer conception of duty would help. Initially, he omitted the phrase "What is duty?" from the last line of the poem "because Lucretius nowhere I think makes any mention of Duty in that sense," but he later decided that that was the very point and put it back in.[38]

10

Idylls of the King

> "It does you credit," said Zarathustra gloomily, looking aside to the
> ground, "it does you credit that you sought greatness, but it also
> betrays you. You are not great. You wicked old magician, this is what
> is best and most honest about you, and this I honor: that you wearied
> of yourself and said it outright: 'I am not great.' "
>
> Nietzsche, *Thus Spoke Zarathustra*, part IV

At the opening of the *Idylls of the King*, Leodogran, king of
Cameliard, is debating whether to give his daughter, Guinevere,
in marriage to Arthur. Arthur desires her so that he may realize
himself in the world,

> 'for saving I be join'd
> To her that is the fairest under heaven,
> I seem as nothing in the mighty world,
> And cannot will my will nor work my work
> Wholly.'

Leodogran would gladly accede to his request, for Arthur has just
put down the anarchy of wild beast, heathen horde, and Roman
legion with which his kingdom has been ravaged. But there is
doubt whether Arthur is truly king, and Leodogran, being a king
himself and having but one daughter and she the "fairest of all
flesh on earth," would not give her to him if he is not. The theme,
then, of this opening idyll, written in 1868 immediately after the
passage of the Second Reform Bill, is precisely that with which
Newman was concerned in the *Apologia pro Vita Sua* (1864) and
Arnold in *Culture and Anarchy* (1867–68). What is the spiritual
authority by which we can regulate our society, and what are the
grounds for giving it our allegiance? Are there absolute values, or
is it true, as Bentham and Mill had said, that doing as one likes is
the only rule? If this or that "visible church" presents itself to us
for our acceptance, how do we know whether or not it is the true
one? The marriage of Guinevere to Arthur would be the realizing
in the world of the spiritual authority which Arthur represents,

214

and Leodogran has the responsibility of deciding whether this authority is the true one. The inquiries which he makes are arranged in what seems to be a hierarchy of the different kinds of inquiry one might make on such a subject. First, he asks the hoary chamberlain, who, declaring that all will be made clear by and by, represents the lowest form of mere incompetence and spiritual evasion. If Arthur had helped me no better than you have done, says Leodogran, I should be the prey of wolves ere now. Then he turns to Sir Bedivere, who, calculating the times and circumstances of Arthur's birth and concluding that he is the son of King Uther born "before his time" and not the son of Gorloïs born after death, gives the empirical and naturalistic solution to the problem. Leodogran is not satisfied, however, and so, debating which story is true or "whether there were truth in anything," he turns to Bellicent, supposed half sister of Arthur, and to her puts the question in a slightly different form—not, "Hold ye this Arthur for King Uther's son?" but "think ye this king . . . Hath body enow to hold his foemen down?"—that is, is he pragmatically and in his own nature a king? Bellicent, answering him in the sense in which he has inquired, emphasizes the human and inward qualities of Arthur, his gentleness to her and especially the spiritual authority by which he bound his knights to himself and inspired in them a momentary likeness of their King. At this Leodogran rejoiced, but then, thinking to sift his doubtings to the last, returned to the objective question of Arthur's parentage. "These be secret things," said Bellicent, and then, sending her sons from the room, proceeded to develop the arcane answer in a way which obviously corresponds to supernatural revelation. Old Bleys, the master of Merlin, told her just before his death that in a night in which "the bounds of heaven and earth were lost," a ship, so high upon the dreary deep it seemed in heaven, and all bright with shining people, loomed through the dark, and, as the great waves rolled in, on the ninth was borne, all in flames, a naked babe—not, by implication, the son of Uther or of Gorloïs, but divine. Such an apocalyptic vision should settle the matter, but the usual difficulty with revelation infects this, that Bellicent herself had it merely upon hearsay from Bleys, and when she went to Merlin to confirm it, he answered in a riddling way which half confirmed and half denied the "tale." "Tale" is the word which Broad Church theologians used of the Gospel story, and Merlin's riddle explicitly associates him with that school. For the concluding line, "From the great deep to the great deep he goes," can be taken either mythically, of the birth of a god, or more generally, of the divine origin and end of every man. "Truth is this to me, and that to thee; / And truth or clothed or naked let it be." Truth "clothed" would be the mythical form of Arthur's godhead, truth "naked" the essential spiritual fact of his kingly nature. So Leodogran, musing is ultimately left to the highest kind of evidence, that of his own heart as illumined by spiritual intuition. Dreaming, he saw

> a slope of land that ever grew,
> Field after field, up to a height, the peak
> Haze-hidden, and thereon a phantom king,
> Now looming, and now lost.

Around him battle raged and the smoke of battle mingled with the haze,

> Till with a wind his dream was changed, the haze
> Descended, and the solid earth became
> As nothing, but the King stood out in heaven,
> Crowned. And Leodogran awoke, and sent
> Ulfius, and Brastias and Bedivere,
> Back to the court of Arthur answering yea.

Leodogran does right to act instantaneously upon the momentary intuition of the heart, for this vision, which he "saw, / Dreaming," of a mountain peak in haze, with the haze lifting only for an instant, is all that man has by way of spiritual revelation. Leodogran made the venture of faith, and though he is not one of the major heroes of the *Idylls*—rather is the ordinary sensual man— still in his acceptance of Arthur he performed a truly heroic act. For it was by this means that Arthur was able, in words repeated at the beginning and the end of the idyll, to "make a realm and reign."

He reigned for twelve years and then at the end of the *Idylls*, in a precisely parallel action, another ordinary man, Sir Bedivere, is entrusted with the equally heroic task of relinquishing this spiritual authority and attempting to live on into a new world of anarchy. We have already examined the ordeal of Sir Bedivere in its original manifestation in the *Morte d'Arthur,* but it is remarkable how different is the meaning it takes on in its new context at the end of the *Idylls of the King.* In 1842, when it was set in the framework of *The Epic*, it was a much less dark and pessimistic poem. There was relatively more emphasis upon the rebirth of Arthur, and this was intensified by being repeated in modern dress in the framework of the poem. But in the *Idylls* the passing comes at the end of a long process of disintegration and decay, and there is no frame, set in the future, to suggest that life will go on. The structure, in other words, is apocalyptic rather than elegiac, linear rather than cyclical. What was originally written as an elegy for Arthur Hallam has been transformed, simply by its setting, into a prophecy of doom for Victorian society. Moreover, whereas the *Morte d'Arthur* was distinctly a work of art, a poem being read by a college youth to his friends at Christmastime, *The Passing of Arthur* is a historical narrative, told by one of the actors in the event, of the death of a king. The very archaic style which, in the former setting, seemed to label it art, in this setting labels it Scripture.[1] For whereas it previously seemed less real than its surrounding frame, it now embodies a spiritual reality which is far more intense than that of the other idylls. And whereas the *Morte d'Arthur* was enclosed within a frame, *The Passing of Arthur* is part of a frame which encloses "The Table Round." The poem is thus inverted upon itself, and is changed from a work that was peculiarly open to one which is peculiarly closed. Instead of the play of myth upon the mind of society as an ever-living process, we have only the one-time movement of that society from its Golden Age to its Age of Iron, from Genesis to Revelation.

The Coming and *The Passing of Arthur*, then, stand like twin pillars at the beginning and the end of the poem establishing the authority of Arthur as a spiritual absolute. In the rest of the poem Arthur is a remote and shadowy figure, present only as Gloriana is present in the *Faerie Queene*, but here, though the central dramatic actions are performed by other characters, Arthur is the great spiritual authority that dominates the poem.

It follows that the structure of the *Idylls of the King* is very different from that of Tennyson's other composite poems, particularly *In Memoriam*. *In Memoriam* is a poem in process, whose very essence is its hesitancy, its tentativeness, its continual striving for something it never reaches. The *Idylls of the King*, on the other hand, is bound from the very first by inviolable vows of loyalty to the King, and since, as Merlin says, these are vows which it is "a shame / A man should not be bound by, yet the which / No man can keep," there is nothing that can be done but fall away. Tenny-

son has not previously written such a somber poem. His earlier
thought was upon the far distant future and upon the process of
change, growth, and aspiration that can bring one there. But from
the moment that Arthur bound Lancelot and Guinevere and all
his knights by "deathless vows" no further aspiration was possible.
Merlin says to the young Gareth and his followers, who see
Camelot through the shimmering haze, that

> 'an ye heard a music, like enow
> They are building still, seeing the city is built
> To music, therefore never built at all,
> And therefore built for ever.'

This is the ideal, that the city is in process, constantly being built
by each man for himself. But in the *Idylls of the King* the city,
insofar as it is ever built at all, is built at the end of the first idyll or
in between the first and the second. There are two supreme
moments. The first is when Arthur was crowned. Then, says
Bellicent,

> 'the King in low deep tones,
> And simple words of great authority,
> Bound them by so strait vows to his own self,
> That when they rose,'

some were pale, some flushed, and some dazed as by a great light.

> 'But when he spake and cheer'd his Table Round
> With large, divine, and comfortable words,
> Beyond my tongue to tell thee—I beheld
> From eye to eye thro' all their Order flash
> A momentary likeness of the King:'

The other moment is the marriage with Guinevere when the
knights sing, "Let the king reign," but even there there is foreboding, for the Queen swore her deathless love with "drooping eyes,"
and we know that Arthur's sentence, "The old order changeth,
yielding place to new," will all too soon be applied to his own.
Indeed, the kingdom lasts in full perfection for only five lines.

> And Arthur and his knighthood for a space
> Were all one will, and thro' that strength the King
> Drew in the petty princedoms under him,
> Fought, and in twelve great battles overcame
> The heathen hordes, and made a realm and reign'd.

The third and fifth line of this passage are repeated from the early part of the idyll, where they describe Arthur's conquests before his marriage with Guinevere. Now, with one line inserted to describe the twelve great battles against the heathen, they are reapplied to his year-long conquests after the marriage. It was in these heathen wars that Arthur was at his greatest. Then, as Lancelot told Elaine, "the fire of God / Fills him: I never saw his like; there lives / No greater leader." Yet these wondrous exploits which, had Tennyson intended an Arthuriad, would have been his subject, are reduced to a single line, and from this point on the kingdom disintegrates.

Indeed, we do not always realize how late in Arthur's reign are the events which Tennyson has chosen to describe. It is usually said that Gareth, in the second idyll, represents the fresh idealism of youth when the kingdom has not yet begun to decay, and it is true that, so far as Gareth himself is concerned, this is the case. But it is clear that a good many years have elapsed since the previous idyll. For one thing, Gawain, who was a wild lad in *The Coming of Arthur,* is now a "proven knight," and Modred, who was described as "young" in the *Coming,* is now old enough so that his blank shield is a source of shame. Gareth, the youngest of the three brothers, is now a stalwart youth ready to do battle and to wed a lady. Moreover, Tristram, who, according to *The Last Tournament,* "came late" to Arthur's court and "sware but by the shell," is already a knight at the time that Gareth came to court. In other words, Gareth also came late and although he did not swear by the shell, his youthful idealism was already an anomaly in that jaded court.

The principal evidence for dating the events in the idylls is the passage in *Lancelot and Elaine* where we learn that Arthur established the tournament of diamonds shortly after he became king and that that tournament is now in its ninth year.[2] Moreover, it was ten years before that he broke the heathen on Badon Hill, and therefore the events of *Lancelot and Elaine* must take place in the tenth year of his reign. This means that the last six of the idylls are crowded into the last three years of the kingdom, and of these the last four—*Pelleas and Ettarre, The Last Tournament, Guinevere,* and *The Passing of Arthur,* which form an unbroken series—into the final year. But *Merlin and Vivien,* which immediately precedes *Lancelot and Elaine,* must also be placed decidedly late because Merlin refers to the founding of the Round Table as an event long past and it is now a time of golden ease. *Balin and Balan* is directly connected to *Merlin and Vivien* by Vivien's journey from Cornwall to Arthur's court, but we learn independently of its lateness from the fact that Balin, like Tristram, arrived late at the court and that it has been three years and three months since he was knighted. Moreover, we are told of Arthur that "One fair dawn / The light-wing'd spirit of his youth return'd," as if he were now in middle age or at least tired. *Geraint and Enid* and *The Marriage of Enid*, which between them occupy a year, cannot easily be dated, but there is every reason to suppose that *Gareth and Lynette* does not begin before about the seventh or eighth year of Arthur's reign. Tennyson has simply left a blank of that length between the first idyll and the second.[3]

It is not merely chronology, however, which makes us feel the lateness of the events but also the general atmosphere of the kingdom. For if Gareth is the very spirit of youthful idealism, the whole point of the idyll is that he is almost alone in exemplifying this spirit. It is not merely that Bellicent is motherly and Arthur mildly tolerant, but that a man like Kay, cynical and materialistic, should be the seneschal of Arthur's court and that the great Lancelot should have nothing better to do than go baby-sitting. Moreover, the mood of the idyll is largely determined by Lynette, whose unpleasant raillery combines the worst features of Shakespeare's Shrew with those of Benedict and Beatrice. Indeed, the central dramatic action of the idyll is not Gareth's persisting in knightly behavior in the face of this raillery but Lynette's conversion from the habit of judging by appearances to that of judging by inner worth. But Gareth's own ordeal is singularly anticlimactic and unworthy. For the three knights, Morning-Star, Noon-Day Sun, and Evening-Star, whom he overthrows, do not really represent the sins of Youth, Manhood, and Old Age, the last two of which he would have had no opportunity of knowing. They are simply three "fools" who have dressed themselves up to imitate the allegory of a dead hermit. Thus, the fact that the fourth knight, Death, turns out to be a blooming boy does not indicate that the fears of Death are groundless once one has conquered the sins of this life but merely indicate the anticlimactic character of the whole enterprise. In other words, Lynette's rationalizing intellect has infected the whole world of Tennyson's idyll, and it is clear that although the moral of the allegory does remain available for Gareth and doubtless will be kept in mind when he reaches manhood and old age, still at this point we find ourselves in a world where, unlike that of Spenser and Malory, there are no supernatural beings against whom one does battle. Indeed, even the hermit's allegory is regarded as the relic of a former belief. Tennyson distinctly compares the rock carvings in which the hermit has depicted "the war of Time against the soul of man" with some carvings left by the vexillary or standard bearer of the Roman legion on a crag by the river Gelt. They are, in other words, of purely antiquarian interest, and the spiritual accomplishment of Gareth was less in having triumphed over these "fools" than in having kept his temper with Lynette and laughed good-naturedly when he was overthrown by Lancelot. Tennyson wrote the idyll, he said, to provide an example for his "boys,"[4] and the whole episode does have a kind of Boy Scout character about it.

The point in thus emphasizing the lateness of the events in *Gareth and Lynette* is to show that Tennyson is not giving us the whole story of Arthur's reign but only its final days. The *Idylls of the King* is Tennyson's *Decline and Fall of the Roman Empire,* and he is distinctly writing with the somber, the saturnine spirit of Gibbon. This, indeed, affects the very form of his work, for there is a close analogy between the belatedness of the events that Tennyson is describing and his own feeling of belatedness as a poet. Just as Arthur finds, after a very brief moment, that the realm he has created is beginning to decay, so Tennyson finds that his ability to re-create that ordered realm is decaying. Indeed, given his firm persuasion that Camelot is, and must be, a city built to music, if that city cannot be built, it must be because he cannot build it. Arthur's failure is his failure, Merlin's seduction is his seduction, and the *Idylls of the King* is a triumph only because it sings so seductively the story of its own demise.

One may validate this thesis in several ways. For although it is clear that Tennyson has not shown us the city built to music in its prime but has only given us its decline and fall, there are three passages in which characters describe it retrospectively as it existed between the end of *The Coming of Arthur* and *Gareth and Lynette.* These passages, in turn, indicate the kinds of poems which Tennyson might have written in order to create Camelot but which, because of his own belatedness, he could not write.

The first passage is that in which Lancelot, in response to the request of Lavaine, the bashful young brother of Elaine, tells of Arthur's "glorious wars."

                    And Lancelot spoke
And answer'd him at full, as having been
With Arthur in the fight which all day long
Rang by the white mouth of the violent Glem;
And in the four loud battles by the shore
Of Duglas; that on Bassa; then the war
That thunder'd in and out the gloomy skirts
Of Celidon the forest; and again
By castle Gurnion, where the glorious King
Had on his cuirass worn our Lady's Head,
Carved of one emerald cent'red in a sun
Of silver rays, that lighten'd as he breathed;
And at Caerleon had he help'd his lord,
When the strong neighings of the wild white Horse
Set every gilded parapet shuddering;
And up in Agned-Cathregonion too,
And down the waste sand-shores of Trath Treroit,
Where many a heathen fell; "and on the mount
Of Badon I myself beheld the King
Charge at the head of all his Table Round,
And all his legions crying Christ and him,
And break them; and I saw him, after, stand
High on a heap of slain, from spur to plume
Red as the rising sun with heathen blood,
And seeing me, with a great voice he cried,
'They are broken, they are broken!' for the King,
However mild he seems at home, nor cares
For triumph in our mimic wars, the jousts— . . .
Yet in this heathen war the fire of God
Fills him: I never saw his like: there lives
No greater leader."

These are the twelve great battles against the heathen, and their
sonorous names afford Tennyson an opportunity to simulate the
style of Milton or of Virgil or perhaps of Homer. Had he wanted
to write an Arthuriad, this is what he might have written, and we
may perhaps be glad that, having expanded it from a single line in
The Coming of Arthur to twenty-five or thirty in *Lancelot and Elaine*,
he did not expand it any further. And yet something like this
might have loomed large in Tennyson's original plans. When he
published the first installment of the *Idylls* in 1859, he was ex-

tremely annoyed with those critics who spoke of the work as an epic. "I wish that you would disabuse your own minds and those of others, as far as you can," he wrote to Ticknor and Fields, "of the fancy that I am about an Epic of King Arthur. I should be crazed to attempt such a thing in the heart of the 19th Century."[5] This was in 1858, and many years later he reiterated his view that "calling the Idylls an Epic, which they are not, is to me a misnomer."[6] Yet in 1837, when he wrote the frame to the *Morte d'Arthur*, he himself called the poem of which the *Morte* was a part an "epic," and it is virtually certain that an entire poem on the subject of King Arthur did exist, at least in his head, at that time. In 1870 when *The Passing of Arthur* assumed its proper place at the end of the *Idylls*, Tennyson's advertisement noted that it was "here connected with the rest in accordance with an early project of the author's."[7] Twenty years later he said, "I had it all in my mind, could have done it without any trouble. The reviews stopped me."[8] When the duke of Argyll reported to him that Macaulay was urging him to do a Sangraal, he wrote, "Many years ago I did write 'Lancelot's Quest of the Grail' in as good verses as I ever wrote, no, I did not write, I made it in my head, and it has now altogether slipt out of memory."[9] Exactly what this poem of the 1830s was like we shall never know. But one may be reasonably sure that it would have been quite different from the *Idylls of the King*. Probably it would have focused more upon King Arthur and would have been more in the archaic style of the *Morte*. But Tennyson was stopped by the reviews, particularly by Sterling's, which told him to treat topics of current interest, and so was diverted into works like *The Princess* and *Maud*. By the time he got back to the subject he realized that the reviews were right in one respect at least, that he would have been crazed to write an epic in the heart of the nineteenth century.

He had already decided that he would have to make his mark by shortness, and he reaffirmed that decision now. "I thought that a small vessel, built on fine lines, is likely to float further down the stream of Time than a big raft."[10] He was, in other words, reaffirming himself as a Victorian Alexandrian, and just as the Alexandrians had rejected the long-winded epic in favor of the highly wrought epyllion, so too did Tennyson. The passage in which Lancelot recounts Arthur's "glorious wars," which is the model of what an Arthuriad might have been, is based on Nennius's *Historia Britonum*,[11] the British equivalent of Ennius among the Romans or the cyclic epics of Homer among the Greeks. Tennyson's decision not to write an epic but to write a series of idylls was a decision in favor of a modern form that would be appropriate to his own postclassical, decadent civilization. But that meant a loss of that very unity which was being lost by Arthur in his Table Round. For just as Tennyson's poem does not center on Arthur, so neither does it center on Arthurian society. The section called The Round Table does not deal with the Table Round in any collective sense. The episode of the Holy Grail is perhaps a group endeavor, but all the other idylls deal with individual knights who pursue their own affairs in the forests of Wales, Cornwall, or Brittany. Critics have devoted so much attention to the patterns of imagery, mood, and theme that unite the *Idylls* precisely because those are the things that are not obvious. But it does not do to neglect the obvious fact that the fragmentation of Arthurian society is reflected in the very structure of its poem. Tennyson elects to tell of the disintegration of a society in a form in which that disintegration has already occurred.

The second passage in which a character describes retrospectively the golden time of Arthurian society is that in which the little novice tells Guinevere that before the coming of the sinful Queen all the land was full of magic.

> 'Yea, but I know; the land was full of signs
> And wonders ere the coming of the Queen.
> So said my father, and himself was knight
> Of the great Table—at the founding of it;
> And rode thereto from Lyonnesse, and he said
> That as he rode, an hour or maybe twain
> After the sunset, down the coast, he heard
> Strange music, and he paused, and turning—there
> All down the lonely coast of Lyonnesse,
> Each with a beacon-star upon his head,
> And with a wild sea-light about his feet,
> He saw them—headland after headland flame
> Far on into the rich heart of the west:
> And in the light the white mermaiden swam,
> And strong man-breasted things stood from the sea,
> And sent a deep sea-voice thro' all the land,
> To which the little elves of chasm and cleft
> Made answer, sounding like a distant horn.
> So said my father—'

But now, since the coming of the sinful Queen, the elves and fairies have departed, and what is more, they have also departed from Tennyson's poem. One would not have thought it possible, but Tennyson has written an entire poem on King Arthur and his knights without one single instance of magic or the supernatural offered on the poet's own authority. We have already seen one instance of the avoidance of the supernatural in *Gareth and Lynette*, where the three knights, Morning-Star, Noon-Day Sun, and Evening-Star, are not supernatural figures, as they would have been in Malory or Spenser, but are simply "fools" masquerading as such. But there is an even more dramatic instance earlier in the poem. When Gareth and his two rustic companions first see Camelot shimmering through the mists, the city appears to move so weirdly that his companions think it a City of Enchanters. This king, say the rustics, is not a true king,

> 'But only changeling out of Fairyland,
> Who drave the heathen hence by sorcery
> And Merlin's glamour.'

The old religion obviously lingers longest in the countryside, for Gareth, who is better educated than they, is above all this and assures them that the true "glamour" is his own youthful strength wherewith he will "plunge old Merlin in the Arabian sea." Still, the effect *is* very uncanny, and so when Merlin himself appears Gareth asked him to tell them "the truth." To which Merlin, riddling, replies, "Son, I have seen the good ship sail / Keel upward, and mast downward, in the heavens / And solid turrets topsy-turvey in air—" to which Tennyson adds the gloss, in the Eversley edition, "refraction by mirage." Merlin, in other words, is giving them a lesson in optics and physics and is simply telling them that the city is distorted by the mists in the distance so that it appears to move. It is true, they ought to derive therefrom the moral lesson that things are not always what they appear and that the invisible King within themselves may be more real than the city of bricks and mortar. Still, it is a little disconcerting to learn that the old wizard himself does not believe in magic and that his orientation is that of a nineteenth-century sage. Yet this technique of either providing an alternative rationalistic explanation of magic or else attributing it not to the poet but to one of the characters in the poem is Tennyson's practice throughout, and he evidently regarded it as a valuable feature of his work. James

Knowles, who usually voices Tennyson's own opinion, indicates in his letter on the *Idylls* in the *Spectator* that the entire poem is capable of a symbolic interpretation but also that this interpretation is not forced. There is a "thread of realism which is preserved throughout, and which, whether intentionally or not, serves the double purpose of entirely screening any such symbolic under-meaning from all who do not care to seek it, and also of accounting naturally for all the supernatural adventures and beliefs recorded in the story itself." In *The Coming of Arthur,* for example, "the marvellous story of [Arthur's] birth, as told by Bleys, might simply have been founded on a shipwreck when the sea was phosphorescent, and when all hands suddenly perished save one infant who was washed ashore. Or, again in the same poem, the three mystic Queens at the Coronation . . . derive their import in the eyes of Bellicent simply from the accident of coloured beams of light falling upon them from a stained-glass window."[12] No wonder that Tennyson said that the three Queens are, and are not, Faith, Hope, and Charity, that they are, and are not, the Three Graces, since they derive their potency from the same warm gules that fell on Madeline's fair breast.

A fine instance of Tennyson's rationalizing technique is found in *Balin and Balan,* where the "demon of the woods" is capable of a naturalistic, a psychological, and a supernatural interpretation. The last is offered by a woodman who reported to Arthur's embassy that the demon was a man

> 'who driven by evil tongues
> From all his fellows, lived alone, and came
> To learn black magic, and to hate his kind
> With such a hate, that when he died, his soul
> Became a Fiend, which, as the man in life
> Was wounded by blind tongues he saw not whence,
> Strikes from behind. This woodman show'd the cave
> From which he sallies, and wherein he dwelt.'

It so happens that this cave yawns over an abyss, and with its rocks pendent from the roof and others arising tusklike from the floor looks like the mouth of Hell, which the woodman belives it is. Balin, however, scoffs at these "fancies" and is astute enough to recognize in the woodman's tale the story of his own life. For Balin, in contrast to his more balanced brother Balan, represents the dark underside of the personality, suspicious, resentful, combining the tendency to over-idealization of the Super-Ego with the dark violence of the Id. Some three years before he had struck a servant whom he had suspected of speaking evil of him and had been exiled by Arthur for three years—"three kingless years" in which he would often have wrought some fury on himself had it not been for the restraining influence of Balan. In other words, he himself became a kind of fiend or demon of the woods, and it is that term that Balan uses, when he has to separate from his brother for a time, in warning him against himself.

> 'Let not they moods prevail, when I am gone
> Who used to lay them! hold them outer fiends,
> Who leap at thee to tear thee.'

As a result, when Balin, enraged at the destruction of the impossibly exalted ideal of the Queen and Lancelot which he has allowed himself to construct, rushes out into the woods and is told by the woodman that he is strong enough to "lay the Devil of these woods," Balin replies, "To lay that devil would lay the Devil in me." He correctly sees that the deepest meaning of the demon is psychological and that it has bearing upon himself. But the reader is gradually made aware that there is also a naturalistic explanation. Garlon and Vivien, both of whom speak evil of Arthur and his knights behind their back, dally in this Mouth of Hell, and Garlon it is who issues thence on horseback and spears unwary knights from behind. The woodman, whether out of ignorance or a genuine mythopoeic imagination, interprets their activities supernaturally. Balin, with more depth of insight, interprets them psychologically; but Tennyson cannot rest easy until he has also provided a naturalistic explanation.

The most notable instance of this rationalizing is, of course, *The Holy Grail*. Tennyson long deferred the writing of this idyll because, as he said, "I doubt whether such a subject could be handled in these days, without incurring a charge of irreverence. It would be too much like playing with sacred things. The old writers *believed* in the Sangreal."[13] The implication of this remark is that Tennyson himself did not believe in it, and yet, as we have already seen, many years before he had written a poem on " 'Lancelot's Quest of the Grail' in as good verses as I ever wrote," though "it has now altogether slipt out of memory." Presumably Tennyson did not feel that this poem had incurred a charge of irreverence, and the reason must have been that there he had simply accepted the Grail at face value as being what it was. But now he feels he cannot do that, and his problem is how to avoid committing himself to the Grail as a sacred object and yet not give offense.[14] Ultimately, he saw his way. His main device was to place the entire narrative in the mouth of Sir Percivale so that he, rather than the poet, would have the responsibility for it, and then, within that narrative, to provide alternative, naturalistic explanations of which Sir Percivale would not be aware. "A. read 'The Holy Grail' to the Bradleys," says Mrs. Tennyson's journal for January 1869, "explaining the realism and symbolism, and how the natural, if people cared, could always be made to account for the supernatural."[15] Whether people cared or not we do not know, but Tennyson was immensely proud of this solution and simply could not believe Palgrave's report that Max Müller had found a medieval poem which anticipated him. "I can't conceive how the Grail M. M. mentions can well be treated by a poet of the 13th century from a similar point of view to mine, who write in the 19th."[16] One may well agree. A poet of the thirteenth century treating the Grail as Tennyson does would surely have been burned at the stake. And that Tennyson was not severely censured in his own day can only be due to the strong anti-Catholic bias of the poem.

For Tennyson treats the quest for the Holy Grail as an example of mass hysteria. The whole thing originated, he makes perfectly clear, in the frustrated sexual desires of a young woman who had been disappointed in love and gone into a nunnery. It was the sister of Sir Percivale who "first saw the holy thing," and, as Percivale says, though she was indeed a holy maid, in her earliest maidenhood she glowed with "a fervent flame of human love, / Which, being rudely blunted, glanced and shot / Only to holy things." From her the faith spread to others purely by psychological means, the intensity of one person's belief communicating it to another. Galahad, the Shelley of the Table Round, was her first victim. Cutting off her hair and plaiting out of it a sword-belt with the device of the Grail woven into it with silver thread, she imbued him with a similar unearthly passion.

> ' "I, maiden, round thee, maiden, bind my belt.
> Go forth, for thou shalt see what I have seen,
> And break thro' all, till one will crown thee king
> Far in the spiritual city:" and as she spake
> She sent the deathless passion in her eyes

> Thro' him, and made him hers, and laid her mind
> On him, and he believed in her belief.'

From Galahad it was communicated to Percivale, for just as Galahad believed, not in the Grail itself but in her belief in the Grail, so Percivale was drawn by the hypnotic power of Galahad into his belief. From him it spread to the entire Round Table aided by meteorological phenomena. For Tennyson so describes the manifestation of the Grail in Arthur's hall that it might be explained, as Knowles observes, "by passing meteors or sudden lightning flashes seen in a season of great tempests and thunderstorms."[17]

> 'And all at once, as there we sat, we heard
> A cracking and a riving of the roofs,
> And rending, and a blast, and overhead
> Thunder, and in the thunder was a cry.
> And in the blast there smote along the hall
> A beam of light seven times more clear than day;
> And down the long beam stole the Holy Grail
> All over cover'd with a luminous cloud,
> And none might see who bare it, and it past.'

This is Percivale speaking, of course, not Tennyson, for when Tennyson speaks it is more bluntly. When Sir Bors describes the appearance of the Grail to him, "in color like the fingers of a hand / Before a burning taper," Tennyson appends the note: "It might have been a meteor." Finally, it is not merely that everything recounted about the Grail is placed in the mouth of Percivale but also that his belief is counterpointed by the earthy skepticism of the monk Ambrosius, who keeps saying that it is odd—he has read many books of holy miracles but they say nothing of this miracle of the Grail. Ambrosius is a simple man who knows nothing save the gossip of his village, but he is a monk and deeply religious and very sensible, and his stubborn insistence that there is nothing about this miracle in the holy books reminds us that it is not biblical. For a Protestant audience that is tantamount to saying that it need not be believed.

Tennyson, of course, does not leave us in this low descendental view. He is perfectly clear that none of the knights, neither Galahad nor any others, saw an objective spiritual vision of the cup into which Christ's blood was shed, for even the prophets of old time and the inspired bards of antiquity see only according to their own nature. Whether such visions are good or ill, then, depends on the nature of the individual. For a Shelleyan figure like Galahad they are good, but most of the other knights would have been better employed in practical works at home.

One wonders why Tennyson insisted on this thoroughgoing rationalization of his poem. It is understandable that in a modern, personal work like *In Memoriam* he would insist that he will not see the ghost of Hallam and that if he should think he did, there would be a natural, psychological explanation. But in a romance about King Arthur and his knights one would think that magic and the supernatural might be allowed their play. In earlier years Tennyson did not feel a need to provide an alternative explanation for the Sea-Fairies or the Kraken or to assert that the Hesperides were three African ladies who had a pet lizard. But now it is as though a Connecticut Yankee has got into King Arthur's court and is not going to allow anything to happen that is not up to date. For in the poem itself Tennyson gives a history of the miraculous. The Grail, we are told by Sir Percivale, though brought by Joseph of Arimathea to Glastonbury, ceased to be seen by men when the times grew evil, and though when Arthur's realm was established it was thought that it would reappear and apparently did to some, Percivale himself says that it will never be seen again by later times. Arnold said in *Literature and Dogma* (1873) that the age of miracles is past, and Tennyson seems to agree. With the coming of the sinful Queen the fairies departed, and with the coming of modern biblical criticism the miraculous departed. Tennyson is writing in that postmiraculous age, and so, although his work is a kind of *Paradise Lost*, which explores how Guinevere, like her predecessor Eve, brought death into the world and all our woe, still Tennyson, far more than Milton, writes from a sinful or postlapsarian point of view.

This is apparent in the third passage in which Tennyson depicts, retrospectively, the Arthurian order before the fall. Vivien is trying to seduce Merlin with the song "Trust me not at all or all in all." Any lack of trust, she sings, is

> 'the little rift within the lute,
> That by and by will make the music mute,
> And ever widening slowly silence all.'

For a moment Merlin half believed her, so tender was her song, but then he answered, half indignantly.

'Far other was the song that once I heard
By this huge oak, sung nearly where we sit;
For here we met, some ten or twelve of us,
To chase a creature that was current then
In these wild woods, the hart with golden horns.
It was the time when first the question rose
About the founding of a Table Round,
That was to be, for love of God and men
And noble deeds, the flower of all the world;
And each incited each to noble deeds.
And while we waited, one, the youngest of us,
We could not keep him silent, out he flash'd,
And into such a song, such fire for fame,
Such trumpet-blowings in it, coming down
To such a stern and iron-clashing close,
That when he stopt we long'd to hurl together,
And should have done it; but the beauteous beast
Scared by the noise upstarted at our feet,
And like a silver shadow slipt away
Thro' the dim land; and all day long we rode
Thro' the dim land against a rushing wind,
That glorious roundel echoing in our ears,
And chased the flashes of his golden horns
Until they vanish'd by the fairy well.'

Vivien has asked Merlin for the secret of the charm whereby, "with woven paces and with waving arms," a man might be imprisoned as in a tower and "lost to life and use and name and fame." The means by which a man might be so imprisoned, we know, is sexual passion, and that Vivien already possesses this secret is darkly suspected by Merlin.

'But Vivien, when you sang me that sweet rhyme,
I felt as though you knew this cursed charm,
Were proving it on me, and that I lay
And felt them slowly ebbing, name and fame.'

It is by means of their song contest that Merlin and Vivien principally contend with one another, and it is by the triumph of her kind of poetry over his that she finally wins. Her poem is "like the fair pearl-necklace of the Queen," of which the thread broke so that the pearls were scattered.

> 'so is it with this rhyme:
> It lives dispersedly in many hands,
> And every minstrel sings it differently;
> Yet is there one true line, the pearl of pearls:
> "Man dreams of Fame while woman wakes to love." '

Fame as opposed to love seems to be the issue between them, but the question is, what is meant by these terms? To Vivien love is pure sexual passion. "Yea! Love, though Love were of the grossest, carves / A portion from the solid present," whereas Fame, if it be in the next world, is an illusion, and if it be in this, is half disfame. Merlin explains that it is for Use that Fame is valued. "Fame with men / [Is] but ampler means to serve mankind," and the song, "fired with fame," which the young knight sang was prompted by "love of God and men / And noble deeds." On the other hand, it was also the means whereby men were incited to noble deeds, and one may almost believe that the hart with golden horns was created by that song. At least it started up at their feet scared by the song, and was pursued by them, "that glorious roundel echoing in our ears," though the dim land. The flashes of its golden horns are clearly the "gleam" which, in *Merlin and the Gleam*, typifies the poetic ideal that Tennyson pursues.[18] "By our own spirits are we deified," says Wordsworth, and in those glorious days when the Table Round had not yet been founded but was only an ideal in the minds of the young knights, such too was the feeling. Who can doubt but that Tennyson is here re-creating the spirit that animated the Cambridge Apostles in the days when another Arthur listened to the songs of another Merlin and the two hoped, through idealism and poetry, to create a Camelot of their own?

With such a "noble song" to offer, why does not Merlin win the song contest? The answer surely is that he does not sing it. Had he sung it, in all its original fire and glory, Vivien would have slunk off through the woods and Merlin, reinspired, would have returned straight to Camelot to reinspirit the king. But only Vivien actually sang her song, which, like her love, was "from the solid present," whereas Merlin could only re-create a faint memory of the poetry that once had been. To what poetry was he referring? The nearest thing to the young knight's song in Tennyson's works is the war song sung by the knights at Arthur's marriage in *The Coming of Arthur*. That certainly is full of "trumpet-blowings" and does come down "To such a stern and iron-clashing close." But then it was deliberately inserted into *The Coming of Arthur* in 1873, many years after *Merlin and Vivien,* to provide a song that would be appropriate to the high point of the kingdom, and although Tennyson thought it rang "like a grand music,"[19] poetically it is nothing. More impressive and more suitable in date are the political poems of the 1830s, *Hail Briton!* and *Love thou thy land,* but these are not animated by a glorious fire—rather they are prudential and cautious. Probably we have to turn to the militaristic poems, *Hands All Round!* and *Britons, Guard Your Own,* which Tennyson wrote in 1852 in response to the coup d'état of Louis Napoleon and which he signed "Merlin." He even wrote a poem about these poems which he contributed to the newspapers and signed with the name of the other Welsh bard, "Taliessen." It began, "I love this writer's manly style." These, however, are even more wretched performances, and the melancholy conclusion to which one comes is that Tennyson did not give Merlin's "glorious roundel" because he could not give it and that he did give Vivien's "tender rhyme" because that was the sort of poetry he habitually wrote. In other words, he was seduced in the sense that he had become Vivien and had betrayed the ideal he had set up for himself in his youth. As a poet who ought by the force of his imagination to have created a vision which would have given rise to the city built to music, he had failed. No wonder that "a great melancholy" had come over him, and no wonder that the wave of evil which seemed about to break over the kingdom appeared, in his presageful thoughts, to take the form of Vivien. " 'For shall I tell you truth?' " says Merlin to Vivien.

> 'You seem'd that wave about to break upon me
> And sweep me from my hold upon the world,
> My use and name and fame.'

Use and name and fame are what ebbed from him as she sang, and that Merlin was thus inhibited from singing is indicated by the little novice in *Guinevere.* Asked by Guinevere why, if the Queen's coming were such an evil, that evil was not predicted, the little novice replied that it was. Her father told her that in those early days there was a bard (presumably Merlin) who, like the young knight, sang "many a noble war song" and, like the novice herself, "many a mystic lay" and, like Lancelot, "Arthur's glorious wars." He sang, in other words, precisely the kind of vital, heroic poetry

appropriate to that era. But one day when he was singing of
Arthur himself, he said that if Arthur could find "A woman in her
womanhood as great / As he was in his manhood, then . . . , /
The twain together well might change the world."

> 'But even in the middle of his song
> He falter'd, and his hand fell from the harp,
> And pale he turn'd, and reel'd, and would have fallen,
> But that they stay'd him up; nor would he tell
> His vision; but what doubt that he foresaw
> This evil work of Lancelot and the Queen?'

The story of the Fall is reduplicated in the *Idylls of the King,* once in
the case of Lancelot and Guinevere and once in the case of Merlin
and Vivien, but the failure in vision preceded the failure in fact. It
was Merlin's foreboding of evil which caused him to falter then
and which inhibits his singing now. Like Coleridge in *Dejection: An
Ode* he has lost Joy, that active, sacred power wherewith he created
worlds about him. His imagination is tainted by the fact that when
he looks into the future he can imagine not only Arthur but also
Lancelot and Guinevere. He has lost faith in Camelot and as a
result he has very quickly become an old man. There is no
chronology that can reconcile the sense of extreme antiquity
which we feel about Merlin both in this idyll and *Gareth and Lynette*
with the youthfulness he manifested only eight years before in the
chase of the hart with the golden horns. He has aged more rapidly
than Ulysses or Tithonus or Tiresias, and he is far less happy than
they in that he has no Telemachus or Menœceus to act for him.
The contest between him and Vivien is the crucial contest in the
poem. As the great artificer of Camelot, the whole society depends
on him. As one who masks under her hedonism the fact of Sin
and spiritual Death, Vivien, "born from death . . . among the
dead," can accomplish the destruction of Camelot. Guinevere is
merely the weak vessel who will illustrate the truth of her vision of
the world, as Lancelot is the vessel who will fail to illustrate
Merlin's. Modred is Vivien's Enactor, translating into fact the
conception she has, as Arthur, by the very character of his other-
worldliness, cannot translate into fact Merlin's.

Most readers feel that the crucial contest between Merlin and
Vivien comes very early in the poem, and Tennyson himself felt it
came too early. He wrote *Balin and Balan* to insert before it and
make it come later, but in truth it came early in his own experi-

ence. Apart from the *Morte d'Arthur*, it was the first idyll he wrote, and so it may be said that, as in the case of *Maud*, he wrote the poem backward, beginning with the tragic catastrophe and then proceeding to its tragic cause. Apart from these two idylls and the necessary preliminary, *The Coming of Arthur*, he was merely filling in interstices, adding inert matter in *Gareth and Lynette* and the two *Geraint* idylls and providing social, psychological, and religious illustrations in most of the others. *Guinevere* is, of course, central. It corresponds to book X in *Paradise Lost* as *Merlin and Vivien* corresponds to book IX. But if one were to take these two idylls with their surrounding frame, one would have a very concentrated short epic on the failure of poetry in the modern world. All the other idylls are very pleasant, but they are the work of a poet on whom a great melancholy has fallen, and in their lack of unity they remind us of Vivien's pearls that "live dispersedly in many hands."

Vivien and Merlin are not the only poets in the *Idylls of the King*: there is also the Fair Maid of Astolat, Elaine, who sings of Love and Death from her lonely tower. She was formerly known as the Lady of Shalott and then was a "faery" creature who possessed a magic mirror and a magic web. Now, in this demythologized world, she has exchanged her magic mirror for Lancelot's shield and her magic web for the silk case she has fashioned for it. She is still a poet in the sense that she lives "in fantasy," but her imagination is now exercised in fashioning a "pretty history" of the dents in Lancelot's shield, in guessing a "hidden meaning" in his arms, and in adding "of her wit, / A border fantasy of branch and flower" to the devices emblazoned on his arms. She is a sweet and lovely maid, and it is a pity that Lancelot is not free to marry her. But she has none of the spiritual power which made her such an impressive figure in the 1830s, and which made Lancelot merely stupid to ignore her. Poetry, if she be a poet, speaks with a diminished voice in her, and her final staged exit on the black-clad barge has less affinity with the dying swan than with Victorian melodrama.

There is one more person who lives "in fantasy," and that is Arthur. On one occasion, observes Guinevere, "there gleamed a vague suspicion in his eyes." Otherwise he is

> 'Rapt in this fancy of his Table Round,
> And swearing men to vows impossible,
> To make them like himself.'

Arthur is the great problem in the *Idylls of the King*, for though one
quite understands that he represents a quasi-divine figure, is
assimilated to Christ when he denounces judgment upon Guinevere, and generally represents the voice of conscience within man,
still the legend makes him a human figure with a human role to
play. Hence, we sympathize with Guinevere when she says,

> 'but, friend, to me
> He is all fault who has no fault at all:
> For who loves me must have a touch of earth;
> The low sun makes the colour.'

Arthur has no touch of earth and indeed is placed in the same
impossible position in the *Idylls of the King* that God the Father is
placed in in *Paradise Lost,* that of presumably foreknowing evil and
yet taking no steps to prevent it. In *Paradise Lost* the explanation is
that man must have free will, and that is the explanation too in the
Idylls of the King. The allegiance of Lancelot and Guinevere would
be worth nothing if it were forced. Arthur is active enough against
the heathen (just as Christ is against the fallen angels), but within
the Christian world of the Table Round he can do nothing but
give his subjects a sharp glance now and then. Indeed, for him
even to suspect them of evil would be to be guilty of that very
failure of trust which is the principal error of people like Geraint.
When evil openly avows itself, as it does in Modred, then he can
act against it, but otherwise it is by the power of their "word"—the
deathless vows they all have sworn—that he holds them to himself.

The power of the word is central in the *Idylls.* In *The Coming of
Arthur* God has told Arthur "a secret word," has breathed into him
"a secret thing." Arthur transmits this word to Lancelot and
Guinevere through their deathless vows, for "Man's word is God
in man." When we ultimately learn the content of these vows, in
Guinevere, they seem trivial, but their importance lies not in what
they bind the knights to but in the process of binding. They are
the incarnation of thought into language, a process analogous to
the Incarnation of the Deity in Christ. For just as the Logos is
incarnate in Christ the Word, so Arthur "honours his own
word / As if it were his God's," and he expects others to do so
too.[20]

There is considerable doubt in the *Idylls* whether this process of
binding men through vows is entirely desirable. It is not merely
Guinevere who finds the vows impossible; Merlin also says they

are "such vows as is a shame / A man should not be bound by, yet the which / No man can keep." They do seem too high for human nature and, like Balin's idealization of Lancelot and the Queen, have the effect of discouraging people by the knowledge that they cannot succeed. Thus, when the King "in low deep tones, / And simple words of great authority, / Bound them by so strait vows to his own self," the effect is paralytic. "Some / Were pale as at the passing of a ghost, / Some flush'd, and others dazed." But immediately afterward "when he spake and cheer'd his Table Round / With large, divine, and comfortable words," then, says Bellicent, "I beheld / From eye to eye thro' all their Order flash / A momentary likeness of the King." There seems to be an effort here to distinguish between a more humane use of language, which leads the knights to aspire, and a legalistic or religious use, which leads them to despair. The latter corresponds to the absolutes of the framing idylls, as the former could correspond to the more humane values of The Table Round. The problem is why it does not. Why does language not continue to be employed to encourage the knights to a likeness to their King? That Arthur cannot compel we understand, that he or Merlin could not persuade we fail to see. Yet they do not. When Gareth comes to the court, full of idealism, instead of being met by Merlin with "large, divine, and comfortable words" that would have confirmed his idealism, he is met by quibbling riddles that inspire his contempt. And Arthur, though not absolutely mute, seems to move around the periphery of the idylls scrutinizing people with his searching glance. Arthur's voice, which is so potent in *The Coming of Arthur* that it can both set the heathen flying and stop the battle instantly, has entirely lost its authority in *The Last Tournament.* In the precisely parallel situation where the Round Table is fighting against the followers of the Red Knight, he is powerless to stop the carnage. Arthur is clearly a kind of poet, an apocalyptic or visionary poet, for in *The Coming of Arthur* he is given the same hyper-acute power of vision that was claimed by the young prophet in *Armageddon:*

> the world
> Was all so clear about him, that he saw
> The smallest rock far on the faintest hill,
> And even in high day the morning star.

But by the end of *The Holy Grail* he is saying that such visions are to be indulged in only after the world's work has been done. This was not Ulysses' view, who was a quester all his life and who delegated to others the task of realizing his visions in the world. Had Tennyson followed his earlier paradigm, he would have made Merlin the seer and Arthur the administrator, but as it is he has given Arthur the double function of both envisioning a new society and also bringing it into being. The one step he has omitted is that of poetry, for Arthur does not incarnate his vision in language, he incarnates it in Guinevere.

Guinevere, like Arthur, is a puzzle in the poem. Arthur wishes to marry her so he can realize himself in the world:

> 'for saving I be join'd
> To her that is the fairest under heaven,
> I seem as nothing in the mighty world
> And cannot will my will, nor work my work
> Wholly.'

It is not apparent why this is true. One would have thought that Lancelot and the Table Round were the means by which Arthur would realize himself in the world. What does he mean by saying he can do this only through marriage with Guinevere? He does not seem to be thinking of getting an heir and establishing a dynasty, which would be the obvious answer. Neither does he seem to mean merely that he can work effectively only if happily married—that a good woman is the sweet supportive influence which enables him to bear the cares of office—though on one level something like this is doubtless implied. Mythically, he means that woman is the material principle as man is the spiritual—that she is a kind of Earth Mother as he is a Sun God—and on a second level that may be the answer. But the question arises, by virtue of what characteristics of woman is this true? In the *Idylls of the King* it is by virtue of her beauty. It is because she is "the fairest under heaven" or, as Leodogran says, "the fairest of all flesh on earth," that Arthur must be joined to her. She is the beauty that the Arthurian ideal must clothe itself in if it is to be accepted by the world, and Tennyson's problem, in this decade of the 1850s, is that this beauty has become corrupt. This is doubtless the reason why he shifts his stance and presents in Guinevere and Vivien corrupt women who contrast so strikingly to the pure maidens of his earlier days. The apocalyptic poet who has clothed himself in the garment of fleshly beauty finds that that beauty is corrupt and that poetic language is in itself an insidious vessel for conveying the ideal. In the Epilogue (1873) to the *Idylls of the King* Tennyson will speak of "Art with poisonous honey stolen from France," and, although the major thefts had not yet occurred, it is no accident that Vivien takes Merlin to Brittany to seduce him or that Lancelot has his castle in France. Tennyson could not wholly approve the direction that poetry was taking in the 1850s, and he must have been depressed by the attacks on *Maud* as a poetry of sensation. *Merlin and Vivien* was written in February and March 1856, just when these attacks were at their height, and although Tennyson indignantly repudiated them as wrongheaded, he may not really have believed they were unjustified. He could hardly not have known in his heart of hearts that his style had acquired an automatic facility that Gerard Manley Hopkins would later condemn as "Parnassian." Hence, in the first installment of the *Idylls* (1859) he contrasted two groups of ladies whom he called "The True and the False." But Guinevere is more attractive to Lancelot than Elaine, and Vivien is far more powerful than Enid.

Vivien, indeed, has a power of language of her own which is in sharp conflict with that of Arthur and Merlin. That power is the power of language to deceive and corrupt. It begins, in the very first idyll of the Round Table, with the simple tendency of men to pay too much attention to language, as when Lynette is more impressed by Gareth's description of himself as a "knave" than by his intrinsic qualities as a knight. It grows into rumor, "the world's loud whisper," which too easily affects Geraint, so that he was led to misinterpret his wife's words that she is "no true wife." It gradually swells and grows into scandal, which is the instrument whereby Vivien poisons the wells at Camelot, and is ultimately seen, in the image of the Mouth of Hell where Vivien and Garlon dally in their unholy loves, to emanate directly from the Father of Lies. Tennyson is deeply perturbed about the power of language to corrupt, and there is a real ambiguity in the poem as to whether the rumors about Guinevere and Lancelot do not in some sense create their infidelity. Certainly they are still innocent when Vivien is spreading scandal about them, and it is Merlin's inability to counter this scandal that leads to his defeat by Vivien. The "secret word" of the Father of Lies ultimately triumphs over God's word in the poem. Vows are broken, rumor increases, scandal flies, and even the mystic talk of Merlin is described as "babble." In his early poems Tennyson uses the word *babble* primarily of streams and babies, but in his later poetry it is applied to the discourse of men. "Babble, babble; our old England may go down in babble at last." So says the speaker in *Locksley Hall Sixty Years After*. In the final idyll of The Round Table, when Dagonet the Fool is the most intelligible person around, Merlin's hall has turned into a Tower of Babel, and by that its destruction is assured.

Camelot is transformed into the Tower of Babel simply because it no longer speaks with the single authoritative voice of Arthur but with the contending voices of the individual knights. In 1868–69, after Tennyson had published the first installment of four idylls but before he launched into the second group of four which would be published in 1873 under the title of *The Holy Grail*, Browning published *The Ring and the Book*. The effect of this was to bring prominently forward a new literary form which both he and Tennyson had been practicing for many years but which had not yet acquired a distinct name or been recognized as a genre—the dramatic monologue. It also gave Tennyson a long poem in twelve books with which he might compete. Tennyson had been held up for years on *The Holy Grail* because he did not know how to handle a theme in which he himself did not believe, but now he wrote it off in "a breath of inspiration," putting it largely in the mouth of Sir Percivale.[21] *Guinevere* he had already treated in that way, counterpointing the harsh voice of judgment of Arthur with the innocent prattle of the little nun, and in *The Last Tournament* he plays off Sir Dagonet against Sir Tristram. Indeed, the narrative structure of the idylls becomes increasingly complex as the kingdom disintegrates. *Gareth and Lynette* is the only one that is told straightforwardly from beginning to end. The two *Geraint* idylls begin *in medias res*, focusing on the symbolic image of the faded silk dress and then flashing back to the earlier episode of the marriage. The three central idylls, *Balin and Balan*, *Merlin and Vivien*, and *Lancelot and Elaine*, are all more complicated than these in structure, though still told in the authorial voice. But with the last four, except *Pelleas and Ettarre*, which has its own kind of disorder, the voice of the authoritarian poet—or at least the voice of "he that tells the tale," for that is as authoritative as Tennyson allows himself to be—is abandoned for the voices of the various characters. Moreover, in turning to a group of "innocents"—the earthy monk Ambrosius, the little novice, and the Fool—Tennyson gives us the impression that the higher chivalric generation is played out and he is having to start afresh with a new generation of the common people. We have already seen that in refashioning the *Morte d'Arthur* into *The Passing of Arthur* he made it into a kind of dramatic monologue as told in retrospect by Sir Bedivere.

In one sense all the idylls are dramatic monologues. Just as Browning has given us, framed by his opening and closing books, ten different versions of a single event, so Tennyson has given us ten different events which are themselves but versions of the Arthurian ideal. It is as if Gareth, Geraint, Balin, Lancelot, Percivale, Pelleas, and Tristram each stepped forward and gave his version of what it was like to be a member of the Table Round. They are as different as Guido's and Pompilia's versions of the Roman murder story. Thus, both poems are concerned at once with unity and multiplicity, but though Browning, in his concern with knowledge, is more relativistic than Tennyson, Tennyson, in his concern with society, is more disparate than Browning. Both feel that they have come upon the world very late. God revealed himself long ago and has now withdrawn and remains silent. But whereas for Browning this very condition of doubt provides an incentive for striving, and he takes as his myth that of St. George and the Dragon, Tennyson finds that the great wars against the heathen are over and that the basic problem for Camelot is that there is nothing for the knights to do. Lancelot goes baby-sitting, Gareth rides forth in irritation to avenge a trivial insult to the queen, an embassy is sent to collect taxes from a moth-eaten king, Merlin goes sailing off the Isle of Wight, and the others tilt in tournaments for diamonds, pearls, or a golden sparrow hawk. Lancelot, who is very good at these things, admits himself that Arthur cares nothing for these "mimic wars, the jousts," and yet that and the great delusion of the Holy Grail are the most that the knights have to do. Browning saw himself at the beginning of a new heroic age, with a new knight-errant arising out of frivolity to fight against incarnate Evil. But Tennyson's Pompilia really was corrupt, his Caponsacchi had committed adultery, and his Pope was an old magician who had allowed himself to be seduced by Vivien. Thus, whereas Browning put himself into the frame and wrote a poem which is essentially about the power of the imagination to extract the pure gold of truth from the crude ore of fact, Tennyson put himself into the middle of the poem and wrote about the failure of the imagination to live up to its poetic ideal.

11

Late Lyrics and Earlier

> to the land's
> Last limit I came—
>
> *Merlin and the Gleam*

After the publication of the first installment of the *Idylls of the King* in 1859 there is very little that is novel in Tennyson's poetic career. This does not mean that there are not good poems—there are a great many—but most of them are in forms or modes already explored. *Demeter and Persephone* and *The Death of Œnone* are fine examples of the epyllion, but they do not represent new poetic ground. The English Idyls are further exemplified, but not further developed, in *The Brook, Sea Dreams, Enoch Arden,* and *Aylmer's Field.* The dramas, the historical ballads, the dialect poems, and perhaps some others do represent genuinely new trends, but even these seem to be new uses to which Tennyson's talent is put rather than new forms of that talent itself. They are less a part of the progress of the poetical spirit in Tennyson than an application of that spirit to new subjects. Therefore, in this final chapter it seems best to focus on two forms which Tennyson practiced supremely well during all periods of his life, but particularly during the last period, the lyric and the occasional poem or poem of social converse. Let us begin with the lyrics.

Tennyson's more meditative lyrics normally explore some relation between the natural and the spiritual world, and their success depends not only on the depth and validity of the relation but also on the degree to which the poet is willing to allow the metaphor to speak for itself. The problem was peculiarly difficult for Tennyson because it is precisely here that the Victorian habit of arguing from analogy comes into conflict with the poetic resource of metaphor, the one sometimes triumphing over the other. In the early poem *The Eagle,* for example, there is nothing but a sharply etched image.

> He clasps the crag with crookèd hands;
> Close to the sun in lonely lands,
> Ringed with the azure world, he stands.
>
> The wrinkled sea beneath him crawls;
> He watches from his mountain walls,
> And like a thunderbolt he falls.

Possibly if the poem had not been a fragment, Tennyson would have spoiled it, but as it is the image reverberates in our minds, generating its own human analogies, whether of a robber baron, an apocalyptic poet, or any bold imperious spirit. In *Flower in the crannied wall,* on the other hand, the poet himself is speculating.

> Flower in the crannied wall,
> I pluck you out of the crannies,
> I hold you here, root and all, in my hand,
> Little flower—but *if* I could understand
> What you are, root and all, and all in all,
> I should know what God and man is.

The simplicity and unpretentiousness of the poem is highly attractive, and yet it is not thoroughly successful, for it lacks felicity of phrasing and ultimately the poet's inability to understand the mystery he contemplates is a little anticlimactic. The best line is the first, in which the homeliness of the crannied wall contrasts with the beauty of the flower, which has miraculously emerged out of so unpromising an environment. And as the poet plucks the flower out of the cranny and holds it in his hand, "root and all," presumably with some of the dark earth clinging to the root, he is aware that he is confronted with the mystery of flesh and spirit, of God and man, in their separateness and their relationship. Quite honestly, he does not solve the mystery, though the answer, that somehow the logical "understanding" must be transcended by the Reason, is implied in the metamorphosis of "root and all" into "all in all," and also by the use of the singular verb "is" for the ostensibly plural subject, "God and man."

A much more complex prolem is presented by *Break, break, break,* an early poem on the death of Hallam.

> Break, break, break,
>   On thy cold gray stones, O Sea!

> And I would that my tongue could utter
>   The thoughts that arise in me.
>
> O well for the fisherman's boy,
>   That he shouts with his sister at play!
> O well for the sailor lad,
>   That he sings in his boat on the bay!
>
> And the stately ships go on
>   To their haven under the hill;
> But O for the touch of a vanish'd hand,
>   And the sound of a voice that is still!
>
> Break, break, break,
>   At the foot of thy crags, O Sea!
> But the tender grace of a day that is dead
>   Will never come back to me.

The important thing in reading this poem is not to reify the waves but to allow the "Break, break, break" to remain a purely verbal utterance. Tennyson tells us that he wrote the poem in a Lincolnshire lane on a spring morning,[1] and thus the words are something that passed through his mind, not something that beat upon his ear. They are the kind of incantation which, under other circumstances, might have induced a trance. It is not, then, that the poet wishes he could express himself as well as the waves, for he has expressed himself very well. By means of a powerful rhythm and a powerful image he has voiced the wild, tumultuous sorrow in his own heart. The true contrast is between that kind of expression and rational discourse, for when it comes to his tongue's articulating "thoughts," the shift to the light, tripping measure of lines 3 and 4 shows that he cannot do it. These "thoughts" evidently have something to do with the obliviousness of human beings to impending sorrow, for the three figures, graduated in age and distance from the shore, who pursue their serene untroubled lives, are caught up in an "O well" formula which seems to betoken doom. But the stately ships escape from that formula, and, in any case, this whole painted world, which floats on quite a different sea from that pounding on the cliff below, is so irrelevant that he dismisses it with the cry, "But O for the touch of a vanish'd hand, / And the sound of a voice that is still." This is the central lyric cry of the poem. It receives the greatest emotional and rhetorical stress, and it is one of the two lines which break out of the metrical form of the poem with four feet rather than three. The fourth foot occupies the rest which otherwise appears at the line's end, so that lines 11 and 15 spill over with a rush of anapests that contrasts powerfully with the slow beat of "Break, break, break." As a result, when the poet returns to the refrain at the end of the poem, he pronounces it more softly, thus distancing the waves to "the foot of thy crags, O Sea!"

The Bugle Song in *The Princess* illustrates precisely the danger eluded by *Break, break, break,* for, lovely as it is, its third stanza presents a problem. It begins:

> The splendour falls on castle walls
>   And snowy summits old in story:
> The long light shakes across the lakes,
>   And the wild cataract leaps in glory.
> Blow, bugle, blow, set the wild echoes flying,
> Blow, bugle; answer, echoes, dying, dying, dying.

The first stanza beautifully expresses the sense of life and vibrancy in nature as manifested in the echoes or reverberations in light, water, time ("story"), and sound, and it participates in these reverberations by means of its internal rhymes and its repetitions, particularly in the refrain. Then in the second stanza we get the dying away of these sources of life and movement till the bugle sounds not like a real horn but like the horns of Elfland, and this is done by the incremental repetition of phrases so that, as the sound fades, through its very faintness there is an intensification of the Romantic. The wild cataract is pursued into the purple glens, the echo into the infinite distance. But then in the third stanza this movement is reversed, for the poet now turns to his beloved and states, with some complacency, that while the echoes of nature die away, their more spiritual echoes "roll from soul to soul, / And grow for ever and for ever." They presumably do this by virtue of the soul's immortality, or possibly by virtue of the "child" on which each one of these songs in *The Princess* is supposed to focus. In either case, the question is not so much whether this kind of *un*simile is permissible ("Just as echoes in the natural world grow fainter, so our spiritual echoes grow louder"), as it is whether the echoes repudiated are not more attractive than those by which they are replaced. Would we really like echoes that grow continuously louder? There is also the problem of the refrain:

"dying, dying, dying" goes well with the first two stanzas but not with the third. The "trick" in this kind of poem is to have a refrain sufficiently ambiguous so it can take on a new meaning with the development in sense, but Tennyson's refrain simply contradicts the third stanza. His only alternative would be to rewrite it somewhat as follows:

> Blow, bugle, blow, set the wild echoes flowing,
> And answer, echoes, answer, growing, growing, growing.

But this is simply to make obvious the unsatisfactoriness of the stanza.

Much the same sort of difficulty occurs in *Crossing the Bar*. It is not merely that there are logical objections to the Pilot in the fourth stanza, who is normally put off a ship after it has cleared the harbor and so would be seen at first or not at all, but also that the problem of the poem has already been solved in the first three stanzas and the fourth seems to be unconscious that this has occurred. The first three stanzas of the poem render death, not fearful and horrible, but beautiful and awesome, purely in naturalistic terms. There is, in the first place, the imagery of the voyage with its sense of a beginning ("embark") rather than an ending and of water as a source of life. Then, there is the beauty of the natural scene—the sunset, the evening star, the twilight bell, and the one "clear" call. Even the dark is rendered mysterious! Finally, there is the serenity achieved through a balance of opposing qualities: the tide which "moving seems asleep, / Too full for sound and foam," and the paradox that to move out into the "boundless deep" is to turn again "home." All these images of plenitude and power, of fullness without terror or doubt, make death acceptable simply as a natural process, so that there is no need for the supernatural apologetic which follows. Yet the fourth stanza offers such an apologetic, and in terms entirely incompatible with the rest of the poem. For whereas the first three stanzas have been conducted entirely in terms of the natural scene and in pure natural language, now we have the capital letters of Pilot, Time, and Place, which take us into the world of moral abstractions, and "bourne," which takes us into the poetic diction of *Hamlet*. A poem which seemed absolutely authentic in the first three stanzas has somehow lost that quality in the fourth.

In the Valley of Cauteretz, which Tennyson wrote in 1861 while

visiting a valley in the Pyrenees that he had visited with Arthur
Hallam in 1830, offers a perfect fusion of landscape and theme.

> All along the valley, stream that flashest white,
> Deepening thy voice with the deepening of the night,
> All along the valley, where thy waters flow,
> I walked with one I loved two and thirty years ago.
> All along the valley, while I walked today,
> The two and thirty years were a mist that rolls away;
> For all along the valley, down thy rocky bed,
> Thy living voice to me was as the voice of the dead,
> And all along the valley, by rock and cave and tree,
> The voice of the dead was a living voice to me.

The alternation of a line about the stream with a line about
Hallam—of symbol with what it symbolizes—and the perfect ap-
propriateness of this symbol to its object—its continuousness
through the valley of the years, the deepening of its voice with the
darkening of the poet's grief, the rocky bed of the stream and yet
its white, flashing water, the mists of the past that roll away, and
the voice that insensibly becomes the voice of Hallam—all these
make for a highly unified poem. The poem is unified, moreover,
in that its own rhythms, repetitions, and structures perfectly reproduce the correspondences in time, and between nature and
man, that it is the purpose of the poem to effect. The various
elements in chiastic order, as when the "living voice" of the stream
becomes the "voice of the dead" and then the "living voice" of
Hallam, prefigure the pattern of loss and recovery which is the
theme of the poem. Most delicately managed, perhaps, are the
metrical effects, in which the odd lines are of six feet, but with a
caesura that occupies the time of a seventh, whereas in the even
lines the caesura is filled up with sound, but the stressed syllables
are alternately heavy and light so as to produce two rhythms, one
superimposed upon another. This slower rhythm, additionally
slowed by the occasional omission of unstressed syllables so as to
place greater weight and emphasis upon rhetorically important
words, is the key to the peculiar music of this most musical of
poems.* "Altogether," said Tennyson, "I like the little piece as
well as anything I have written."[2] It is, indeed, very nearly perfect.

* All along the valley, / stream that flashest white,

Deepening thy voice [x] with the deepening of the night.

So too is *Frater Ave atque Vale,* written while Tennyson was on a visit to Lake Garda, in Italy, in June 1880. Tennyson's brother Charles had just died, and so Tennyson was peculiarly sensitive to the beauty of the place, which was associated with Catullus, whose elegy for his brother Tennyson regarded as one of the most pathetic expressions of pagan sorrow. The poem is thus suffused with a tender melancholy which expresses the double sense of death and life-in-death, of a new vigorous Italian civilization that is shooting up through the fissures of the Roman past. This is the meaning of the first line, "Row us out from Desenzano, to your Sirmione row!"—to what *you* call Sirmione but which I, with my classical education, know as Sirmio. So the dusky groves of olive mingling with the summer glow, the purple flowers pushing up through the Roman ruin, the lament "Ave atque vale" countered by the Lydian laughter of Lake Garda, the old and the new, the English poet and the Roman, Hail and Farewell, all come together in this "all-but-island,"—*paene insula*—"olive-silvery Sirmio." The meter is the same as that of *Locksley Hall,* but few readers are aware of the fact, so capable is it of varied expression.

Frater Ave atque Vale is partly a memorial poem to Tennyson's brother and partly a tribute to Catullus. In either case the intimate and personal tone is perfectly appropriate. *To Virgil,* on the other hand, is a public tribute prepared at the request of the Mantuans for the nineteenth centenary of Virgil's death, and for that reason the note of majesty and stateliness, of lofty dignity appropriate to the imperial theme, is struck at once.

> Roman Virgil, thou that singest
>   Ilion's lofty temples robed in fire,
> Ilion falling, Rome arising,
>   wars, and filial faith, and Dido's pyre.

The poet then proceeds to what is the heart of his tribute, that Virgil is a "lord of language,"

> All the chosen coin of fancy
>   flashing out from many a golden phrase.

But not merely is he master of the aureate language, in the more humble *Georgics* we see "All the charm of all the Muses / often flowering in a lonely word." In brief compass Tennyson touches upon all the major works and alludes both to the Virgilian faith in the future and also to his sense of eternal sadness. Then, gracefully turning from the Roman past to the Italian present and paying tribute to the newly won freedom of the Italian nation, Tennyson addresses his master not as Roman Virgil but as native of Mantua and offers his personal tribute.

> I salute thee, Mantovano,
> > I that loved thee since my day began,
> Wielder of the stateliest measure
> > ever moulded by the lips of man.

This measure Tennyson had sung in his heart all along the shores of Lake Como in a trip taken with his wife in 1851.[3] He recaptures something of its "ocean-roll of rhythm" in this poem by wedding a four-foot unrhymed trochaic line with a five-foot line into a single nine-foot unit. Except perhaps in the *Ode on the Death of the Duke of Wellington* Tennyson has never achieved a more stately measure.

In the elegy to Sir John Simeon, Tennyson speaks of his friend as the Prince of Courtesy and says that only two other men has he known "in courtesy like to thee." One would like to appropriate that title to Tennyson himself, for there are a group of poems, poems of social converse we might call them, which express the highly civilized intercourse of this group of noble men. In so much of his poetry Tennyson is so obviously the heir to the Romantic tradition that one forgets he is in some aspects a classic poet and that he deeply assimilated the Horace whom in his schoolboy days he hated. Most of the poems come from his later years, as is most natural, but a few of them are early and show that the grave courtesy, the dignity, the quiet grace and tenderness that make for a deep and abiding friendship were his from the first. Indeed, among all the stances which he assumed as a poet, of apocalyptic prophet or revolutionary, of isolated maiden or ancient sage, one feels that that which also appears in the idyls, of a civilized Englishman speaking in his own voice to civilized peers, is most naturally his own. It would have been well had circumstance and the proprieties of his time allowed him to write more of these poems, for in their own way they are nearly perfect. Many are verse epistles, others are dedications accompanying the present of a poem, some are invitations to stay at Farringford, others thanks for a present or kindness to a son. The characteristics of the poems in all cases are propriety of sentiment, delicacy of feeling, the play of fancy, exquisite craftsmanship, and a delightful intimacy that need not hesitate to make itself public.

Everyone will have his own favorites, but among those that

should not be omitted is *To J.S.*, written to James Spedding in 1832 on the occasion of the death of his brother. Tennyson was such an indifferent letter writer in prose that it is a miracle he can perform the same task so perfectly in verse. He begins with a beautiful analogy from nature which perfectly sets the tone of gentleness, offers some wise reflections on the loss of a loved one, notes that he too has recently experienced sorrow in the death of a father, but that his friend's loss, that of a younger brother, is more rare, tactfully refrains from offering advice to weep or not to weep, and then closes with a benediction. It is the kind of letter that might appear in a letter book as a model for this kind of social task, and, though consummate art, it both is and appears to be perfectly sincere.

The Daisy was written at Edinburgh in 1853 when the poet, alone in the dark northern city, finds a daisy pressed in a book he had carried with him and is reminded by it of the Italian tour which he and his wife had taken two years before. The poem lovingly re-creates the sights and sounds and sentiments of that tour, from the time they arrived in Genoa, swung down by Pisa and Florence, returned by Milan and Lake Como, and then mounted up the Splügen, where Tennyson plucked the daisy, which "told of England then to me, / And now it tells of Italy." Through it the poet is able to forget his loneliness, to imagine his wife again beside him, and in fancy to re-create this pleasant tour. Several of the social poems depend on travel, *To E[dward] L[ear]*, *on his Travels in Greece,* in which the poet, reading Lear's *Journals of a Landscape Painter in Albania and Illyria,* is transported in spirit to the Golden Age and makes a poem out of the scenes which pass before him, and *To Ulysses,* in which he similarly thanks W. G. Palgrave for his essays on exotic lands. The latter is the more complex poem because Tennyson, though conceding that in youth he was "half-crazed" for tropical vegetation, finds now that in the winter of his age he is more "tolerant of the colder time" and discovers a beauty in his own Isle of Wight which he modestly sets in competition with Ulysses' scenes. It is appropriate that to the friend who paid him the compliment of taking *Ulysses* as the title of his volume Tennyson should, in this classic poem, find himself playing a Telemachean role.

To Ulysses and *To E.L.* are both written in the *In Memoriam* stanza, *The Daisy* in a meter which Tennyson invented, as "repre-

senting in some measure the grandest of metres, the Horatian
Alcaic."[4] A quatrain, its character is determined by the little tripping or skipping effect of the anapest in the last line, aided by an
unrhymed feminine ending in the preceding line which, with the
unstressed syllable that follows, gives the effect of another anapest. It is this little skipping movement which, mixed with the more
regular iambic movement of lines one and two, gives the
sense of tenderness and lightness that is so appropriate to the
poem. Tennyson experimented with the meter again in *To the Rev.
F. D. Maurice* and *To Professor Jebb,* where the reversal of the initial
foot in the last line makes for an even more spirited and lively
effect. The poem to Maurice, in particular, is a triumph. It is an
invitation to the liberal churchman, who has just been expelled
from his professorship at King's College for nonorthodoxy, to
come to Farringford, where he will find a welcome free from the
petty spite of theological controversy. The Horatian mode has
seldom been so beautifully employed as in Tennyson's description
of the "lay-hearth" and "careless-order'd garden," where

> You'll have no scandal while you dine,
> But honest talk and wholesome wine,
>   And only hear the magpie gossip
> Garrulous under a roof of pine:

But lest this social converse be thought trivial, the poem then
moves on to more serious matters, the Crimean War, the social
wants of the poor, which will all be discussed in that large and
humane spirit appropriate to liberal minds.

The invitation *To Mary Boyle,* though very different in tone, is
equally fine. Mary Boyle was an elderly lady, an aunt of Hallam
Tennyson's wife, who, on leaving Farringford the previous year
had said she would return with the spring flowers. But since then
a relative has died and she has been immersed in grief. Tennyson's intention in this letter is to wean her from her grief by
urging her to make the proposed visit. By a lucky coincidence he
has just come upon an old poem, written "more than half a
hundred years ago," when both he and Mary were young, *The
Progress of Spring,* and so he sends her this "spring flower" as a
reminder of her promise. The gift enables him to reminisce about
his own part in those early days and so to allude to his own loss of
Arthur Hallam, but to urge that while youth may mourn the dear

one, the silver year hardly has time. We prize the poem today for its personal reminiscence about rick-burning days, but never has a poem been so delicately attuned to the needs of its hearer.

Finally, there is the pleasant piece to Edward FitzGerald, which also accompanies the present of a poem, in this case *Tiresias*, also resurrected from "some forgotten book of mine" half a hundred years ago. The present was appropriate in this case because FitzGerald prized only those poems of Tennyson which had been written when he knew him well and gruffly considered everything done since a declination. Even this work Tennyson fears his crotchety friend will consider too opulent, not classically austere, and so the whole poem turns on a playful allusion to FitzGerald's vegetarianism and to Tennyson's one attempt to imitate him. Momentarily, he felt like "a thing enskied," but then fell from grace, and the animal heat engendered in his blood by the illicit indulgence released his imagination in riotous dreams of tropical vegetation. Yet Fitz's Lenten fare, the poet courteously acknowledges, did not make for Lenten thought in the case of his own *Rubáiyát,* to which Tennyson pays a fitting tribute. The epistle is so charmingly casual in form that it meanders idly through fifty-six lines with no proper transitions and with a syntax that defies analysis. Indeed, the entire poem consists of a single sentence which yet seems to be a fragment! Unhappily, FitzGerald died before he could receive his present, and so Tennyson is constrained to add an epilogue in which he compares his own gift to would-be guests, idling along the road, who arrive too late and find the gate bolted and the master gone. It is just such an image as Old Fitz would have liked, homely and apt, and yet the impressive thing is that Tennyson can combine an informal style with deep feeling and a perfectly serious assertion of the immortality of the soul.

Several of these poems of social converse accompany the present of a poem and so constitute a dedication or introduction. In the case of *To E. FitzGerald* there are also lines following the poem and commenting retrospectively upon it. Thus, these poems correspond to the frame device which Tennyson employed from the midthirties through *The Princess* but not thereafter. They mediate between the poem and the reader, but in this case the prospective reader is not the general public, whose attitude is thought to be hostile or uncomprehending, but a dear friend whose love and sympathy are already assured. The reading of the poem, dramatized in the frame of the *Morte d'Arthur,* will very likely take place in reality when FitzGerald or Maurice or Mary Boyle or Professors Jebb or Jowett accepts the invitation to Farringford and there finds his life enriched by poetry, conversation, good fellowship, and wine. One has the feeling that this association of poetry with social life and manners is more in accord with Tennyson's deeper instincts than the disjunction of poetry from society which he asserted for so many years. The city built to music never arose in Tennyson's day. The Telemachus, the Menœceus who might have created it did not arrive, and perhaps ultimately Tennyson felt that it did not matter. For in the final image that he gives us of himself as poet, in *Merlin and the Gleam,* written three years before his death, he tells us that what he wants is someone to carry on. The poem is addressed to a young Mariner who, from the safety of the haven under the sea cliffs, is watching the gray Magician with eyes of wonder. Who this gray Magician is we would like to know. Swinburne? Zola? Presumably no one in particular but all the false magicians of the modern movement whose art Tennyson has already denounced in *Locksley Hall Sixty Years After.* Hence he cries out to the youth:

> *I* am Merlin,
> And *I* am dying,
> *I* am Merlin
> Who follow the Gleam.

By "the Gleam" Tennyson explains that he means "the higher poetic imagination,"[5] and in the stanzas which follow he chronicles his efforts to pursue it through its various manifestations and under the difficulties of incomprehension and sorrow. But now he has come to the "land's / Last limit," and so he calls on the young Mariner to launch his vessel and follow the Gleam "ere it vanishes / Over the margin"—presumably the same margin that in *Ulysses* "fades / For ever and for ever when I move." It is curious that Tennyson has chosen to make the youth a sailor, for elsewhere in the poem he does not employ a seafaring image. Merlin was taught his art by the Mighty Wizard "There on the border / Of boundless Ocean," and he has now come "to the land's / Last limit"—from the great deep to the great deep he has come. That the next phase of the quest is over the sea suggests that Tennyson deliberately wanted to recall his own Ulysses and to note that, at this stage in his life, what he wants is not a young Telemachus to realize the Ideal but a young Ulysses to pursue it.

Notes

CHAPTER 1. "Tennyson, Tennyson, Tennyson"

1   *Alfred Lord Tennyson: A Memoir,* ed. Hallam Tennyson (London, 1897), II, 473–74 (hereafter cited as *Memoir*).

2   [Hallam Tennyson], *Materials for a Life of A.T.* Collected for my Children [n.p., n.d.], II, 29 (hereafter cited as *Materials*). This was a preliminary version of the *Memoir* which Hallam Tennyson had printed up and circulated among friends and members of the family. A version of the passage also appears in *Memoir,* I, 320. The original source is apparently a letter which Tennyson wrote to Benjamin Paul Blood on May 7, 1874. The passage begins, "I have never had any revelations through anesthetics: but 'a kind of waking trance' (this for lack of a better word) I have frequently had," etc., as in the *Memoir*. The passage concludes, "I am ashamed of my feeble description. Have I not said the state is utterly beyond words?" (Harvard MSS).

3   See Maggie Scarf, "Tuning Down with TM," *New York Times Magazine,* February 9, 1975, pp. 12-13, etc.

4   James, *The Varieties of Religious Experience* (New York, 1902), pp. 382–84; Wilson, *To the Finland Station* (New York: Doubleday Anchor, 1953), p. 158.

5   The standard and indispensable edition of Tennyson's poems is *The Poems of Tennyson,* ed. Christopher Ricks (London: Longmans, 1969) (hereafter cited as Ricks). I will actually quote the text of the Eversley edition (Tennyson, *Works,* ed. Hallam Tennyson [London: Macmillan, 1907–08], 9 vols.) since Ricks's text is slightly modernized.

6   *French Revolution,* pt. II, bk. III, chap. 4; pt. I, bk. IV, chap. 4.

7   Walt Whitman, "A Word about Tennyson," *The Critic,* 7 (January 1887), 1-2, quoted in John D. Jump, ed., *Tennyson: The Critical Heritage* (London: Routledge & Kegan Paul, 1967), pp. 349–50.

8   Richard Henry Horne, *A New Spirit of the Age,* ed. W. Jerrold (Oxford; Oxford University Press, 1901), p. 247. Elizabeth Barrett Browning collaborated with Horne on this work, and thus this passage may be hers. See *The Letters of Robert Browning and Elizabeth Barrett Barrett,* ed. E. Kintner (Cambridge: Belknap Press, 1969), I, 67; II, 727.

9   *Memoir,* I, 268; see also I, 381.

10 *Materials,* I, 28; *Memoir,* I, 11.

11 *Memoir,* I, 7.

12 Ovid, *Fasti,* IV, 428.

13 Sir Charles Tennyson, *Alfred Tennyson* (London: Macmillan, 1950), p. 26.

14 Ricks, p. 161.

15 *Memoir,* II, 319.

16 *Memoir,* I, 154, 81. This is the meaning attached to the phrase in James Kissane, "Tennyson: The Passion of the Past and the Curse of Time," *ELH,* 32 (March 1965), 85–109. Tennyson, however, speaks of the Passion of the

Past as "the abiding in the transient," which suggests that the passion is *in* the past. *Memoir,* I, 253.

17 *Materials,* III, 146–47; *Memoir,* II, 83.

18 *Materials,* I, 28–29; *Memoir,* I, 11–12. See also Hallam Tennyson, ed., *Tennyson and His Friends* (London, 1911), p. 263.

19 *Memoir,* I, 10.

20 *Trinity Notebook* 19 (hereafter cited as *T.Nbk.* 19). The abbreviations used in Ricks are followed.

21 W. D. Paden, "MT. 1352: Jacques de Vitry, The Mensa Philosophica, Hödeken, and Tennyson," *Journal of American Folklore,* 58 (1945), 46–47.

22 The words are actually Magus's but the sentiment is Amoret's (I, iv, 97, 82–85).

23 Alfred Lord Tennyson, *The Devil and the Lady and Unpublished Early Poems,* ed. Sir Charles Tennyson (Bloomington, Ind.: University of Indiana Press, 1964), p. vii.

24 *In Memoriam,* xcv; *The Two Voices,* 380–84.

CHAPTER 2.   The Poetry of Apocalypse

1 Sir Charles Tennyson, "Tennyson's Conversation," *Twentieth Century,* 165 (1959), 35.

2 *Memoir,* I, 15.

3 See Charles Coulston Gillispie, *Genesis and Geology: A Study in the Relations of Scientific Thought, Natural Theology, and Social Opinion in Great Britain, 1790-1850* (Cambridge, Mass.: Harvard University Press, 1951), chaps. 4 and 5.

4 *Memoir,* I, 497–98.

5 *Table Talk,* August 18, 1833.

6 See the revised version of *Armageddon* (*T. Nbk.* 18) mentioned below.

7 *T.Nbk.* 18. Extracts from this notebook were published by Christopher Ricks in the *Times Literary Supplement,* August 21, 1969, pp. 918–22. See also Ricks, "Tennyson: 'Armageddon' into 'Timbuctoo,' " *MLR,* 61 (1966), 23–24.

8 See Thomas Balston, *John Martin, 1789-1854: His Life and Works* (London: Duckworth, 1947).

9 *Charlotte Brontë: The Evolution of Genius* (Oxford, 1967), pp. 43–45.

10 Published by Ricks, *Times Literary Supplement,* August 21, 1969, p. 919.

11 The topic was announced in the *Times* for December 13, 1828 (p. 3, col. 4); entries were to be submitted by March 31, 1829.

12 See Brian Gardner, *The Quest for Timbuctoo* (London: Cassell, 1968), p. 120 and passim; *Times,* March 30, May 4, October 24, 1827; April 25, May 3, May 5, October 30, 1828; "Clapperton's Second Expedition into the Interior of Africa," *Quarterly Review,* 39 (January 1829), 143–83; Review of M. Caillié, *Travels through Central Africa to Timbuctoo* (1830), in *Quarterly Review,* 42 (March 1830), 450–75.

13 [John Wright], *Alma Mater; or, Seven Years at the University of Cambridge.* By a Trinity Man. (London, 1827), I, 33n. See Jerome H. Buckley, *Tennyson: The Growth of a Poet* (Boston: Houghton Mifflin, 1960), pp. 25–26.

14 Abner W. Brown, *Recollections of the Conversation Parties of the Rev. Charles Simeon, M.A.* (London, 1863), p. 62. R. C. Trench wrote to his fiancée in May 1832: "Simeon is worn out, and, moreover, spoiled by being at the head of a

set who have fed him with that religious adulation which is the least suspected, and yet most puffing up of all kinds of flattery." (*Letters and Memorials,* ed. M. Trench [London, 1897], I, 114). Tennyson apparently did not
know much about the figure who purports to be the original of his poem.
W. E. H. Lecky wrote, "He once confessed to me that when he wrote his
'Simeon Stylites' he did not know that the story was a Syrian one, and had
accordingly given it a Northern colouring which he now perceived to be
wrong." (*Materials,* III, 324; omitted from *Memoir,* II, 206; see also *Memoir,*
I, 265.)

15 John Allen, MS Diary, February 3, 1830 (Trinity College Library).
16 *Memoir,* I, 497.
17 *Memoir,* I, 170. Hallam Tennyson noted, "He thought with Arthur Hallam
that 'the essential feelings of religion subsist in the utmost diversity of forms,
that different language does not always imply different opinions, nor different opinions any difference in *real* faith.' 'It is impossible,' my father said,
'to imagine that the Almighty will ask you, when you come before Him in
the next life, what your particular form of creed is.' " *Materials,* II, 18–19;
cf. *Memoir,* I, 309. Some rejected stanzas for *The Palace of Art* show the
"secret entities of Faith" as "blind and vague in form and face, / Not yet mixt
up with human deeds, / But always waiting in a dusky place / To clothe
themselves in creeds." Ricks, 413n.
18 *Edinburgh Review,* 42 (August 1825), 316, 318–20.
19 *The Voice and the Peak,* lines 9–12. In the manuscript the meaning is more
explicit: "And I roar because I fall." Ricks, p. 1222 n. 12.

CHAPTER 3.   The Solitary Singer

1 Alfred Tennyson, *Unpublished Early Poems,* ed. Sir Charles Tennyson (London, 1931), p. 27.
2 The manuscript in *T.Nbk.* 18 has the stanzas in the following order: v, i, ii,
iii, iv, suggesting that Tennyson began the poem with the fresh personal
experience of v and then went back and developed the material of i–iv.
3 In his review of the 1842 volume John Sterling read the "friend" of line 119
as Memory. He had no inkling that it was supposed to be an individual.
Sterling, "Poems by Alfred Tennyson," *Essays and Tales,* ed. J. C. Hare
(London, 1848), I, 446–47.
4 An entry in the Journal of Emily Tennyson, the poet's wife, for January 25,
1868, says: "We begged him to lose no time in beginning to remould 'The
Lover's Tale.' He said, 'Oh no, it is a Poem written at 19. I'm past that now,
besides, it's pirated.' E.T. thought he might reset the Poem, adding to the
fragment a sequel as heard from other lips in after years, or something of
the sort" (*Materials,* III, 74–75). This suggests that *The Golden Supper* was
Emily Tennyson's idea, not Alfred's. On the other hand, a note to II, 129, of
the 1832 proof of *The Lover's Tale* (Lincoln) says: "This & some few other
passages in the Poem allude to a circumstance in the sequel, which is in a
great measure founded on the beautiful tale of Gentil Carisendi in the
Decameron." This seems to be in A.T.'s hand and to be intended as a note to
be printed in the 1832 edition. If so, the present sequel was, of course,
planned from at least that date. Perhaps the solution is that in 1868 Tenny-

son felt he could not recapture his earlier luxuriant manner and accepted his wife's suggestion that he put the sequel in the mouth of another speaker, who would tell it more objectively.

5   Preface to *Prometheus Unbound,* in *Complete Poetical Works,* ed. T. Hutchinson (Oxford, 1952), p. 205.

6   *Materials,* I, 37; *Memoir,* I, 20–21.

7   *The "How" and the "Why,"* 11–12.

8   Most of the engravings in the Annuals are of scenes from Scott, Byron, or Shakespeare, or from foreign countries, and the text, usually in prose, is normally related thereto. Of course, there was a great interest in "beauties" at this time, as witness Heath's *Book of Bauties* (1833), ed. L.E.L., with 19 plates, and Mrs. Anna Jameson's *Beauties of the Court of King Charles the Second* (1833), with 21 engravings of miniatures of Sir Peter Lely's "Windsor Beauties." The main influence on Tennyson's "lady" poems may well have been the many female portraits of Reynolds, Gainsborough, Romney, Lely, and others.

9   Tennyson's sister, Emily, wrote to Ellen Hallam (postmarked Spilsby, April 14, 1835): "We had a party to dinner last Thursday, and finished the day with dancing. . . . A Miss Rawnsley who was here, is the lightest and most indefatigable dancer I ever saw. . . . Alfred is delighted with her. I some-times fancy she is the prototype of his 'Airy Fairy Lilian.' " (Trin. Coll. MSS) See also H. D. Rawnsley, *Memories of the Tennysons* (Glasgow, 1900), p. 64.

10 *Works* (Eversley ed.), I, 335.

11 "The 'High-Born Maiden' Symbol in Tennyson," *PMLA, 63* (March 1948), 234–43.

12 Slip case for *Baroque Music for Recorders* (Nonesuch Records).

13 It is preserved in the Trinity College Library with the note (I, 7 of the 1842 ed.): "Of the tiresome Gallery of Ladies in this Vol. I—the Adelines, Madelines, Eleanores & c. I only care to preserve this *Isabel:* which was said to be a Reflection of AT's Mother: one of the most innocent and tender-hearted Ladies I ever saw."

14 World's Classics ed., pp. 249–50.

15 *Literary Essays,* ed. Edward Alexander (New York: Bobbs-Merrill, 1967), p. 103.

16 *Works* (Eversley ed.), I, 337.

17 See Carol Christ, *The Finer Optic: The Aesthetic of Particularity in Victorian Poetry* (New Haven: Yale University Press, 1975), pp. 18–20.

18 *Memoir,* I, 500–01.

19 *Memoir,* I, 116–17.

20 Alfred Ainger, ed., *Tennyson for the Young* (London, 1891), p. 113.

21 *Materials,* I, 135–36.

22 Ainger, *Tennyson for the Young,* p. 113. R. C. Tobias rejects Ainger's state-ment as a basis for interpreting the poem in "The Year's Work in Victorian Poetry: 1964," *Victorian Poetry,* 3 (1965), 126–27.

23 MS note in his copy of Tennyson's *Poems* (1842), I, 86 (Trin. Coll. Lib.).

24 "Tennyson's 'The Lady of Shalott': The Ambiguity of Commitment," *Cen-tennial Review,* 12 (1968), 415–29.

25 See my *Imaginative Reason: The Poetry of Matthew Arnold* (New Haven: Yale University Press, 1966), pp. 68–79.

26 Ricks, pp. 502–03.
27 *A Handbook to Greek Mythology* (London, 1964), p. 216.
28 Apollodorus, *The Library*, trans. J. G. Frazer (Loeb Classical Library, 1921), II, v. 11–12.
29 "Tennyson's *The Lotos-Eaters:* Two Versions of Art," *Modern Philology*, 62 (1964), 118–29.
30 *Sonnet [Check every outflash, every ruder sally]*.
31 *Tennyson and His Friends*, p. 310.
32 D. G. Rossetti, *Letters*, ed. O. Doughty and J. R. Wahl (Oxford, 1965), I, 106.
33 *Materials*, III, 349.
34 *Materials*, IV, 91.
35 *Memoir*, I, 209.
36 Washington Irving, *The Life and Voyages of Christopher Columbus* (London, 1830), p. 150.
37 Ibid., pp. 159–60.
38 Ibid., p. 194.
39 *Life, Journals, and Letters of Henry Alford* (London, 1873), p. 60.

CHAPTER 4. "O Civic Muse"

1 *Memoir*, I, 44n.
2 *Memoir*, I, 41–42, 83.
3 Frances M. Brookfield, *The Cambridge "Apostles"* (London, 1906), p. 10. One wonders whether there was not also some allusion to the class list. In the 1820s at Cambridge the highest ranking scholar was called the Senior Wrangler, then came about twenty Wranglers, then the Senior Optimes, the Junior Optimes, and the *Hoy Polloi*, of whom the last twelve were called "The Apostles." [Wright], *Alma Mater*, I, 3n.
4 Brookfield, *The Cambridge "Apostles,"* p. 8.
5 The first is cited by Stevenson, "The 'High-Born Maiden' Symbol in Tennyson."
6 *Memoir*, I, 68.
7 Ricks, pp. 287, 352, 457–58, 470–71; *Memoir*, I, 89–90.
8 Ricks, pp. 166–67.
9 [James Spedding], *Apology for the Moral and Literary Character of the XIXth Century* (n.p., 1830), pp. 7–9.
10 There seems to be no doubt that the remark was made, for in a brown notebook at the Tennyson Research Centre (Lincoln) we find the entry: "The Palace of Art, 'Tennyson we cannot live in art' Trench (afterwards Archbishop) said to me when we were at Trinity Cambridge together. This Poem is the embodiment of my own belief that the godlike life is with & for man." See also *Memoir*, I, 118–19, and *Works* (Eversley ed.), I, 363–64. I have treated the subject somewhat more fully in my article, " 'Tennyson, we cannot live in art,'" *Nineteenth-Century Literary Perspectives: Essays in Honor of Lionel Stevenson* (Durham: Duke University Press, 1974), pp. 77–92.
11 For an account of this episode see John Bromley, *The Man of Ten Talents: A Portrait of R. C. Trench, 1807-86* (London, 1959), pp. 29ff.; also Carlyle, *The Life of John Sterling*, in *Works*, Centenary ed. (London, 1897), XI, 62–66.
12 Trench, *Letters and Memorials*, I, 31–37.

13 Ibid., I, 16.
14 Ibid., I, 28.
15 Ibid., I, 47.
16 Ibid., I, 46.
17 R. C. Trench, *The Story of Justin Martyr, and Other Poems* (London, 1835), p. 166.
18 Trench's brother, Francis, gives an account of their visit to these ruins in late April 1830, in *A Few Notes from Past Life: 1818-1832* (Oxford, 1862), pp. 175–88.
19 Trench, *The Story of Justin Martyr,* pp. 17–18, 20–22. The theme is also developed in other poems by Trench, e.g., *Anti-Gnosticus.*
20 Trench, *Letters and Memorials,* I, 48, 50.
21 Ibid., I, 59.
22 Ibid., I, 65. Tennyson and Trench never became intimate. In mid-March 1832 Tennyson wrote to W. H. Brookfield: "You and Trench, I am told, grew very intimate with one another before he left Cambridge: it is impossible to look upon Trench and not to love him, though he be, as Fred says, always strung to the highest pitch. . . . Trench is a bold truehearted Iconoclast—yet I have no faith in any one of his opinions" (Lang). About the same time Hallam wrote to Trench: "I regret, with you, that you have never had the opportunity of knowing more of him [Tennyson]" (Trench, *Letters and Memorials,* I, 111). In view of this, it seems possible that the introductory poem to *The Palace of Art* was addressed not to Trench but to Hallam or Spedding.
23 Brookfield, *The Cambridge "Apostles",* p. 256.
24 Ibid., pp. 262–63.
25 Trench, *Letters and Memorials,* I, 84.
26 Ibid., I, 84.
27 Alford, *Life, Journal, and Letters,* p. 61. A.T. wrote: "I remember seeing thirty ricks burning near Cambridge, and I helped to pass the bucket from the well to help to quench the fire." *Works* (Eversley ed.), IV, 259.
28 *Memoir,* I, 66–68. A. C. Howell, in "Tennyson's 'Palace of Art'—an Interpretation," *Studies in Philology,* 33 (1936), 507–22, notes the architectural resemblance between the Palace and Trinity College but illegitimately extends this to say that Tennyson is taking a fling at his college out of pique at having been unable to take a degree. There is no evidence for this.
29 Trench, *Letters and Memorials,* I, 50, 58, 63. FitzGerald called Sunderland "very plausible, Parliament-like, & self-satisfied." (Trin. Coll. Lib.)
30 *Works* (Eversley ed.), I, 367.
31 FitzGerald noted in his copy of Tennyson's *Poems* (1842), I, 144 (Trin. Coll. Lib.): "In this Advancement of Livy [in *The Palace of Art*] I recognize the Fashion of AT's College Days, when the German School, with Coleridge, Julius Hare, &c. to expound, came to reform all our Notions. I remember that Livy & Jeremy Taylor were 'the greatest Poets next to Shakespeare'—I am not sure if you were not startled at hearing that *Eutropius* was the greatest Lyric Poet except Pindar—'You had not known he was a Poet at all.' " Cf. *Materials,* I, 49–50.
32 *Defence of Poetry,* in *Literary and Philosophical Criticism,* ed. J. Shawcross (London, 1907), pp. 150–51. Although Shelley's *Defence* was not published

until 1839, the manuscript was in the hands of Leigh Hunt and Thomas Love Peacock from 1822 on and so may have come to the attention of the Apostles.

33   *Memoir,* I, 85–86.
34   Hazlitt, *Sketches,* pp. 4–5, 29, 51, 52–53, 129.
35   Thomas Babington Macaulay, *Works* (London, 1875), VIII, 24–25.
36   *Memoir,* I, 98–99. For an account of the Saint-Simonians in England, see Richard K. P. Pankhurst, *The Saint Simonians, Mill and Carlyle: A Preface to Modern Thought* (London, n.d.), pp. 37–60.
37   Trench, *Letters and Memorials,* I, 16.
38   *Memoir,* I, 81.
39   Trench, *Letters and Memorials,* I, 73–74.
40   See Spedding's authoritative comment in the *Edinburgh Review,* 77 (1843), 383–84: "The 'Palace of Art' represents allegorically the condition of a mind which, in the love of beauty and the triumphant consciousness of knowledge and intellectual supremacy, in the intense enjoyment of its own power and glory has lost sight of its relation to man and to God. . . . The sin of self-absolution from human cares and duties, finds its appropriate retribution in the despair which the sense of being cut off from human sympathy, when it once forces itself on the mind, inevitably brings; . . . the concluding stanzas (as conveying the moral, and especially as showing that it is not the enjoyment, but the *selfish* enjoyment, of her intellectual supremacy—not the gifts, but the gifts as divorced from charity—which he holds to be sinful) must find a place."
41   Spedding, *Apology,* p. 11.
42   Edgar Wind, *Pagan Mysteries in the Renaissance* (New York, 1967), p. 82.
43   Ricks, p. 298.
44   *Memoir,* I, 140–41. The Greek is from Dionysius of Halicarnassus, *Opera Omnia* (Lipsiae, 1773–77), V, 420–21. Dionysius was included in the 1832 version of *The Palace of Art.*
45   *Memoir,* I, 97.
46   *Memoir,* I, 209.
47   *Tennyson and His Friends,* p. 331.

CHAPTER 5.   From Ulysses to Sir Bedivere

1   James Knowles, "Aspects of Tennyson, II," *Nineteenth Century,* 33 (1893), 182.
2   *Memoir,* I, 459.
3   Emily Tennyson to Edward Lear, August 14, 1883, as quoted in Ricks, p. 568. Hallam Tennyson also says it was "partly written at the same time" as *Ulysses. Works* (Eversley ed.), VI, 395.
4   *Memoir,* I, 305.
5   *The Poetry of Experience: The Dramatic Monologue in Modern Literary Tradition* (London, 1957), chap. 2.
6   See my article, "Monodrama and the Dramatic Monologue," *PMLA,* 90 (May 1975), 366–85.
7   Donald L. Clark, *Rhetoric in Greco-Roman Education* (New York, 1957), pp. 199–201. See also the same author's *John Milton at St. Paul's School: A Study of*

Ancient Rhetoric in English Renaissance Education (Hamden, Conn., 1964), pp. 189–90, 242–43; Quintilian, III. viii. 49–53; IX. ii. 29–32.

8   *Memoir,* I, 140–41.

9   *Memoir,* I, 166.

10 For the Alexandrians and Neoterics see Brooks Otis, *Virgil: A Study in Civilized Poetry* (Oxford, 1963), pp. 8–31; Tenney Frank, *Vergil: A Biography* (New York, 1922), pp. 38–48; W. F. Jackson Knight, *Roman Vergil* (London, 1944), pp. 47–49, 120–28; J. W. H. Atkins, *Literary Criticism in Antiquity* (Gloucester, Mass., 1961), I, 166–67; Bruno Snell, *The Discovery of the Mind: The Greek Origins of European Thought* (Oxford, 1953), p. 267.

11 The most comprehensive study of the epyllion is that of M. Marjorie Crump, *The Epyllion from Theocritus to Ovid* (Oxford, 1931). Its thesis, however, has been controverted by Walter Allen, Jr., "The Epyllion: A Chapter in the History of Literary Criticism," *Trans. Amer. Philol. Assn.,* 71 (1940), 1–26; and John F. Reilly, "Origins of the Word 'Epyllion,' " *Classical Journal,* 49 (December 1953), 111–14.

12 *Memoir,* I, 40.

13 *Works* (Eversley ed.), VII, 361; see also *Memoir,* II, 13.

14 See W. B. Stanford, *The Ulysses Theme: A Study in the Adaptability of a Traditional Hero* (Oxford, 1954), pp. 87–89, 181; J. E. Harrison, *Myths of the Odyssey in Art and Literature* (London, 1882), pp. 111–12; Apollodorus, *The Library,* trans. Sir James G. Frazer (London, 1921), II, 303, 305–07 and notes; Pausanius, viii, 12, 5ff.; Sextus Empiricus, *Against the Professors (Adversos Grammaticos),* I, 267: Plutarch, *Quaest. Graec.,* xiv.

15 Tasso, *Ger. Lib.,* xv, 25; Pulci, *Morg. Magg.,* xxv, 130. Tennyson's attention would have been directed to these references (as mine was) by the note in H. F. Cary's translation of Dante, *The Vision* (London, 1819), I, 228n.

16 Bacon, *Works,* ed. J. Spedding, R. L. Ellis, and D. D. Heath (London, 1857), III, 319. Cicero alludes to Ulysses' preference in *De Grat.* 1. 44 and Plutarch in *Gryll.* 1.

17 *Semele,* a fragment of a classical dramatic monologue written c. 1835, illustrates the same theme as *Tithonus* or *Tiresias* of the mortal who is destroyed by her vision of the divine. "I wished to see Him. Who may feel / His light and live?" But though she herself was destroyed, out of her union with Zeus came the child Bacchus, who, with his clangorous music, will "delight the world." He is a comic or hedonistic version of the deputy or mediator who transmits the divine vision to the people.

18 Ricks, p. 1464; *Memoir,* II, 128.

19 *Memoir,* I, 83.

20 *Memoir,* II, 127.

21 *Memoir,* II, 133: "Arthur's death takes place at midnight in mid-winter."

22 W. D. Paden, *Tennyson in Egypt* (University of Kansas Publications, Lawrence, Kansas, 1942), p. 81.

CHAPTER 6.   The English Idyls

1   FitzGerald's copy of Tennyson's *Poems* (1842), II, verso of last page (Trinity). On another occasion FitzGerald wrote, "I well remember that when I was at Merehouse (as Miss Bristowe would have us call it), with A. Tennyson

in 1835, Mr. Spedding grudged his Son's giving up much time and thought to consultations about Morte d'Arthur's, Lords of Burleigh, etc., which were then in MS. He more than once questioned me, who was sometimes present at the meetings, 'Well, Mr. F., and what is it? Mr. Tennyson reads, and Jem criticizes:—is that it?' " (*Tennyson and His Friends*, p. 402.)

2   "Morte d'Arthur when read to us from MS in 1835 had no Introduction, or Epilogue; which were added to anticipate or excuse the 'faint Homeric Echoes' &c." (FitzGerald's copy of *Poems* [1842], II, 1). See *Materials*, I, 237; *Memoir*, I, 194.

3   "The Prologue & Epilogue were added after 1835, when we first heard it read in Cumberland; I suppose for the same reason that caused the Prologue &c. to Morte D'Arthur; giving a *Reason* for telling an Old-World Fairy Tale." MS note in FitzGerald's copy of Tennyson's *Poems* (1842), II, 148.

4   *T.Nbk.* 26.

5   *Church of England Quarterly Review* (October 1842), quoted in Ricks, pp. 731–32.

6   For a good account see Walter E. Houghton, *The Poetry of Clough: An Essay in Revaluation* (New Haven: Yale University Press, 1963), pp. 93–99.

7   *Letters of Robert Browning and Elizabeth Barrett Barrett*, ed. E. Kintner, I, 427.

8   *Westminster Review*, 14 (January 1831), 212.

9   *Poetical Works*, ed. C. B. Tinker and H. F. Lowry (Oxford, 1953), pp. xix–xx.

10   Wilfred Ward, *Aubrey de Vere: A Memoir* (London, 1904), p. 74.

11   William Empson, *English Pastoral Poetry* (New York, 1938), pp. 23, 137.

12   Quoted in Douglas Bush, *Mythology and the Romantic Tradition* (Cambridge, 1937), p. 204n.

13   M. J. Chapman, the translator of Theocritus, Bion, and Moschus (1836), and Henry Alford, author of *Chapters on the Poets of Ancient Greece* (1842).

14   J. W. Robberds, *A Memoir of the Life and Writings of the Late William Taylor of Norwich* (London, 1843), I, 213.

15   *A New Spirit of the Age* (Oxford, 1909), pp. 132–33.

16   Arnold, *On Translating Homer*, in *Complete Prose Works*, ed. R. H. Super (Ann Arbor: University of Michigan Press, 1960), pp. 206–07.

17   *T.Nbk.* 17 (23).

18   See Kirsten Gram Holmstrom, *Monodrama, Attitudes, Tableaux Vivants: Studies on Some Trends of Theatrical Fashions, 1770–1815* (Stockholm, 1967), pp. 110–208.

19   The note is in FitzGerald's copy of Tennyson's *Poems* (1842), II, 32.

20   FitzGerald in his copy of *Poems* (1842) gives readings "from the MS as it stood for a long time, & so was known among us. In some respects I must like the old Reading best, though the Whole Poem is undoubtedly improved in Form & Matter. In particular, I never liked to lose the bit of Autumn landscape noted at p. 28—which I remember to have guessed—and rightly—to be taken from a Background of a Titian: I think, Lord Ellesmere's 'Ages of Man.' " The lines are given in Ricks, p. 517: "Her beauty . . . fallows."

21   Sir Charles Tennyson, "Tennyson Papers, I: Alfred's Father," *Cornhill Magazine*, 153 (January–June 1936), 291.

22   *Memoir*, I, 87, 103, 104, 175–76, 276–77.

23 Edmund C. Stedman, *Victorian Poets* (Boston, 1876), pp. 211–12; see Ricks, p. 731
24 Stedman, *Victorian Poets,* p. 233.
25 *Materials,* I, 239–40; *Memoir,* I, 196. One wonders whether the title of the poem was not suggested by the well-known country house of Lord Braybrooke, Audley End, at Saffron Walden near Cambridge. In 1836, just two years before the poem was written, Richard Lord Braybrooke published *The History of Audley End,* a topographical description and history, with plates, in which William Whewell and J. S. Henslow of Cambridge assisted.
26 *T.Nbk.* 26 (26).

CHAPTER 7. *The Princess*

1 John Killham, *Tennyson and "The Princess": Reflections of an Age* (London: Athlone Press, 1958), pp. 56, 67, 113. In my account of the feminist background of the poem I am indebted to Killham's comprehensive survey.
2 Ibid., pp. 148–49.
3 *Memoir,* I, 248n.; *Works* (Eversley ed.), IV, 246; Sir Charles Tennyson, "Tennyson Papers, IV. The Making of 'The Princess,'" *Cornhill Magazine,* 153 (June 1936), 673.
4 Killham, *Tennyson and "The Princess,"* p. 165.
5 *Westminster Review,* 14 (January 1831), 221, quoted in Killham, pp. 89–90.
6 Killham, *Tennyson and "The Princess,"* p. 51.
7 Ibid., pp. 130–33.
8 [John Richardson], *The Eglinton Tournament* (London, 1843), pp. 1–6. See Killham, *Tennyson and "The Princess,"* pp. 272–74.
9 *Memoir,* I, 251.
10 *Works* (Eversley ed.), IV, 238, 242.
11 See Bernard Bergonzi, "Feminism and Femininity in *The Princess,*" in *The Major Victorian Poets: Reconsiderations,* ed. Isobel Armstrong (London: Routledge & Kegan Paul, 1969), p. 47.
12 Killham, *Tennyson and "The Princess,"* p. 54.
13 Ricks, p. 838n.
14 *In Memoriam,* cix; *Memoir,* I, 326n.; II, 69, quoted in Killham, *Tennyson and "The Princess,"* p. 260n.
15 *Memoir,* I, 282.
16 Ricks, pp. 1768–69.
17 *Memoir,* I, 233–34.
18 *Letters of Matthew Arnold to Arthur Hugh Clough,* ed. H. F. Lowry (Oxford, 1932), p. 92.

CHAPTER 8. *In Memoriam*

1 A. C. Bradley, *A Commentary on Tennyson's "In Memoriam,"* 3rd ed., rev. (Hamden, Conn.: Archon Books, 1966), p. 30; see also Carlisle Moore, "Faith, Doubt, and Mystical Experience in 'In Memoriam,'" *Victorian Studies,* 7 (1963), 158–69.
2 *The Writings of Arthur Henry Hallam,* ed. T. Vail Motter (New York: Modern Language Association, 1943), p. 196.

3 *Memoir*, I, 193n.
4 Ricks, p. 522.
5 *Materials*, I, 246; *Memoir*, I, 139, 142.
6 *Faust*, 1112.
7 *Memoir*, I, 304–05; see also *Materials*, II, 13.
8 "In Memoriam," *Selected Essays* (New York, 1960), p. 291.
9 *The Language of Tennyson's "In Memoriam"* (Oxford: Blackwell, 1971), pp. 26–27.
10 *Thomas Carlyle: A History of His Life in London* (New York, 1910), p. 248, quoted by E. E. Smith, *The Two Voices: A Tennyson Study* (Lincoln: University of Nebraska Press, 1964), p. 95.
11 *The Christian Year: Thoughts in Verse for the Sundays and Holidays Throughout the Year*, advertisement.
12 Froude, *Thomas Carlyle*, p. 248.
13 *Guesses at Truth*, 3rd ed., First Series (London, 1847), p. iv.
14 Ibid., p. vii.
15 We are told, however, that he did not admire Coleridge's prose (*Memoir*, I, 50).
16 *Kingdom of Christ; or, Hints on the Principles, Ordinances, and Constitutions of the Catholic Church* (London, 1838), II, v; see also Everyman ed., I, 17.
17 *Kingdom of Christ* (Everyman ed.), I, 238.
18 Arnold, *Culture and Anarchy* (New York: Macmillan, 1896), p. 56.
19 *Memoir*, I, 393n.
20 A *catena* is series of passages from Scripture or the Fathers so linked together as to form a connected argument or illustration of doctrine. Aquinas's *Catena Aurea* was a commentary on the four gospels collected out of the Fathers. The term had recently been brought into prominence by the authors of *Tracts for the Times*, who published four of the tracts as a *Catena patrum*.
21 *Memoir*, II, 391. It is possible that Tennyson was alluding to Goethe's remarks to Eckermann on June 6, 1831, about the lines at the end of *Faust*, "Wer immer strebend sich bemuht, / Den konnen wir erlösen" (11936–37): "In these verses is contained the key to Faust's redemption: within Faust himself an ever loftier and ever purer activity to the very end, and from above the eternal Love coming to his assistance" (Passage translation).
22 *Faust*, part II, 11918–25, 11934–41, 11981–88, 12104–11; see Lore Metzger, "The Eternal Process: Some Parallels between Goethe's *Faust* and Tennyson's *In Memoriam*," *Victorian Poetry*, 1 (1963), 189–96.
23 *Memoir*, I, 60; Ricks, pp. 282–83, 864n.
24 Knowles, in *Nineteenth Century*, 33 (1893), 182. This division was used by Martin J. Svaglic in "A Framework for Tennyson's *In Memoriam*," *Journal of English and Germanic Philology*, 61 (1962), 810–25.
25 *In Memoriam*, x, xviii, xxi. Tennyson wrote to a Mr. Malan, November 14, 1883: "It is news to me that the remains of A.H.H. were landed at Dover. I had always believed that the ship which brought them put in at Bristol" (*Memoir*, I, 305n.).
26 Tennyson was reading a great deal of Wordsworth in 1835 (*Memoir*, I, 151; W. F. Rawnsley, *Tennyson, 1809–1909* [Ambleside, 1909], p. 17). See also

Eleanor B. Mattes, *Tennyson's "In Memoriam": The Way of a Soul* (New Haven; Yale University Press, 1951), pp. 37–39.

27   Wordsworth, *Prose Works*, ed. Alexander B. Grosart (London, 1876), II, 36.
28   Ibid., II, 36–37.
29   Knowles, in *Nineteenth Century*, 33 (1893).
30   *Varieties of Religious Experience* (New York, 1902), p. 524.
31   *Works* (Oxford, 1836), I, 361, 13.
32   MS note by Edward FitzGerald in his copy of Tennyson's *Poems* (1842), II, 147.
33   *Critique of Practical Reason*, trans. T. K. Abbott, 6th ed. (London: Longmans, 1919), pp. 218–19.
34   *Memoir,* I, 321.
35   *Prose Works*, ed. Grosart, II, 29.
36   A MS of *The Two Voices* (*T.Nbk.* 15) has the passage: "They say, when your best friend is about to die, make a compact with him that he will appear to you again. 'Is that his footstep on the floor / Is this his whisper at the door / Surely he comes. He comes no more.' "
37   *An Essay on the State of the Soul after Death* (Edinburgh, 1825), pp. 20, 23.
38   Whately, *A View of the Scripture Revelations Concerning a Future State* (London, 1829), pp. 41, 45, 73–75.
39   Ibid., pp. 217–18.
40   *Immortality or Annihilation?* (London, 1827), p. 109.
41   Ibid., p. 159.
42   Ibid., p. 183.
43   Ibid., pp. 185–86.
44   Ibid., p. 252.
45   For a full account of the doctrine of the plurality of worlds see Ralph V. Chamberlain, *Life in Other Worlds: A Study in the History of Opinion*, Bulletin of the University of Utah, vol. XXII, no. 3. Salt Lake City: University of Utah, 1932.
46   Chalmers, *Discourses on the Christian Revelation Viewed in Connexion with the Modern Astronomy* (Andover, Mass., 1818), p. 14.
47   *Memoir*, I, 379; see also II, 96, 336. For allusions to the plurality of worlds in Tennyson's poetry, see Ricks, pp. 883, 975, 1017, 1099, 1204, 1300, 1308–09, 1346, 1366–67, 1385. There are also references to the doctrine in Newman's *Grammar of Assent*, 4th ed. (London, 1874), pp. 181, 201, 383.
48   *Prose Remains* (London, 1888), p. 224.
49   Sir David Brewster, *More Worlds Than One* (London, 1854), pp. 256–59.
50   Quoted by A. C. Bradley, *Commentary*, p. 122.
51   *Memoir*, I, 102.
52   *Memoir*, I, 223 and n.; Thomas Malthus, *An Essay on the Principle of Population*, 3rd ed. (London, 1806), I, 2–3; see Eleanor B. Mattes, *Tennyson's "In Memoriam,"* pp. 58–59.
53   *Memoir*, II, 239; see Ricks, p. 913.
54   *Immortality or Annihilation?*, pp. 186–90.
55   Ibid., p. 190.
56   *Materials*, quoted in C. Ricks, *Tennyson* (New York: Macmillan, 1972), p. 28; see also *Memoir*, I, 72–73.

57 *Works* (Eversley ed.), III, 251–52; Ricks, p. 946n.; Knowles, in *Nineteenth Century*, 33:186.

58 *Works* (Eversley ed.), III, 256.

59 *Memoir*, II, 474.

60 *Faust*, 11934ff.; see Metzger, in *Victorian Poetry*, 1:189–96.

CHAPTER 9. "Maud or the Madness"

1 *Memoir*, I, 294.

2 Knowles, in *Nineteenth Century*, 33:182; see also Gordon N. Ray, *Tennyson Reads "Maud"*, Sedgewick Memorial Lecture, University of British Columbia, Vancouver, 1968, pp. 41–42; *Memoir*, I, 304; *Materials*, II, 13. Tennyson himself said of *In Memoriam*, "It was meant to be a kind of *Divina Commedia*, ending with happiness" (*Memoir*, I, 304), or, as reported by Knowles, "It begins with a funeral and ends with a marriage— . . . a sort of Divine Comedy, cheerful at the close" (p. 182).

3 James Russell Lowell called it "The antiphonal voice to 'In Memoriam.'" (*Memoir*, I, 393).

4 *Memoir*, I, 396; see also Ray, *Tennyson Reads "Maud"*, p. 43, and Knowles, in *Nineteenth Century*, 33:187.

5 *Memoir*, I, 304–05.

6 Knowles, in *Nineteenth Century*, 33:182.

7 The first form of *Firmilian*, a burlesque review with copious extracts, appeared in *Blackwoods* in May 1854, the poem itself in late July. Tennyson was writing *Maud* by March 1854, and he had evinced an intention of writing it by October 1853, when he sent to the Sellwood's requesting a copy of "O that 'twere possible." See Ralph Rader, *Tennyson's "Maud": The Biographical Genesis* (Berkeley: University of California Press, 1963), pp. 2–11.

8 *Memoir*, I, 264, 468; II, 73, 506. See also Mark A. Weinstein, *William Edmondstoune Aytoun and the Spasmodic Controversy* (New Haven: Yale University Press, 1968), pp. 82, 173–74; Jerome H. Buckley, *The Victorian Temper* (Cambridge: Harvard University Press, 1952), p. 63, and *Tennyson: The Growth of a Poet* (Cambridge: Harvard University Press, 1961), p. 141; Edgar F. Shannon, "The Critical Reception of Tennyson's 'Maud,'" *PMLA*, 68 (1953), 397–417; Joseph G. Collins, "Tennyson and the Spasmodics," *VNL*, no. 43 (Spring 1973), pp. 24–28.

9 Sir Charles Tennyson, *Alfred Tennyson*, pp. 3–116; Rader, *Tennyson's "Maud"*, passim.

10 Rader, *Tennyson's "Maud"*, p. 88.

11 Ray, *Tennyson Reads "Maud"*, p. 43. For a fuller account of the form see my article, "Monodrama and the Dramatic Monologue," *PMLA*, 90:366–85.

12 R. H. Horne, *A New Spirit of the Age*, p. 253; *Eclectic Review*, 26 (August 1849), 211.

13 *Memoir*, I, 195; *Materials*, IV, 297; *Works* (Eversley ed.), II, 341.

14 *Works* (Eversley ed.), II, 341.

15 *Memoir*, II, 329.

16 *Memoir*, II, 330.

17 AT to Archer Gurney, December 6, 1855 (Lang).

18 *Works* (Eversley ed.), II, 341; *Memoir*, I, 402. It is curious that this passage

appears almost verbatim in a letter of Mrs. Tennyson to her son Lionel (March 12, 1874) with regard to his school paper on Browning. Whether she was paraphrasing something her husband had said or whether Hallam, in editing the *Memoir* and the *Works*, simply attributed the remark to his father is uncertain. It undoubtedly does represent Tennyson's view. (*Letters of Emily Lady Tennyson*, ed. James O. Hoge [University Park: Pennsylvania State University Press, 1974], p. 305.)

19 AT to Archer Gurney, December 6, 1855 (Lang).
20 *Materials*, III, 201; VI, 193.
21 AT to Emily Tennyson, [n.d.] (Lang); see also *Memoir*, I, 383–84, 406; *Materials*, II, 109; IV, 74.
22 AT to Dr. Mann, October 9, 1855 (Lang).
23 Emily Tennyson to James Spedding, June 27, 1856 (*Letters of Emily Lady Tennyson*, ed. Hoge, p. 101).
24 *Materials*, IV, 74.
25 *Materials*, IV, 74; *Memoir*, I, 405.
26 *Tennyson's "Maud" Vindicated: An Explanatory Essay* (London, 1856), reprinted in part in *Tennyson: The Critical Heritage*, ed. John D. Jump, pp. 198–99.
27 *Memoir*, I, 396–97.
28 *Memoir*, I, 404.
29 *Memoir*, I, 396.
30 MS copy of *Riflemen, Form:* c. January 9, 1852 (Lang).
31 *Memoir*, I, 402; Ricks, p. 1038; *Materials*, III, 201.
32 *Memoir*, I, 398; AT to Charles Weld, October 1855 (TRC); AT to Mann, October 9, 1855 (*Materials*, IV, 74). It was doubtless the doctor who wrote the review in the *Asylum Journal of Mental Science*, 2 (October 1855), 95–104.
33 *Tennyson and His Friends*, p. 408.
34 AT to Archer Gurney, December 6, 1855 (Lang).
35 Ricks, pp. 600, 602.
36 Ricks, p. 1206.
37 *Roman Poets of the Republic* (Edinburgh, 1863), p. 312; see also Sellar, "Lucretius and the Poetic Characteristics of His Age," in *Oxford Essays* (London, 1855), p. 45. Arnold also emphasized Lucretius's modernity in his lecture, "The Modern Element in Literature."
38 AT to B. P. Blood, May 7, 1874 (Harvard). Sellar says that in Lucretius's philosophy "there is no thought of progress, no sense of duty, no sympathy with human activity" (*Roman Poets of the Republic*, p. 306). That Tennyson read Sellar's work is apparent from *Materials*, III, 365.

CHAPTER 10. *Idylls of the King*

1 *Memoir*, II, 133.
2 M. W. Maccallum, *Tennyson's Idylls of the King and Arthurian Story from the XVIth Century* (Glasgow, 1894), pp. 423–28.
3 In justifying the mention of the heathen in the war song at the end of the first idyll Tennyson says, "It is early times yet, and many years are to elapse before the more settled time of 'Gareth' " (*Memoir*, II, 117).
4 *Memoir*, II, 83.

5   AT to Ticknor and Fields, December 11, 1858 (Lang); but cf. *Memoir*, II, 89–90.
6   C. L. Graves, *Life and Letters of Sir George Grove* (London, 1903), pp. 197–98.
7   *The Holy Grail and Other Poems* (London, 1870), advertisement facing the title page.
8   Quoted in Kathleen Tillotson, "Tennyson's Serial Poem," in Geoffrey and Kathleen Tillotson, *Mid-Victorian Studies* (London: Athlone Press, 1965), p. 89.
9   *Memoir*, I, 457; see also II, 124–25.
10 Quoted by Hallam Tennyson, ed., *Idylls of the King* (London, 1908), p. 436.
11 Ricks, p. 1629n.
12 Quoted in Jump, ed., *Tennyson: The Critical Heritage*, p. 316.
13 *Memoir*, I, 456–57; II, 126.
14 *Memoir*, I, 459; *Materials*, II, 342.
15 *Memoir*, II, 63.
16 *Memoir*, II, 61; *Materials*, III, 95–96.
17 Quoted in Jump, ed., *Tennyson: The Critical Heritage*, p. 316.
18 *Memoir*, II, 366.
19 *Memoir*, II, 117.
20 I am indebted for several points in this and the next paragraph to an unpublished paper by Robert M. Scavone.
21 Ricks, p. 1660n.

CHAPTER 11.   Late Lyrics and Earlier

1   *Memoir*, I, 190.
2   *Memoir*, I, 492
3   See *The Daisy*, lines 73–77.
4   Ricks, p. 1019; see also *Memoir*, I, 341.
5   Ricks, p. 1412.

Index

Aeschylus, 204
Ainger, Canon, *Tennyson for the Young*, 44
Alcaeus, 81, 83, 90, 250–51
Alexandrian poetic, 90–92, 113–14, 223
Alford, Henry, 57, 70
Allen, John, 24
Allen, Dr. Matthew, 190, 193, 207
Anacreon, 119
Apocalyptic poetry, 14–28
Apollodorus, 50
Apollonius of Rhodes, *Argonautica*, 91
"Apostles," The, 58, 59–60, 61, 64–69, 72, 75, 131
Arabian Nights' Entertainments, 32, 33
Aristotle, 95, 173
Arnold, Matthew, 44, 91, 159; *The Strayed Reveller*, 46, 47–48; and modern subject, 113; *Empedocles on Etna*, 147, 168; *Thyrsis*, 149–50; *Culture and Anarchy*, 213, 214; *Literature and Dogma*, 230
Arnold, Thomas, 6
Atherstone, Edwin, 21
Auden, W. H., 95
Augustine, Saint, 3
Aytoun, William Edmondstoune, 192

Bacon, Francis, 60, 71, 75, 76, 93, 158
Bailey, John Philip, *Festus (1846)*, 192
Baring, Rosa, 193
Barmby, John Goodwyn, 143
Barrett, Elizabeth, 112, 113
Beckford, William, 72
Benda, Georg, 195
Bentham, Jeremy, 60, 159, 214
Bible: Book of Revelation, 15; Song of Songs, 209
Bion, 149
Blakesley, J. W., 61, 66, 67
Boccaccio, Giovanni, 35
Bourne, Marty (AT's aunt), 14
Boyd, Robert, 69, 81
Boyle, Mary, 251, 253
Bradley, Mr. and Mrs. Granville, 228
Brandes, Johann, Christian, 195
Brewster, Sir David, *More Worlds Than One (1854)*, 174
Brontës, the, 22
Browning, Robert, 43, 97, 117, 152, 168,

195; and dramatic monologue, 85; *Ring and the Book*, 240, 241
Bruno, Giordano, 173
Buckland, William, 15
Bulwer-Lytton. *See* Lytton
Burke, Edmund, 15
Butler, Joseph, 153, 166, 177
Byron, George Gordon, Lord, 9, 60, 173; *Manfred*, 147, 192

Caillé, René, 23
Calderón de la Barca, Pedro, 60
Callimachus, 90–92
Calvus, 91
Cambridge University, 24, 71–72
Canby, Edward Tatnall, 38–39
Carlyle, Thomas, 4, 15, 55, 97, 127, 156, 157, 185, 188, 213
Carroll, Lewis, 210
"Catastrophism" (vs. "Uniformitarianism"), 14–15, 21–22, 150–51, 160, 191
Catullus, 91, 177–78, 248
Chalmers, Thomas, *Astronomical Discourses (1817)*, 173
Chambers, Robert, *Vestiges of the Natural History of Creation (1844)*, 177
Chaucer, Geoffrey, 23, 130
Chesterton, G. K., 78
Choerilus of Samos, 91
Cicero, 95, 96
Cinna (the poet), 91
Clapperton, Hugh, 22
Clare, John, 40
Clarke, Samuel, 167
Clough, Arthur Hugh, 112, 128
Coleridge, Samuel Taylor, 1, 43, 59, 106, 119, 185; *Aids to Reflection*, 9, 17, 60, 156–57, 158–59; *The Friend*, 75; *Dejection: an Ode*, 85, 87, 88, 234
Collins, Anthony, 167
Collins, William, 33, 40, 196
Constable, John, 34
Cousin, Victor, 65
Crabbe, George, 9, 114
Cuvier, Georges, 15

Dante, 19, 23, 26, 60, 93, 94, 130, 164, 190
Darwin, Charles, 177